DEFENDING
A CONTESTED IDEAL:
MERIT AND THE PSC
OF CANADA
1908–2008

D1568872

HUMBER LIBRARIES LAKESHORE CAMPUS
3199 Lakeshore Blvd West
TORONTO, ON.   M8V 1K8

GOVERNANCE SERIES

G overnance is the process of effective coordination whereby an organization or a system guides itself when resources, power, and information are widely distributed. Studying governance means probing the pattern of rights and obligations that underpins organizations and social systems; understanding how they coordinate their parallel activities and maintain their coherence; exploring the sources of dysfunction; and suggesting ways to redesign organizations whose governance is in need of repair.

The series welcomes a range of contributions—from conceptual and theoretical reflections, ethnographic and case studies, and proceedings of conferences and symposia, to works of a very practical nature—that deal with problems or issues on the governance front. The series publishes works both in French and in English.

The Governance Series is part of the publications division of the Centre on Governance and of the Graduate School of Public and International Affairs at the University of Ottawa. This is the 19th volume published within this series. The Program on Governance and Public Management also publish a quarterly electronic journal: www.optimumonline.ca.

Editorial Committee

Caroline Andrew
Linda Cardinal
Monica Gattinger
Luc Juillet
Daniel Lane
Gilles Paquet (Director)

The published titles in the series
are listed at the end of this book.

Barcode in Back

DEFENDING
A CONTESTED IDEAL:
MERIT AND THE PSC
OF CANADA
1908–2008

Luc Juillet and Ken Rasmussen

UNIVERSITY OF OTTAWA PRESS

OTTAWA

HUMBER LIBRARIES LAKESHORE CAMPUS
3199 Lakeshore Blvd West
TORONTO, ON.   M8V 1K8

© University of Ottawa Press, 2008

All rights reserved.

The University of Ottawa Press acknowledges with gratitude the support
extended to its publishing list by Heritage Canada through its Book Publishing
Industry Development Program, by the Canada Council for the Arts, by the
Canadian Federation for the Humanities and Social Sciences through its Aid
to Scholarly Publications Program, by the Social Sciences and Humanities
Research Council, and by the University of Ottawa.

**LIBRARY AND ARCHIVES CANADA
CATALOGUING IN PUBLICATION**

Juillet, Luc, 1969-
Defending a contested ideal : merit and the Public Service Commission, 1908-
2008 / Luc Juillet and Ken Rasmussen.

(Governance series,ISSN 1487-3052 ; 19)
Issued also in French under title: À la défense d'un idéal contesté.
Includes bibliographical references and index.

ISBN 978-0-7766-0684-2

1. Public Service Commission of Canada--History. I. Rasmussen, Ken A.,
1957- II. Title. III. Series: Governance series (Ottawa, Ont.);19

JL108.J8413 2008   352.2'60971   C2008-904251-4

Published by the University of Ottawa Press, 2008
542 King Edward Avenue
Ottawa, Ontario K1N 6N5
www.uopress.uottawa.ca

HUMBER LIBRARIES LAKESHORE CAMPUS
3199 Lakeshore Blvd West
TORONTO, ON. M8V 1K8

TABLE OF CONTENTS

ACKNOWLEDGMENTS

When we were first approached with the idea of writing a history of the Public Service Commission on the occasion of its centenary, our enthusiasm was initially accompanied by a few doubts. Nowadays, administrative history is not very popular amongst scholars of public administration, but, in this case, the book would necessarily be seen as a follow-up on *The Biography of an Institution: The Civil Service Commission, 1908-1967*, the seminal study published in 1967 by Professor Ted Hodgetts and his colleagues. Given that the book is somewhat of a landmark in the field of Canadian public administration, modesty and good sense seemed to advise against simply attempting to follow in its footsteps: the work would have to be of a different nature. Moreover, writing a serious academic study of an institution at a time when it would be celebrating its anniversary seemed particularly daunting and condemned to disappoint many of those who love the institution and have been part of its history.

In the end, we undertook this project because the Public Service Commission is a unique institution with a history that is intimately intertwined with the evolution of a fundamental principle of Canadian public administration: the principle of merit. Over the years, and still today, as we attempt to ensure competent and efficient management of public resources, provide equality of opportunities in public employment, and ensure a proper balance between preventing patronage and ensuring the public service's responsiveness to elected officials, the principle of merit remains a key part of our debates on the future of the public service. In fact, the principle of merit, and hence the institution designed to protect it and make it an operational reality, occupy an important place in our conception of the role and the constitutional position of the public service in our democracy since the early twentieth century. For this reason, it became apparent to us that an examination of the history of the Public Service Commission and its evolving role in the protection of merit could also be an opportunity to better understand how Canada has addressed some of the difficult questions raised by operating an effective public administration in ways that also meet the broader objectives of democratic government. We hope that the readers will find this work useful in this regard.

In completing this work, we have accumulated a debt of gratitude toward many people. We want to thank the leadership of the Institute of Public Administration of Canada and the Public Service Commission for the trust that they showed in offering us this opportunity. The president of the PSC, Maria Barrados, offered unwavering support throughout the project, while at all times respecting our independence as we crafted the analysis presented in the book. In fact, the Commission has been as scrupulous in its respect of our academic freedom as it has been generous in its support, providing invaluable access to documents and people. For this reason, we express our gratitude to Mme Barrados as well as to Bernard Miquelon and Robert Desperrier. We thank everyone who has read the manuscript, in full or in part, and provided useful comments and suggestions, especially Gilles Paquet, James Iain Gow, Maria Barrados, and Marie Tremblay. We also greatly benefited from the generosity of the many individuals, including the former presidents of the Commission, who agreed to be interviewed for this book.

Many people also provided research assistance and editorial support. Alick Andrews provided with much appreciated assistance in setting up and conducting many of the interviews, but we also benefited from the experience and wisdom that he accumulated over many years in human resource management in the public service. Aaron Hamilton, Travis McLellan, Michael Perry and Marc Gervais provided research assistance on various parts of the manuscript. Louise Normand played a key role in shepherding the manuscript to completion, displaying flawless professionalism in the process. Patricia Balfour provided excellent copy editing, not only helping us to improve our writing but also to clarify our thinking. We thank her for her expertise and hard work. We are also very grateful to the staff of the Public Works and Government Services Translation Bureau in Québec City for the excellent translation of this book. Finally, the team at the University of Ottawa Press deserves special recognition for producing the book with exceptional timeliness and effectiveness. In this regard, we express our heartfelt gratitude to Gilles Paquet, whose continued support was essential in bringing the project to fruition.

As we began our research, we were both offered the opportunity to take on leadership positions at new schools of public policy in our respective universities. While these appointments represented great opportunities, they added considerably to the challenge of finding the time to research and write the book. That we were able to finish it at all was due to the support of our respective institutions. At the University of Regina's Johnson-Shoyama Graduate School of Public Policy, Ken Rasmussen thanks especially Sarina Wowchuk for her support. At the University of Ottawa's Graduate School of Public and International Affairs, Luc Juillet expresses his sincere gratitude to Robert Asselin, France Prud'Homme and Ginette Robitaille for their assistance. Finally, many evenings and weekends were sacrificed to this project, cutting down on time that should have been spent with our families. Luc Juillet wishes to thank Sophie, Véronique and Sacha for their love, unconditional support, and understanding. Ken Rasmussen would like to thank Suzanne, Kaitlin and Jonathan for their love and support over the years.

Luc Juillet and Ken Rasmussen

FOREWORD

The morning of my arrival at the Public Service Commission, my colleagues presented me with a book entitled *The Biography of an Institution*. Written by Professor J. E. Hodgetts et al., it was all about the first sixty years of this organization. The commission is not well known outside of the public service so I was pleased to read such a comprehensive piece of work about the organization for which I had just begun to work as president. It would appear that change and challenge have always been a way of life for the commission, even from its very inception.

One hundred years ago, in 1908, the Civil Service Commission, as it was then called, was born. It is my good fortune to be here for this special birthday. The book you are about to read is a special contribution to the celebration of this event. It is the result of the study by two scholars, Professor Ken Rasmussen of the University of Regina and Professor Luc Juillet of the University of Ottawa.

I want to thank both these authors for their work and their willingness to take on the challenge of exploring the one hundred years of a parliamentary institution—a formidable task by any reckoning.

This project demonstrates the effectiveness of partnership. I refer here to the close working relationships that have always existed among academics, the Institute of Public Administration of Canada and the Public Service Commission.

While reading this book, I could not help but think of the thousands of Canadian men and women who have contributed to the direction of the Public Service Commission during the past century. From clerks to commissioners, they strived to help form and defend the evolution of the core values—merit and non-partisanship—that have helped guide the Canadian public service to this very day.

I hope you enjoy reading this book. I believe it contributes to a better understanding not only of the Public Service Commission but also of the wider field of Canadian public administration.

Maria Barrados, PhD

INTRODUCTION:

DEMOCRATIC GOVERNMENT, MERIT AND THE PUBLIC SERVICE COMMISSION OF CANADA

[D]emocratic government in modern industrial society must be able to command ... the services of a well-trained bureaucracy of good standing and tradition, endowed with a strong sense of duty and a no less strong *esprit de corps*. Such a bureaucracy is the main answer to the argument about government by amateurs.... It must also be strong enough to guide and, if need be, instruct the politicians who head the ministries. In order to be able to do this it must be in a position to evolve principles of its own and be sufficiently independent to assert them. It must be a power in its own right.[1]

Joseph Schumpeter, 1942

The creation of the Civil Service Commission (CSC) in September 1908 represents a milestone in the history of the public service and the development of democratic government in Canada.[2] The establishment of a commission independent from the government with exclusive statutory authority for appointing individuals to the public service, apart from the most senior executives, marked the birth of a non-partisan bureaucracy. By putting in place a system that would appoint and promote public servants on the basis of an independent assessment of their merit, the Government of Canada ended widespread political patronage and made possible the development of a professional public service that would be better able to ensure the effective delivery of public services and advise the government of the day on policy decisions.

In addition to increasing the competence of the public service, the application of the merit principle gave public servants a measure of independence from their political masters. While it was recognized that public servants could never be completely insulated from political pressures, the independent system of appointment and promotion allowed them to remain politically impartial and offer candid advice to ministers guided solely by the public interest and without fear of repercussions on their career prospects. The merit system also gave public servants enough independence and security to resist unscrupulous politicians who might try to pressure them into circumventing laws or disregarding standards of conduct in order to further partisan aims. In sum, in September 1908, the Canadian Parliament took a crucial step toward building a professional public service that could be used by the government as an effective instrument in the pursuit of the public interest, and it also planted the seed of a new national institution destined to become a power in its own right in the governance of Canada.

On the surface, the creation of a staffing agency and the adoption of rules for appointing civil servants hardly seem like crucial matters of state. But a decision to build a professional and impartial bureaucracy is of fundamental importance in the development of a modern democracy. As Professor Ezra Suleiman reminds us, democratic governments require legitimacy, which, in no small measure, is derived from their effectiveness in delivering important public goods and from citizens' ability to trust that they will be treated with fairness and impartiality by the state bureaucracy.[3] Despite some of the potential dangers associated with professional bureaucracies, notably the lack of responsiveness to duly elected governments that can come from too much independence and from the asymmetry of information and expertise that necessarily exists between elected officials and bureaucrats, it remains a fact that the creation of an effective and impartial public service is an indispensable component of democratic government.

In the Anglo-American democracies, including Canada, the development of the professional public service was inextricably linked to the adoption of a staffing system founded on the principle that appointments and promotions should be made only on the basis of an independent assessment of merit as determined through examinations. This merit principle finds its main source in a landmark report written for the British government in 1854: the Northcote-Trevelyan report. Authored by reformers Sir Stafford Northcote and Sir Charles Trevelyan, the report called for a new civil service to help meet the challenges faced by their country:

> It may safely be asserted that, as matters now stand, the Government of the country could not be carried on without the aid of an efficient body of permanent officers, occupying a position duly subordinate to that of the ministers who are directly responsible to the Crown and to Parliament, yet possessing sufficient independence, character, ability and experience to be able to advise, assist, and to some extent, influence those who are from time to time set over them.[4]

The progressive establishment of a merit-based staffing system was the mechanism through which this "independence, character, ability and experience" would be assured.

The Northcote-Trevelyan report was pivotal in the development of the civil services of all the Anglo-American democracies, which were influenced by the report as they reformed their bureaucracies in the late 19th and early 20th centuries. Britain set up its first civil service agency in 1855 and progressively developed its merit-based staffing system over the subsequent decades. It was eventually emulated by the others. The United States started to implement a merit-based system with the adoption of the *Pendleton Act* in 1883.[5] Australia and New Zealand followed suit with the adoption of a merit-based system in 1902 and 1912, respectively.[6] With the creation of the Civil Service Commission in 1908, and the extension of its authority over the entire public service in 1918, Canada was clearly part of this broader wave of reforms. As we will see in our first chapter, the British experience played an important role in the choices made by Canada. Despite significant national variations, by the 1920s, all the Anglo-American democracies had adopted merit systems for staffing their bureaucracies.

However, despite its historical contribution to the development of professional public services in these democracies, the merit principle soon became the target of much criticism. In particular, the commissions established to make the principle of merit an operational reality progressively developed extensive and cumbersome sets of rules that stifled the efficient management of personnel. As the bureaucracies expanded, government became more complex, and societies began to expect faster and more adapted responses to a diverse set of social problems. The merit system came to be seen as excessively unwieldy and burdensome, a poster child for bureaucratic inefficiency.[7] Like United States President Jimmy Carter, commenting on the arcane rules of the American merit system in 1976, many people came to believe that there was "no merit in the merit system."[8] Moreover, in the post-war period, politicians increasingly felt that they lacked control over the policy-making process and they started demanding that their civil service be more responsive to their direction. As a consequence, many democracies witnessed renewed efforts to re-establish political control of the bureaucracy, including through the politicization of appointments.[9] In some cases, public servants themselves came to see the convention of political neutrality of the public service as imposing unwarranted shackles on their legitimate right to fully participate in the political life of their communities. Furthermore, as advanced democracies embraced a fuller conception of democratic equality, concerns about discrimination and the underrepresentation of minorities in state bureaucracies posed additional challenges to the actual operation of merit-based staffing processes.

As a result of this confluence of criticisms, the operation of the merit systems of Anglo-American democracies, if not the principle of merit itself, has changed considerably over the years. In fact, many countries have abolished their independent commissions and modified their staffing systems in the hope of responding to the pressures for greater managerial efficiency and political responsiveness. Canada has not been immune from these pressures. While the Public Service Commission (PSC) continues to play an important role as an independent staffing agency, it has undergone considerable changes over its hundred years of history. Like the personnel management system of the Canadian public service as a whole, it has had to adapt to its changing environment. But how should we characterize the Public Service Commission's evolution over the last century? How can we explain its resilience and longevity despite the growing criticism of the merit system over the years? What were the main trends and pressures that affected the commission and the merit system over time? How did the commission itself seek to respond to its changing environment? What do these changes tell us about the evolution of Canadian public administration over this period? This book seeks to address these questions.

Merit as a Balance of Values and the Value of Institutional Ambivalence

In order to better understand the unique role and origins of the Public Service Commission, its evolution, and the challenges that it has faced, this book provides a brief history of its first hundred years of operation. In recounting this history, we make two broad claims. The first is that the history of the commission can be understood as an evolving struggle to achieve a balance among three competing, and at times contradictory, sets of values at the heart of public service staffing in a liberal democracy: political neutrality and independence; fairness and democratic equality; and competence and managerial efficiency. The second is that the commission's unique institutional position, both as a central personnel agency with authority over staffing and an independent body reporting directly to Parliament on the state of the merit system, has contributed significantly to its longevity and to its ability to ensure a balance among the key values underpinning the staffing system.

Because these values are complex, multi-faceted and ever-evolving, periodic adjustments to the staffing system have been required. A look at the history of the Public Service Commission reveals how a large part of its efforts have been spent trying to make sense of the meaning of these values, adjusting to endogenous and exogenous shocks or pressures that have affected their relative weight or changed their meaning, and searching for a set of rules—the infamous merit system—that could be used to live up to them. In other words, while it is undeniable that the creation and evolution of the PSC has been inextricably linked to the ideal of merit, the exact meaning and practical implications of this ideal have often been ill defined and the object of much controversy. From the outset, the merit system has been contested, and it has attempted to strike an uneasy balance among the competing values that it was meant to embody.

What degree of political rights for public servants should non-partisanship tolerate? At what point does the independence of the bureaucracy, meant in part to ensure professionalism and efficiency, become an obstacle to the effective implementation of the democratic will as legitimately articulated by the elected government? Should fairness and equitable access mean preferential treatment for underrepresented groups? To what extent is preferential treatment compatible with ensuring that the "most qualified" person is hired? At what point does a rigid and cumbersome system meant to ensure the hiring of the best qualified person without political consideration turn in fact into a drag on organizational efficiency and become a straightjacket for managers, hindering the efficient delivery of public services? Conversely, at what point does managerial flexibility in staffing generate discretionary decisions that are incompatible with fairness and endanger the competence of the public service? These types of questions, concerning either the meaning of the three sets of values previously listed or the appropriate balance among them, permeate the history of the commission. And, of course, they have few clear and consensual answers. As the history of the PSC shows, finding answers to these questions is a never-ending struggle.

The task is all the more difficult because it involves shooting at a moving target. Over the course of the last century, Canadian society has changed considerably. For example, the growing emphasis on rights and the rise of identity politics since the 1960s have given unprecedented prominence to issues of employment equity and altered old conceptions of fairness. These social changes are not unrelated to the PSC's renewed venture into the areas of bilingualism and employment equity in the 1960s and 1970s. But responding to these social and political trends has necessitated some adjustments to the commission's operations and to its operational conception of the merit principle. One only has to read the speeches of John J. Carson, PSC president in the 1970s, to measure the difficulties involved in rethinking the traditional meaning of merit in the new social context. A similar story can be told about the changing expectations of public servants with regard to their political rights in the 1980s and 1990s. However, probably the most significant trend to have affected the PSC over the years has been the growing attention paid to efficiency and managerial flexibility. Since the end of the Second World War, demands for more managerial flexibility and greater efficiency in public management have been unrelenting. Over this period, the PSC has worked to meet these demands while continuing to protect the other values that have been integral to its raison-d'être since its inception.

In sum, over the years, more than a simple search for the "best qualified," merit has been an uneasy proxy for different sets of values and aspirations that are themselves not easy to either define or reconcile. As noted scholar Patricia Ingraham puts it, "Merit is related to values, ideals, and ethics, to the appropriate role of the civil service in a democracy and thus to governance in a democratic society."[10] For this reason, at some level, debates about the merit system are not merely technical and administrative in nature. They are also debates about which fundamental values a public service should espouse in a democracy and about how to design a system that can reasonably uphold competing values. In our view, this complex reality involves a difficult balancing act, which inevitably leads to evolving, and never fully satisfactory, compromises. It explains in good part the difficulty experienced in trying to 'fix' the merit system over the years. It explains why the PSC, while actively embracing the need for reform at several points throughout its history, has also often been the voice of caution that sought to temper the zeal of reform advocates more single-mindedly focused on only one dimension of the staffing system. It also helps us understand why, at some stages of its history, the commission has heavily invested itself in activities such as language training, which may have appeared somewhat removed from a more narrow conception of merit-based recruitment, but which were related to the promotion of important values for the Canadian public service.

The commission's longevity and continued influence can also be explained by another of its features: its unique institutional ambivalence. As we will see in Chapter 1, the creation of the Civil Service Commission in 1908 involved an unusual institutional choice. On the one hand, the commission is a central personnel agency, exercising exclusive statutory authority for appointing individuals to the public service, but it is independent from Cabinet and it does not take directions from a minister. On the other hand, it is an agent of Parliament, expected to account directly to Parliament for the use of its executive authority and responsible for the oversight required to guarantee the integrity of the merit system, but it is not represented in the House of Commons by a minister and, historically, it has had only a tenuous relationship with Parliament. In other words, it has a foot on each side of the executive-legislative divide.

The creation of an organization with such characteristics took some creativity and abnegation, especially in the context of the early 20th century. In order to foster the development of a public service characterized by professionalism and a reasonable degree of independence, legislators needed to accept that the commission itself would have an unusual degree of independence and break with the traditional doctrine of ministerial responsibility. It would also mean giving up any involvement in the distribution of patronage. As two of Canada's pre-eminent political scientists noted, selecting who should be appointed to the public service was so important that it required a "self-denying gesture for all MPs, a sort of institutionalized conscience to act on their behalf so that they could no longer be led into patronage temptations."[11] Equally important was the willingness of the Crown to abandon its control over appointments and agree to transfer this authority to an independent agency out of its reach.

This rather remarkable "gesture of self-denial" has had a long-lasting impact on the PSC and its ability to protect the principle of merit. At times, the PSC has exercised leadership within the administrative arm of the executive; at other times, it has played up its privileged relationship to Parliament, asserting its independence and its unique role as a guardian of the merit system. Over the years, parliamentarians, ministers, and public servants have often found this combination of roles to be uneasy, even problematic. Several reform proposals have attempted to do away with this duality, often by transferring the PSC's executive authority to a traditional central agency while transforming it into a pure parliamentary oversight body. But by using the two facets of its institutional personality, by making the most of its ambivalent institutional position, the PSC has been better able to strive for a balance among the competing demands placed on the staffing system. It has been able to remain in closer contact with senior executives and departmental managers as a direct participant in staffing and other personnel management functions, but it has also been able to step back, use its independence to resist political pressures on behalf of departments and sometimes block reforms that might have undermined some of the core values of the public service.

Certainly, living with this ambivalence has not always been easy. Over the years, the PSC has been accused of being both too compliant and insufficiently co-operative. But despite the criticism, this unique position has often served it well. Moreover, with the independence of the PSC inscribed in statute in the name of protecting the ideals of independence and merit, the executive would have difficulty taking it back. Even in an age when many observers worry about the lack of the public service's responsiveness to its political masters, a politician asking Parliament to do away with the commission's independence in the field of staffing would run the risk of being accused of wanting to return to the good old days of political patronage. From this perspective, its institutional ambivalence has undoubtedly contributed to its longevity.

OUTLINE OF THE BOOK

In order to fully capture its evolution and the debates that have shaped it, this book examines the entire history of the Public Service Commission, from its inception at the turn of the 20th century to the reforms of recent years. The focus of our analysis is not so much the detailed organizational changes that have marked the evolution of the PSC as the broad transformations that have affected its role over the years and the debates that have dealt with its raison-d'être. Consequently, our treatment of the history of the PSC gives prime of place to its institutional position in Canada's constitutional order, to its role in promoting some of the fundamental principles underlying Canada's public administration and to its importance for democratic government in Canada. At the same time, given the PSC's inextricable link to the merit principle, we also examine how the understanding of this principle has evolved over time and how the merit system has tried to live up to a changing set of values and objectives over the last century. While the key trends and events that have shaped the commission are described, we endeavour to discuss their significance in the broader context of the evolving nature of Canadian government and public administration.

Chapter 1 retraces the debate concerning the need for an independent Civil Service Commission as a key step in overcoming patronage in the late 19th century and early 20th century. At its heart, the creation of the commission served one primary goal: eliminating patronage by establishing a system of competitive examination for recruitment and promotion on the basis of merit. But, as this chapter demonstrates, a wide range of arguments were raised at the time and, from the outset, the purpose of the merit principle and the need for an independent commission were contested. The need to rid the public service of patronage was associated in large part with the requirement for more professionalism and competency in the management of public affairs. Less political control over staffing would result in a more effective public service, it was argued. In this sense, while it would come to be associated with many criticisms of the commission, efficiency was one of the reasons that the commission was established in the first place. But professionalism and efficiency were not the only objectives. The democratic necessity for more equitable access to public employment, regardless of one's relationship with the governing party, was also a prevalent argument.

However, standing in the way of these goals was a powerful constitutional argument in favour of retaining the Crown's prerogative to make appointments to the public service. Despite the ills associated with it, patronage remained for many politicians and public servants a legitimate use of the Crown's authority, and to place staffing in the hands of an independent commission with a tenuous relationship to Parliament would constitute a serious violation of the fundamental principle of ministerial responsibility. In this period, despite the growing influence of reformers and the precedents set by Britain and the United States, the emerging convention of a non-partisan public service, staffed by an independent commission, remained contested among the governing elite.

Chapter 2 examines the challenges faced by the Civil Service Commission from 1918 to the end of the Second World War. Soon after it gained full authority to staff the entire public service in 1918, the commission came to occupy a central place in the Canadian personnel management regime. Whatever limited ambitions may have existed at the time of its creation in 1908, it was quick to establish itself as an important institution in the creation of the modern professional public service, taking on responsibilities not only for recruitment but also for classification, pay determination, organizational development, training and development and appeals. Moreover, in this same period, the commission began to struggle with the need to balance competing values and demands with regard to staffing the public service. The appealing idea that competitive examination would be the sole means of determining merit soon had to be tempered by the need to take into account other social and political considerations. Throughout this period, the merit system was adapted in order to favour veterans who were seeking public employment, prevent women from obtaining certain positions and entering certain classes of employment and secure better regional and linguistic representation. Furthermore, as it continued to fend off criticism for usurping the power of the Crown and being insufficiently accountable, the commission also had to contend with the disagreement of staff associations and senior management about the best way to put in place a classification system that would underpin the country's merit-based career public service.

Chapter 3 examines the period from the end of the Second World War to the major legislative reforms of 1967. Arguably, this could have been the commission's heyday at the centre of the personnel management system in Ottawa. Having accumulated more responsibilities in the preceding decades, it was now playing the central operational role in staffing and personnel management and, until the end of the 1950s, it even continued to acquire new functions related to training, research and appeals. But, over this period, a growing preoccupation with modern management also led to the emergence of one particularly stinging criticism of the commission: that it constituted a barrier to efficient public management. In particular, three high profile commissions that examined the public service—the Gordon Commission (1946), the Heeney Commission (1959) and the Glassco Commission (1962)—released reports that challenged the authority of the Civil Service Commission in personnel administration. For these commissions, as the public service was becoming a much larger and more complex organization, it needed to embrace more modern approaches to management in order to remain efficient. Excessive central controls over departmental managers and the awkward division of responsibilities for management between the Treasury Board and the Civil Service Commission at the centre were increasingly seen as impediments to good administration. So while this period saw some minor changes to personnel management in the public service, most notably with the adoption of the *Civil Service Act* of 1961, its more significant legacy was that it marked the beginning of what became a strong and lasting criticism of the commission and the merit system in the name of managerial flexibility and efficiency.

Chapter 4 looks at the period from 1967 to 1979, which witnessed the most extensive reforms to the Civil Service Commission (CSC) and personnel management since the beginning of the century. The *Public Service Employment Act*, adopted in 1967, transformed the CSC into a new Public Service Commission (PSC), which lost its responsibilities over matters of pay and classification to the new Treasury Board Secretariat (TBS), formally designated as the 'employer' of public servants. In response to the Glassco Commission's report, the PSC began to extensively delegate its staffing authority to the deputy heads of departments. Despite having to exercise this authority within the policy framework set by the PSC, departmental managers were to gain an unprecedented degree of freedom in personnel management.

However, as this chapter clearly shows, this crucial period in the history of the PSC did not simply result in a curtailment of its responsibilities and authority in favour of the TBS and departmental managers. In fact, the reforms implemented in the pursuit of greater efficiency were sufficiently limited that, by 1979, the Lambert Commission and the D'Avignon Committee were calling for additional changes to ensure better personnel management. Over this period, the PSC also developed new services and policies in response to the rising importance of the concepts of equality and freedom in Canadian society. Taking a leadership role in building a representative public service, it developed programs to improve the bilingualism of public servants and recruit more employees from underrepresented groups, such as women, aboriginal peoples and members of visible minorities. Moreover, the PSC had to respond to changing conceptions of political neutrality and public servants' right to political participation, anticipating further changes that would occur in the following decades. In sum, while the growing importance of managerial flexibility and efficiency led to significant changes over this period, the PSC continued to play a key role in staffing and personnel management and it remained actively committed to a broader set of values, including non-partisanship and equity.

While the growing pressures to redefine the meaning of the political neutrality of public servants were evident in the 1970s, the issue took on greater importance in the following decades. Chapter 5 examines how the PSC struggled to defend the traditional values of neutrality and non-partisanship in the face of changing political and social expectations in the period from 1979 to 2006. As this chapter shows, the debate took two forms. First, two important court decisions forced the commission to rethink the traditional limitations placed on the participation of civil servants in the political process, eventually leading to new legal provisions that were inscribed in the new *Public Service Employment Act* in 2003. Second, following the arrival in power of the Progressive Conservative government in 1984, new concerns were raised about the bureaucracy's insufficient responsiveness to the new government's direction. The creation of larger and more powerful ministerial offices, staffed directly by the government outside the merit system, was one of the means used to re-establish political control over the bureaucracy. However, this novel development gave rise to some concern about the integrity of the merit system, especially since ministerial staff were able to gain priority rights of appointment to the public service. This pathway into the public service was eventually closed by the Conservative government of Stephen Harper in 2006. This chapter clearly illustrates how the commission has had to adapt to a changing social and political environment and how the meaning of even fundamental values such as non-partisanship and political neutrality has evolved over the years.

Chapter 6 looks at the reforms that took place in the period from 1984 to 1993, the years of the Progressive Conservative government led by Brian Mulroney. With a rhetoric hostile to the bureaucracy and an agenda of deficit elimination, the Mulroney government, arriving in office, sent a clear signal to the public service that administrative reforms would soon ensue. Given the government's sympathy for the New Public Management movement and its belief in the superiority of private sector management practices, it is not surprising that the staffing system would again be criticized for its excessive rules and undue constraints on managers. Efficiency, once again, became the order of the day. In this context, the Public Service Commission turned out to be a cautious but dedicated reformer. As this chapter demonstrates, the PSC itself pursued an agenda of administrative and legislative reforms meant to facilitate staffing for departments. Then, when the government launched its own administrative reform process known as Public Service 2000, the PSC worked actively to make more structural improvements, not only defending the government's legislative proposals but also proposing some of the new flexibilities that were ultimately included in the *Public Service Reform Act* of 1992. However, as this chapter also shows, while the commission embraced the need for more managerial flexibility and efficiency, it remained careful to seek a balance between this objective and other traditional objectives of the merit system, such as non-partisanship and equity. Integral to this balance, the commission believed, was its own independent authority over staffing. For this reason, while the Mulroney years saw the commission embrace the need for reform, they also saw the commission successfully defend itself against another attempt to curtail its direct and independent authority over staffing.

Finally, Chapter 7 examines the period from 1993 to the present. Over this period, the human resources management framework of the public service, including the PSC, underwent its most profound transformation since the reforms of 1967. Throughout the 1990s, as the Canadian public service continued its transformation, seeking to become leaner, more strategic, more results oriented and more flexible, the PSC itself began to re-examine its raison-d'être. As the public service was trying to move away from the traditional forms of bureaucratic organization, the PSC increasingly felt the need to focus on its core mandate: the guardianship of some of the foundational values of a professional public service. It progressively modernized its approach to delegation, placing more emphasis on accountability for results and respect for key values, and it came close to withdrawing almost completely from service delivery in order to better focus on staffing oversight.

But, ultimately, it was the adoption of the *Public Service Modernization Act*, which included a new *Public Service Employment Act*, in 2003 that significantly transformed both the PSC and the merit system. The law enacted a new definition of merit that was clearly meant to deliver the kind of staffing flexibility that managers and reformers had demanded over the years. Moreover, under the new framework, the commission retained its authority over staffing and even saw its independence reaffirmed, but it also divested itself of a large part of its human resources services in favour of a clearer focus on the oversight of departmental staffing. In effect, as it approached its centenary, the PSC repositioned itself to better focus on fulfilling its essential mandate—ensuring merit-based appointments—at a time when the meaning of merit was being radically changed.

Over the last century, the Public Service Commission has been much more than a simple staffing agency recruiting competent employees for careers in the public service. Its direct involvement in the various facets of human resources management has waxed and waned over time, but it has always remained a significant force in the development and preservation of a professional public administration in Canada. More importantly, the PSC has occupied a unique position in our national institutions, using its dual status as an independent agent of Parliament and a central personnel agency within the executive branch to defend the ideal of an efficient, representative, non-partisan and responsive public service that is able to serve the government of the day with a required measure of independence. As the following story will make clear, defending this ideal has not always been easy and the PSC has certainly faced much criticism. Over the years, the merit system—an often cumbersome set of rules meant to achieve an uneasy mix of competing values—and the PSC itself have had to be significantly transformed in response to the changing environment. But, throughout this never-ending search for a proper balance among efficiency, equity and non-partisanship, the Public Service Commission has played an invaluable role in the development of a national public service that continues to serve as an important cornerstone of democratic government in Canada.

ENDNOTES

[1]   Joseph A. Schumpeter (1942), *Capitalism, Socialism and Democracy*, New York, Harper and Row, 293.

[2]   The name of the Civil Service Commission was changed to the Public Service Commission in 1967. In this book, we will use Civil Service Commission (CSC) when discussing the period from 1908 to 1967 and Public Service Commission (PSC) when discussing the post-1967 period or when referring to the commission generally across historical periods.

[3]   Ezra Suleiman (2003), *Dismantling Democratic States*, Princeton, Princeton University Press, 2.

[4]   Quoted in Peter Hennessy (1989), *Whitehall*, London, Fontana, 38.

[5]   Patricia Wallace Ingraham (1995), *The Foundation of Merit: Public Service in American Democracy*, Baltimore, The Johns Hopkins University Press, 25–27.

6   John Halligan (2003), "Anglo-American Civil Service Systems: Comparative Perspectives," in John Halligan (ed.), *Civil Service Systems in Anglo-American Countries*, Cheltenham, Edward Elgar, 196–197.

7   Robert Best (1982), "The Meaning of Merit," in Robert F. Adie and Paul G. Thomas, *Canadian Public Administration: Problematical Perspectives*, Toronto, Prentice Hall, 183–222; and Hugh Heclo (2000), "The Future of Merit," in James P. Pfiffner and Douglas A Brook (eds.), *The Future of Merit: Twenty Years After the Civil Service Reform Act*, Baltimore, The Johns Hopkins University Press, 226–238.

8   Patricia Wallace Ingraham (1995), *The Foundation of Merit: Public Service in American Democracy*, Baltimore, The Johns Hopkins University Press, xvii.

9   Ezra Suleiman (2003), *Dismantling Democratic States*, Princeton, Princeton University Press, especially 209–278. See also B. Guy Peters and Jon Pierre (eds.) (2004), *Politicization of the Civil Service in Comparative Perspective: The Quest for Control*, London, Routledge.

10 Patricia Wallace Ingraham (2006), "Building Bridges over Troubled Waters: Merit as a Guide," *Public Administration Review*, July/August, 487.

11 C. E. S. Franks and J. E. Hodgetts (2001), *Parliament and Human Resources Management: The Role of the Public Service Commission as an Agent of Parliament*, Ottawa, Canadian Centre for Management Development, December 14, unpublished manuscript, 8.

CHAPTER

THE ORIGINS OF
THE PUBLIC SERVICE
COMMISSION:
1867–1918

It would have been much wiser to have framed the measure so as to give the members of the Civil Service Commission absolutely independent status similar to that enjoyed by the Auditor General.

Robert Borden, *Debates*, June 29, 1908

I would also point out that these commissioners are to be appointed as though they were judges.

Sidney Fisher, *Debates*, June 29, 1908

There shall be a Commission, to be called the Civil Service Commission consisting of two members appointed by the Governor-in-Council. The rank, standing and salary of each commissioner shall be those of a deputy head of a department; and each commissioner shall hold office during good behaviour, but shall be removable by the Governor General on address of the Senate and House of Commons.

Civil Service Amendment Act, September 1, 1908

The Public Service Commission today is the legitimate heir to the civil service reform movement of the 19th century, which dedicated its efforts to creating an independent public service that would improve the quality, fairness and morality of government by eliminating the patronage and associated corruption that had plagued the public service since Confederation.[1]

Reformers at the time felt that the best way to bring about positive reform was to create a public service staffed on the basis of merit as determined through a process of competitive examination. Such a reform would enhance efficiency by ensuring that only the competent would be appointed, and it would enhance equity by making sure that all Canadians had fair and reasonable access to public employment. Moreover, by largely removing staffing from the purview of politicians, the introduction of the merit principle would also enable public servants to play a legitimate constitutional role in providing the Crown with honest, fearless and confidential advice.

It is worth noting at the outset that those advocating reform were not of a single mind and that they were often promoting different aspects of the reform agenda. Some were more concerned about morality and patronage. Others mostly wanted to bring about a more professional and managerially efficient public service. Some cared primarily about fairness in public employment and wanted to see a public service that was open to all Canadians. Still others wanted to have the public service play a more effective role as a neutral and non-partisan adviser to the Crown and focused on the idea of creating a new independent public service that would have professional autonomy to serve the nation as a whole, rather than any particular group or political party. Yet the concerns and arguments of all reformers culminated in the same solution: an independent commission that would appoint individuals to the public service after a process of examination.

When the reforms eventually occurred in 1908, they resulted in the establishment of a Civil Service Commission (CSC) that had to engage in a complex balancing act to keep its various objectives in play. The CSC had to balance a desire for a more professional and managerially effective public service, the need to ensure greater fairness in staffing to account for geographical and linguistic differences and the wish to protect the constitutional conventions of neutrality and anonymity, which had been weakly observed by politicians in the past. While the term "merit" would often be used as a shorthand for a new method to staff the public service, the principle was never easily defined and it was often an amalgam of conflicting values and objectives embodied in the reforms.

In fact, once the CSC was established, it would become clear just how flexible, or multi-faceted, the definition of merit would need to be to allow the new CSC to reconcile its competing objectives. And in pursuing this balancing act, the CSC would also have to play, and use to its own advantage, its ambiguous institutional role as both an executive and a parliamentary agency in order to keep both parliamentarians and Cabinet engaged with, but not in control of, staffing in the public service. This chapter will examine the origins of this defining balancing act by exploring the nature of the arguments used to create the original commission and will take a look at how, in the early years directly after 1908, the CSC struggled with limited authority and jurisdiction.

THE INTELLECTUAL FOUNDATION OF THE CIVIL SERVICE COMMISSION

What stood in the way of the reform of the public service for the first forty years of Canadian history was the self-interest of the political parties, which did not want to relinquish their power to appoint partisans to the public service. Adding legitimacy to this purely partisan argument was the fact that an independent CSC would require Cabinet, and the Prime Minister, to abandon prerogative powers that supported patronage appointments. In Canada, since Confederation, it had been generally understood and accepted that, once appointed, public servants should not use their office for directly partisan purposes, but the method of appointment had always raised concerns about their ability or willingness to abide by this standard of behaviour. Given also that pensions were not guaranteed but required the support of Cabinet upon retirement, the neutrality of the public service was an open question. As though to prove the point, there were numerous scandals in the late 19th and early 20th centuries surrounding public servants who had provided untendered contracts to firms connected with the party in power at the time, purchased supplies at above-market values and acted to ensure that those in the private sector contributing to election funds received favourable treatment. While it had been an established principle, before and after Confederation, that active political partisanship on the part of a civil servant would constitute official misconduct leading to dismissal, instances of such partisanship were rarely acted upon by the party in power.[2]

As with many other ideas in good standing in Canada in the 19th century, concepts of administrative reform were imported from Britain. In particular, the ideas were taken from the renowned Northcote-Trevelyan report of 1855, which was referred to endlessly in Canadian debates about reform and was even appended in its entirety to one 19th century inquiry. The central concepts of the Northcote-Trevelyan inquiry were open competitive examination and selection and promotion by merit. The language of the report doubtless seemed like a manifesto for a rising middle class: it spoke of meritocracy and technocracy, and it was flattering to the ethic of self-made urban professionalism and hard work.[3] Armed with a body of ideas legitimated in the mother country, a growing group of reformers, both inside and outside government, began to agitate for the establishment of an independent CSC that would conduct examinations to serve as the basis of appointment.

While political parties were obviously self-interested when it came to the issue of patronage appointment, the practice did have some legitimacy, making it more difficult to abandon. During much of this period, the prevailing view was that appointment to the public service was a legitimate part of the Crown prerogative. With the advent of responsible government in 1848, Canada's political elite and much of the administrative elite had comfortably accepted the idea that staffing the public service through the practice of ministerial nomination was simply part of a comprehensive theory of the sovereignty of the Crown. In fact, the idea of an independent CSC was seen by many within government as something that would be constitutionally illegitimate and a violation of the tenets of responsible government. The practice was described in an 1882 royal commission on the civil service in the following manner:

> In the spirit and practice of the English constitution, the Crown
> is the fountain of all appointments, and among the duties and
> responsibilities of its advisers stand the proper and responsible
> selection of servants of the State. If it be, at times, expedient for
> Constitutional Government to institute Commissions to investigate,

it is repugnant to them to devolve on such bodies, the duties of governing and administering, for which appointment and promotions form an essential part.[4]

This simple statement captures in essence the problems confronted by those who were advocating the creation of an independent CSC. The existing constitutional model justified patronage in terms of the Crown prerogative, making patronage more than just a synonym of corruption. It was a constitutionally legitimate form of action for the executive to engage in. This interpretation of Crown privilege was used to keep the idea of an independent CSC illegitimate. An independent organization would violate both the Crown prerogative as well as the conventions surrounding ministerial responsibility, including the need for ministers to be able to report to Parliament on the conduct of the affairs of their departments, specifically in regard to the manner in which individuals were appointed. This situation

was only possible if the government could freely place its own appointments within the administrative system. In this view, the Minister being responsible for the effectiveness of his department would ensure that the most capable person would be placed in the leading posts.[5]

Lending weight to the practice of ministerial nomination was the manner in which the leaders of Canada's political parties acquired the power of the colonial governors: they claimed "that Canada's monarchical constitution validated their comprehensive exploitation of the public service and manipulation of the electoral system."[6] Before the achievement of responsible government, the entire patronage of Upper and Lower Canada was in the hands of the Governor General and his appointed council, and in both colonies powerful networks of local notables were built up by patronage distribution.[7] After responsible government, and then with the achievement of Confederation, Cabinet and more particularly the Prime Minister, began to exercise such Crown prerogatives:

> Macdonald took over the powers exercised by the governors since 1791 and appointed only his party's supporters to posts throughout the public service. He even evolved a constitutional justification for such a thoroughgoing deployment of patronage for party purposes. 'By constitutional practice,' he insisted, 'appointments are vested in the Crown and the whole responsibility of appointments rests with the ministry of the day.'[8]

It should be emphasized that this model regarded the use of the Crown prerogative in this manner as an effective check on democracy, and as a means of enhancing executive authority and bringing about political stability.[9] Of course, it is well known that this privilege was used mostly to help build strong political parties.

At first, the concerns around efficiency that emerged from a patronage bureaucracy were not great, because the early bureaucracy had few responsibilities and little impact on the lives of most Canadians. Indeed, the problems of a bureaucracy staffed exclusively on the basis of patronage only began to present themselves in Britain in the mid-19th century, when that country was experiencing rapid industrial growth.[10] The general response to the problem of bureaucracy that emerged in Britain was to subsume a non-partisan, merit-based public service under the institutions of representative and responsible government. Such a model would be based on a separation between the political party and the public service, a separation of policy and administration and a belief that public servants should loyally execute public policy regardless of personal belief. In short, just as the monarchy moved above the political party, the civil service was to find its new constitutional position below the political party.[11] Just as the Crown had no political positions, the new civil service would have complete neutrality. This new model was part of the establishment of a constitutional monarchy that required

> an unpolitical civil service whose primary connection is with the Crown, and which while subordinated to party government, is unaffected by their changes: the two permanent elements, the Crown and the civil service, which not by chance together left the political arena, supply the framework for the free play of parliamentary politics and governments.[12]

In this interpretation, the public service was no longer a part of a unified executive but served each successive government. To fully realize this vision, a body that would select the new neutral public servants would be essential. Once established, the CSC, according to its advocates, would create a constitutional public service that would become a technical instrument of representative and responsible institutions serving the impartial interests of the Crown and advising and, in some cases, instructing a succession of governments.

A PROFESSIONAL PUBLIC SERVICE: EFFICIENT, REPRESENTATIVE AND NEUTRAL

Arguments favouring an independent CSC began to develop shortly after Confederation, when the first in a series of royal commissions was called to investigate the public service.[13] John Langton, Canada's first auditor general, was asked to "inquire into and report upon the organization of the several branches of the Public Service with a special view to their adaptation to the wants of the new Constitution, and to providing for their efficient and economical performance."[14] The Langton inquiry did not pay much heed to patronage; it was more concerned with creating an effective administrative organization regardless of the method of appointment. This lack of connection between efficiency and patronage is probably explained by the fact that the civil service at the time employed only 250 people in Ottawa and a few thousand others spread out across the rest of Canada.

The absence of any discussion of patronage cannot, however, be seen as an endorsement of patronage by the Langton royal commissioners. Rather, they saw administration as an activity that should be considered separate from politics, and for that reason they wanted to make public administration more efficient by ensuring that the partisans who were appointed were capable of handling the non-political nature of the majority of their tasks. Their concern was therefore directed almost exclusively at eliminating conditions relating to the personnel function that were deterring "young men, who were conscious of energy and ability, from adopting the public service as a profession."[15] In trying to create a strong administrative "cadre," the commissioners felt that steps would have to be taken to ensure that the best young men were recruited, justly rewarded and assured of a fair system of promotion based on merit.

For these early reformers, the emphasis was on the very basic desire to improve the personnel function of the public service. Principally, the commissioners believed strongly that "only young men should be appointed to the service, that they should enter it in the lowest grade, and that before being appointed they should undergo the ordeal of a rigid examination, and also at every step they take upwards."[16] They also hoped to avoid corruption by paying decent salaries. They wanted responsibility rewarded with salary and, of course, they advocated the possibility of an assured pension. If efficiency was to be increased by attracting talented young men and rewarding them fairly, the next logical step was to disencumber "the service from men, who from age and infirmity are no longer efficient for the performance of their duties."[17] The commissioners also advocated a rational system of promotion based on a combination of ability and seniority. While they avoided identifying patronage as the cause of any of the ills afflicting the post-Confederation public service, it seems safe to conclude that this practice was never far from their minds. The central point in many of their recommendations was that the whole efficiency of the service depended upon a rigid adherence to the rules of advancement and promotion.

Immediately after Confederation, we see the beginnings of the assault on patronage. Two different arguments were put forward, both of which would become part of the legacy of the CSC once it was established. First, patronage needed to be replaced because it was unfair and contradicted a central liberal belief that a man should have the opportunity to succeed or fail according to his own abilities. Second, patronage was wrong because it was inefficient.[18] In the context of these early reforms, the public service was considered part of the broader political community; it therefore needed to be organized according to principles that reflected and represented the best of that community. By attempting to make the public service more efficient, by definition reformers were hoping to make it more independent, autonomous and representative. Patronage, then, was both unfair and inefficient. This notion, that the political must be separated from administration, would find its first forceful champion in the person of a Conservative member of Parliament named George Casey.

GEORGE ELLIOT CASEY: AN INDEPENDENT PUBLIC SERVICE FOR CANADA

In the 1870s, George Elliot Casey, a Conservative MP from southern Ontario, was probably one of the first prominent figures in Canada to champion the creation of a CSC based on the need for an administratively efficient public service with autonomy from government. Casey's involvement in the reform movement started almost two years prior to the establishment of the parliamentary inquiry he was to head. Casey had begun "an intelligent and persistent agitation to improve the service along the lines adopted in Great Britain."[19] As a result of his intense activity, a select committee was appointed with him as its head.[20] Casey, along with a growing number of Canadians, regarded the public service as a necessary and vital part of the governmental system that needed to be established on a sound and rational basis of administrative practice. As a strong advocate of the ideas contained in the Northcote-Trevelyan report, Casey was convinced that "no matter how excellent might be the Government of the day, or how wise its administrative acts, it might be spoiled by the faults of the Civil Service."[21] This view would remain at the core of the arguments in favour of an independent public service.

Reformers were now beginning to take dead aim at patronage. For Casey, and the reform movement in general, the public service was imperilled because political nomination did not provide the necessary checks on the quality of the civil servants appointed. Therefore, patronage "was apt to lead to the establishment of what was sometimes called a bureaucracy, or a sort of family compact among the civil servants."[22]

Recognizing the difficulty of persuading party politicians to give up their patronage power on moral grounds alone, Casey's committee proceeded to point out that politics and administration were two separate fields of activity that naturally operated according to different principles. This was perhaps the most convincing of the arguments favouring an independent public service commission. The committee made one of the earliest and most powerful arguments in favour of a separate realm of public administration:

> As general principle appointments, promotions, and the whole management of the Service should be separated as far as possible from political considerations. The Service should be looked upon merely as an organization for conducting the public business, and not as a means of rewarding personal political friends. The attempt should be made to render it a *profession* calculated to attract the best ability available, and to afford a due reward for the possession and exercise of first-class business and administrative capacity.[23]

At the time, patronage made the public service unattractive "to the class of active and intelligent young men who should be obtained for it," and it was not always "able to retain such of that class that do enter."[24] In order to remedy this situation, Casey's committee followed the lead of the Langton inquiry of 1869 and recommended competitive examinations guided by a board of examiners as the first step toward improving the image and quality of the civil service. For the public service to become a respectable middle-class employer, it would first have to free itself from the clutches of self-interested politicians. One deputy minister summed up this concern succinctly in his testimony before the committee: "I should not like to put one of my sons into the Civil Service if I could put him into a profession."[25] When the civil service had become a respectable middle-class profession, a major goal of the reformers would have been met.

To achieve this separation, the Casey committee's chief recommendations were to place the practice of making appointments entirely in the hands of an independent commission, subject applicants to an examination before appointment (although only a qualifying, not a competitive, one), and have them serve a period of probation before their final appointment. The committee also accepted a form of divided service, recommending that it

> would be advisable to grade the service in departments where the nature of the work will permit, in such a manner as to separate the mechanical from the higher duties, and to confine promotion in rank to the class of officers engaged in the performance of the latter.[26]

Promotion in the two grades "should proceed prima facie on the grounds of seniority unless a junior be reported as better qualified for the position, with full reasons for such report."[27] The fact that all these reforms had long been in force in Great Britain, and that they had continued in force under successive governments, was, as far as the committee was concerned, proof of their effectiveness in "purifying" the administrative world.[28]

No new legislation was to emerge from any of this committee's recommendations. This is not surprising, since it was merely a select committee that had spent only one month preparing its report. Yet whatever its shortcomings, the investigation had a positive impact in that it helped spread the idea that an independent CSC was essential to creating a separate sphere of professional public administration. This idea would not disappear; rather it would grow in the years to come, eventually forcing the political parties into relinquishing patronage, if not in the name of democracy then at least for the good of democracy.

FIRST VICTORY IN 1882: A BOARD OF CIVIL SERVICE EXAMINERS

The reform movement gained its first substantial victory in 1882 on the heels of the McInnis Royal Commission.[29] Membership for this commission was drawn mostly from the senior civil service, with the exception of its chairman, Senator D. McInnis. The commissioners "traveled over the Dominion, heard a host of witnesses, asked them more than three thousand questions, received delegations from the lower ranks of employees, investigated the British and American civil services and produced a comprehensive study of superannuation."[30] When it was over, Canada would have a new *Civil Service Act* and, more importantly, an established pattern of administrative reform that would, with a few interruptions, continue to accelerate until 1908.

The McInnis Commission began its report strongly endorsing the reforms that had taken place a decade earlier in Britain. Although they expressed certain doubts "as to whether the public opinion of the Dominion is even now fully alive to the importance of a thoroughly efficient Civil Service,"[31] the commissioners felt there was "nevertheless a feeling in the public mind that the interest of the public service had been subordinated to a greater or less extent to the purposes of political parties."[32] They were of the opinion that politicians, once they realized "how much the prosperity and welfare of the country depends on a pure and efficient Civil Service, will not hesitate to abandon a patronage which is found to be injurious to the best interests of the country."[33] Their optimistic faith in the responsibility of politicians, and the influence of an abstract "public interest," would remain largely unrewarded, and the political parties would continue to make no distinction between their partisan interests and the national interest with regard to the civil service.

While rejecting the division of the service into the British two-tier model, the McInnis Commission did strongly encourage the adoption of the other two main components of the British system: open competitive examinations and promotion by merit. The attractiveness of these features was to be found in their ability to separate politics from administration, creating a neutral bureaucratic apparatus. As the commissioners suggested,

> Men who had obtained their places by merit alone and as the result of impartial examination could not possibly be open to any imputation of political partisanship in office; nor would they be in any degree influenced in the discharge of their duties by political considerations."[34]

From this time forward, merit and impartial competitive examination would become the tools reformers used to "purify" the administrative apparatus, separating it from political control. In short, merit and impartial competitive examination were enshrined as the first new values of a responsible public service and would be the major responsibilities of a CSC when it was established 1908.

The commissioners had great faith in merit and examination as a means of creating an impartial civil service; they also argued that they be used to determine promotions. In the commissioners' view, promotion by examination was almost as important as entrance examinations, because

> the efficiency of the Service so largely depends on a good system of promotion, that we have felt it necessary to emphasize the importance

of avoiding such injustice as we have mentioned, and which can not fail to be injurious to the best interests of the Service. Men whose just claims are thus passed over become discouraged, they lose their self-respect and hope for the future. Such injustice destroys all incentive to emulation and all desire to excel. Nor does the mischief end there. It affects the whole Service. It is destructive for discipline, and it impairs the usefulness of those who witness as well as of those who suffer it.[35]

According to this view, all subjective assessments of a candidate's worth had to be eliminated from the personnel function. Open competitive exams, promotion by merit, and the resulting conventions of neutrality and non-partisanship would combine to remedy the problems plaguing the public service by replacing the subjectivity of patronage with the fairness and democratic egalitarianism of merit. These reforms would also aid in the creation of a more dignified civil service by moving the civil service toward professional status. As the commissioners argued

The public service would, under such a system, be open to the public instead of being, to a large extent, a closed corporation in the hands of political parties. An opportunity would be given to all intelligent and educated young men to obtain by their merits alone, a start in a service in which promotion, by a continuance of intelligent self-improvement and well directed official labour, would be certain.[36]

Again, the key element in bringing all these important innovations to fruition was to be found in the establishment of a CSC that was as free from political influence as the "judiciary happily is." Although the first *Civil Service Act* (1868) had created a Board of Civil Service Examiners, it was easily ignored by ministers, and when it was in fact used it provided an examination so rudimentary that only the completely illiterate failed. The board contemplated by the McInnis Commission, which was eventually established, was to be a precursor to the CSC. It was to provide the public service with a system of competitive examination conducted all across the Dominion that would rigorously test every candidate's character for both intellectual and moral qualities. The establishment of this new Board of Civil Service Examiners would clearly be the first victory and the first real institutional innovation toward the development of a truly independent Civil Service Commission.

Many of the McInnis Commission's recommendations were accepted and appeared in a new *Civil Service Act* (1882), Canada's second to date. The act created the Board of Examiners, which was independent of party control; it limited the age of new employees to those between eighteen and thirty-five; it began the slow process of formally recognizing the deputy head as the administrative head of the department and it authorized appointment to the civil service only after an examination. Unfortunately, this act applied only to the Inside Service, that is, the Ottawa-based public service, and was regarded by politicians, in the words of John A. Macdonald, as merely a means "to provide that men should write in a good hand, should know the principles of arithmetic and possess a good common school education."[37] It was clearly not intended to eliminate patronage, at least from the Prime Minister's point of view.

While the act was largely ignored after its passage, it nevertheless provided a solid basis for the development of the Civil Service Commission. Primarily, it brought a subtle change to the relationship between the public service and the other institutions of government. The public service was slowly gaining increased independence from the older institutions at the same time as it was gaining increased responsibilities. The civil service was coming to be regarded by a growing number of politicians and intellectuals as an administrative means to political ends. In addition, it was beginning to be seen as an important tool in the further development of a national interest, a view that ran up against the prevailing belief in the rightful dominance of vested interests. In the end, the most concrete result of the passing of the *Civil Service Act* in 1882 was the creation of the Board of Civil Service Examiners, the precursor of the CSC that would conduct qualifying examinations and limited promotion examinations. Despite objections on many fronts, the assault on the strictly political model of civil service appointment was gaining momentum.

Scandal and Corruption: The Path to Reform

One of the arguments for creating a CSC was the need to eliminate the ever-present corruption created by patronage. As something that forced politicians to act, the issue of scandal and corruption would prove to be central; indeed, it resulted in another 19th century royal commission ten years after the McInnis Commission.[38] The new royal commission, chaired by George Hague, general manager of the Merchants Bank of Canada, was appointed, all too typically, because "certain officials had been guilty of serious breeches of trust; some had altered accounts, others had accepted bribes; the Government had been defrauded in goods it had bought due to corrupt civil servants."[39] When the burden of scandal proved to be too much for Prime Minister John Abbott to withstand, he met opposition demands for action with the nomination of the Hague Commission.

The Hague Commission's origin in scandal explains the strong emphasis that it placed on developing a sense of the national interest at stake in the debate about how the civil service should be organized and how it should operate. This would be an enduring theme among those advocating for a more powerful public service. In testimony to the commission, Auditor General J. L. McDougal commented that

> the continuance of the notion that the management of public business is the management of what belongs to the Government of the day and not to all the taxpayers of the country

is the biggest defect in the civil service.[40] For McDougal, the first step in creating a public service operating in the public interest was to increase the amount of deputy control; in fact, he felt that the deputy should have "absolute control of every man in the department."[41]

McDougal's point was emphasized by most of the deputies who gave expert testimony. A few senior civil servants expressed their belief that "if the deputy-heads were too independent of the political heads, they would rule the country without being responsible to the House."[42]

But in the end, most agreed with Alexander Burgess, deputy minister of the Interior, that the

> permanent head of a department should be in a position to exercise the functions of his office fearlessly and independently, which he in many instances might not be able to do if his tenure of office were dependent upon the favour of the Government.[43]

A fearless and independent deputy was the first major step towards the ultimate goal of a fearless and independent civil service capable of working in the public interest.

Deputies were clearly interested in acquiring the authority they needed to fulfill their obligations, and deputies were trying to establish an equal but separate relationship with ministers. Deputies wanted to be supreme in administrative matters, with politicians supreme in political matters. In their testimonies, deputies went to great lengths to describe what they thought would be the ideal relationship between themselves and their ministers.

> In countries such as Great Britain where responsible Government has developed into its highest form, the position is this, that while the head of the department directs the policy thereof, the deputy head, subject to such policy, directs its administration.[44]

In Canada, however, the minister was deemed to have excessive control over the details of administration. Such ministerial involvement had the advantage of bringing the administration of public business to Parliament, but for the royal commissioners, it tended "to bring the administration of public affairs somewhat too closely into contact with politics."[45]

This latter view was perhaps best expressed by William LeSueur, an early public servant/reformer who contended that the duty of a deputy minister

> is to furnish his Minister with full and accurate information upon all departmental questions which the Minister may be called upon

> to decide, and to advise the Minister in the public interest. His
> function is not to suggest to the Minister ways and means of turning
> this or that contingency to political account, nor to cover with his
> recommendation things which are advisable solely in a political
> sense.[46]

In short, the deputy was to be completely neutral, like the public service
as a whole. A classic bureaucrat and a classic bureaucracy were to serve as
the norm. "A public servant should not be required to navigate political
shallows, or take political soundings: his business one would suppose,
should be to steer a simple course in the safe waters of public duty."[47]
The desire was for a public service commanded by a deputy minister
who would ensure that it promoted the interest of the nation in an
impartial and efficient manner.

Rather than submitting a long list of recommendations that
might guide the government in pursuing a more rationally organized
civil service, the Hague commissioners chose to submit a draft bill. Its
principle recommendations were the appointment of a Civil Service
Commission to replace the existing Board of Civil Service Examiners,
the adoption of the principle of appointment by open competition
rather than the existing qualifying examination and the clarification of
the role of the deputy as administrative head of the department.[48]

The commissioners admitted that public opinion in Canada might
"not as yet be ripe for open competition." Nonetheless, they firmly
believed that their recommendations would improve the quality of the
civil service. As they put it,

> Doors to appointments and promotions in the service will open only
> to capacity and honesty, and no man or woman who aspires, as all
> have a right to aspire, to any such position, will have occasion to seek
> or use any influence less honourable than his or her own merit and
> fitness for office."[49]

The dignity of the civil service would be improved, and so would that
of the people in it, knowing that their success or failure was related to
their own character, ability and capacity. By championing more rational

methods of selecting and promoting civil servants, the commissioners were also reflecting a changed relationship between individual effort and subsequent success in the job market. Merit in this sense is a classic liberal principle in that it makes people responsible for their own success or failure.[50] Access to positions in the civil service was on the way to becoming a right available to all Canadians with the necessary qualifications. Formal recognition of this right, even in a limited sense, was another fifteen years away, but the ideas paving the way forward were now, at the end of the 19th century, largely in place.

BORDEN, LAURIER AND THE CIVIL SERVICE COMMISSION OF CANADA: 1908

Beginning in the early 1900s, there was a growing sense of frustration among many MPs and, increasingly, among the general public, including many in the business community. Most would have sympathized with John Willison, Wilfrid Laurier's first biographer, who observed that "there is surely a crying need for reform of the Civil Service in Canada and the protection of honest and efficient public officers from the spoils element which corrupts and bedevils the administration of public affairs."[51] This was unquestionably the predominant attitude among most reformers by the early 1900s. The public service was being harassed by selfish, ignorant and short-sighted politicians. What was called for was the complete reform of the personnel system, which would strengthen the hand of the public service through an emphasis on utility and meritocracy, thereby protecting the true guardians of the public interest. Most reformers now sought a new *Civil Service Act* that would "take every place from top to bottom out of the hands of the politicians who, both at Ottawa and Toronto, have shown themselves so unworthy of being trusted with the power."[52] The goal was to free the bureaucracy from the grasp of rapacious politicians, and that required strengthening the public service. Such reform would have to take place even if it meant weakening a fundamental pillar of responsible government: ministerial responsibility to Parliament. Indeed, the creation of the Civil Service Commission implied, and indeed required, that Cabinet relinquish some executive control and that Parliament accept less than complete accountability. Such were the feelings surrounding the need for strong action that, when the time came to debate the proposed legislation, neither Cabinet nor Parliament balked at the idea of losing some of their authority. Indeed, in the debates about the legislation for a new *Civil Service Act*, Conservative Party leader Robert Borden noted that "it would have been much wiser to have framed the measure so as to give the members of the Civil Service Commission an absolutely independent status similar to that enjoyed by the Auditor General."[53] Yet it was clear that the commissioners would be granted a great deal of autonomy and independence, which, while not always used by some of the early commissioners, turned out to be an essential feature of the Public Service Commission as we know it today.

There was a willingness to accept independence for the CSC, because Canadians were becoming more comfortable with growth in government activity. Supporters of this view included the Conservative Party, which was an early proponent of increased government ownership. There was recognition that development of an industrial infrastructure demanded "expert knowledge and technical efficiency of the highest order, with a force trained and organized to handle such intricate questions."[54] The acceptance of a growing state made efficient by the widespread use of experts may be taken as a modern example of the Canadian willingness to use the state to provide direction and assistance to the limited industrial economy that existed at the time. Whatever the reasons, there was a growing consensus that the public service needed to be increasingly independent and that this independence was related to the CSC's independence. The accumulation of public business was a natural and progressive state of affairs; the reforms were simply intended to handle public business more effectively. Thus, public service reform was motivated not only by a sense of moral outrage but also by economic interests, by the business community, which wanted the public service to be better able to manage the economy in the interests of business.[55] There was a general belief that Canadian governments, at all levels, were incompetent and inefficient, that the public was by and large ignorant, and that there was thus a need for a new force that could deal effectively with the various problems facing the state.[56]

Reform would eventually come at the end of a two-year parliamentary session between 1906 and 1908 in which the Liberal government of Wilfrid Laurier had come under constant attack from a Conservative opposition hoping to expose the corruption in the ongoing administration of the government at the time and its inability to move forward. There were of course new demands for new social and economic policies, but both parties were hesitant to act, partly due to the inadequacy of the machinery of administration at the time. But Borden had decided to put the full weight of his party into a new tactic aimed at discrediting the Laurier government.[57] The Conservatives ran a "purity in politics" campaign and continued it throughout the remaining session of Parliament until the general election at the end of October 1908. Of this time, one contemporary observer noted that "it was a stormy Session and filled with angry debate and prolonged discussion and personal charges; it was a scandal Session teeming with Opposition allegations of corruption and maladministration."[58]

This session summed up what had become clear to most Canadians: the public service was corrupt and ineffective due to patronage appointment. The Liberal Party, like the Conservatives before them, had lots of supporters continually clamouring for jobs and private firms expecting rewards for their donations. One of Laurier's early biographers noted that the governing party would not only fill all the postmaster, excise officer and other jobs but participate in activities well beyond: "Supplies must be bought from firms on the patronage list, subsidy hunters, contracts seekers found the way smoother if they subscribed to campaign funds."[59] Indeed the distribution of patronage, broadly defined, had arguably become the most important function of government. It was noted at the time,

> Sir Wilfrid frequently repeated the story of Lincoln, asked during a crisis in the Civil War whether it was a change in the army command or complications with foreign powers that wrinkled his forehead, and replying, "No it is that confounded postmastership at Brownsville, Ohio." No other subject bulked so large in correspondence; no other purpose brought so many visitors to Ottawa. It meant endless bombardment of ministers, ceaseless efforts to secure a work from

the friend of a friend of the premier, bitter disappointment for the ninety and nine who were turned away.[60]

The move to end this system began in 1907 under relentless pressure from the opposition because of the scandals. The Laurier government eliminated all patronage lists for suppliers. An Order-in-Council was passed requiring that timber licences be granted only at public auction and a new *Elections Act* forbid companies from contributing campaign funds and set heavy fines for ballot tampering.

The presence of an increasing number of reform constituencies, demands for more public policy, growing industrialization, immigration, urbanization and ongoing scandals had forced the government's hand beyond its earlier limited reforms. A royal commission was established to investigate the civil service and was headed by John Courtney, the deputy minister of finance.[61] The Courtney Commission was to be the most thorough inquiry to date, lasting ten months, and hearing over 200 officials and publishing 1,900 pages of evidence and appendixes. Strongly dissenting from the Laurier government's view that the civil service was satisfactory, it instead recommended the complete repeal of the existing *Civil Service Act*. It stated what nearly everybody knew: that patronage was alive and well in the civil service and that the 1882 act had done little or nothing to get rid of it.

The Courtney Commission noted the litany of abuses that the previous inquiries had observed and made many of the same recommendations. The most far-reaching were as follows:

> The service should be entirely free from political favouritism or patronage; that appointments should only be made by merit after competitive examination; and that for that purpose, a permanent Commission of three officials should be created to deal with the question of the service; that this Commission should be entrusted with all examinations in connection with the service; that they should cause different examinations to be made in the different subjects required by the several classes employed in the Civil Service.[62]

Like the previous inquiries, the Courtney Commission did not want to develop a two-tier system in the civil service but rather felt that every position should be open to talent. It emphasized that

> the principle should never be lost sight of that promotion and pay
> should in every case depend on individual merit, and that, therefore,
> every individual in the service should, as it were, be under continual
> appraisement and be eligible for promotion to any position in any
> division of the service.[63]

It wanted to make the civil service a career open to talent and representative of the best in Canada.

> When a young man of great efficiency, who gives indication of force
> of character, appears it is surely to the advantage of the country
> that it should get the full benefit of his capacity as soon as possible.
> To secure this he should have swift promotion instead of having
> obstacles thrown in his course by narrow official regulations and
> limitations.[64]

Despite these arguments, the act that eventually did emerge divided the Inside Service in Ottawa into two broad categories, reflecting perhaps the executives' awareness of the political nature of the senior civil service.

Despite recognizing the importance of the formal institutions of government in the creation of administrative responsibility, the Courtney Commission would focus most of its effort on reforming the civil service and not the overhead institutions. The guiding assumption in the other inquiries had been that Parliament was strong enough to withstand a weakening of the convention of ministerial responsibility, especially since this convention had led to the rampant abuse of the civil service for strictly partisan purposes. Like all the other inquiries, the Courtney Commission was most interested in creating an accountable administration, not more parliamentary oversight. It believed that strengthening the civil service and strengthening Cabinet control would result in responsible administration.

The passage of civil service reform legislation took place in the lead-up to a federal election that was held on October 28, 1908, which the Liberal party won again, although with a reduced majority. Even though the election was fought on the Liberal party's substantial record of scandal and Borden campaigned aggressively on clean government and a commitment to greater public ownership, the Liberals still prevailed. Once the election was concluded, not surprisingly the government went on to other matters and lost interest in reform of the public service. But the CSC was created and it did begin its work to improve the quality and professionalism of the public service of Canada, albeit with limited jurisdiction for the Inside Service located in Ottawa. The CSC that was created had a strong legislative basis with substantial autonomy, but it would quickly begin to find out how difficult it was in practice to ensure that patronage appointments did not occur even in the Ottawa public service, let alone in the service outside Ottawa, over which it had no jurisdiction. The CSC was at least potentially powerful, however, in that its strong statutory basis and independence and autonomy would help shield the CSC from its detractors and allow it to create a strong, effective public service in the years to come.

THE EARLY CIVIL SERVICE COMMISSION: 1908–1918

From September 1, 1908, when it was created, until 1918, when its jurisdiction was extended to cover the entire public service, the CSC faced numerous challenges, including regular challenges to its legitimacy and jurisdiction. During this initial period, it consisted of two commissioners appointed by the Governor-in-Council at the rank and salary of a deputy head and a small staff not numbering more than eight. The Laurier government wanted to ensure that the CSC had sufficient status and made sure that those appointed to lead it would be equivalent to deputy heads. A further indication of the independent status of the commissioners was that they were not appointed at pleasure like deputy ministers, but rather were appointed during good behaviour for a fixed term. While they were appointed by the Prime Minister, they were removable only by the Governor General on the joint recommendation of the Senate and the House of Commons.

The creation of the two-person commission was also the first attempt to ensure that the CSC would embody the representative principle in its decision-making process. When introducing the legislation that established the CSC, the minister noted in the House of

Commons, "In this country we have people belonging to two different original races and that fact will be recognized in the appointment of the commissioners."[65] The act came into effect on September 1, 1908, the commissioners were appointed on September 4 and they began their work on September 16. One of the first two commissioners was Michel La Rochelle, a former secretary to Wilfred Laurier who had run as a Liberal candidate in Quebec and who, given that partisan connection, was not an ideal candidate.[66] The other commissioner was Adam Shortt, a well-respected Queen's University professor who had been a strong advocate of civil service reform in the run-up to the legislative changes of 1908. When the two commissioners took office, they inaugurated a stormy decade during which they defended merit appointment within the CSC's limited jurisdiction of the Ottawa-based public service. This two-person structure quickly proved to be problematic and was eventually replaced by a three-commissioner system with one of the commissioners designated as the chair and exercising most of the executive authority. The new three-person system had to wait, however, because when he became prime minister in 1911, Robert Borden chose to leave the old structure in place until Shortt left the Civil Service Commission to become head of the Historical Documents Branch of the National Archives in 1918.

Organizationally, the CSC began its life in 1908 by taking over the activities of the existing Board of Examiners, which had been established in 1882 under the *Civil Service Act*. The Board of Examiners had always been a testing agency whose mandate was to make sure that public servants were minimally literate and capable of the duties that they were to perform. The secretary to the Board of Examiners became the secretary to the CSC, the rest of the board's small staff transferred to the CSC, and they began to hold examinations in Ottawa for a small fee. The new CSC continued the work of the Board of Examiners holding certifying examinations for persons that departments wanted to appoint in the public service based outside Ottawa. But in 1908, a new practice was instituted: when a vacancy became available within the Ottawa-based public service, departments would indicate that they had a vacancy and the CSC would fill the vacancy from its list of successful examination candidates. This practice differed greatly from that in the United States, which had developed what was known as the rule of three, in which the Civil Service Commission would forward three names of qualified candidates to a department and that department would select one of the individuals. In Canada, the CSC was to be more authoritative in the matter of appointments.

The examinations that the CSC organized were, in the first instance, aimed at two classes of entrants. Those at the lower levels needed only to have a good high-school understanding of mathematics, spelling, history and so on, but those at the higher levels needed to meet a much higher academic standard. The examinations were an attempt to test both for the job at hand and the overall academic suitability of the candidate for a career in the public service.[67] In some of its special examinations, the CSC tested only for the specific job, but at the higher levels the CSC clearly attempted to identify those with an ability to progress in their career as a public servant. This approach contained, of course, a not-so-subtle class bias, somewhat like the British model, but it also contained, as would become clear, regional and language biases because of the underdeveloped nature of higher education in most provinces. These various biases were repeatedly criticized by MPs. While the CSC did respond with an attempt to make its examinations representative of the educational system across the entire country and not just the elite universities, the exams continued very much to reflect the Anglo-American tradition, making it difficult for those growing up in the more classic French system in Quebec to compete.

While the CSC that was established in 1908 was an important precedent, it was a limited victory and ministers and departments quickly reverted back to making political appointments, even in the Inside Service, believing that the CSC should function really as a certification agency and not as a central recruitment agency. The CSC's ability to establish itself was further hampered by the coming of the First World War in 1914. During the war, most hiring occurred with no restrictions. As before, across the entire public service, no certificates of qualification were issued, no general examinations were held and no time limits for temporary employment were imposed. The public service was in as much disarray by the end of hostilities in 1918 as it had been at any time in its past, and it was in need of another major jolt of reform.

CONCLUSION: THE CSC AND THE CAREER PUBLIC SERVICE IN CANADA

The CSC that emerged in 1908 was eventually to become an influential participant in the creation of the modern public service as a result of both its structure, which guaranteed its independence, and its desire to ensure that merit drove the recruitment process. Forever eliminated was the view of the public servant as a handmaiden of a political party. The new vision, accepted, endorsed and facilitated by the newly established CSC, was that the public service should become a neutral instrument, impartially serving the various interests of the state. The public service would become the preserve of, if not the virtuous, at least the competent. It would be a mistake, however, to see this triumph of the CSC as a mere accident of fate. Rather, it was largely the product of the strenuous efforts of modernizers, mainly senior public servants, university-based reformers and reform-minded members of Parliament, who saw the creation of a CSC as the precondition for turning public service into a respectable profession and ensuring that public servants would serve the nation as well as act as a valuable resource to a succession of partisan government leaders. While there were few explicit claims that the public service was now a constitutional entity, the fact that the public service was staffed on the democratic principles of fairness and equality, that it had acquired new behavioural requirements and obligations and that it was a statutory body gave the CSC some authority to oppose Cabinet when it came to protecting the public service's new constitutional position. The CSC would therefore be at the heart of the creation of a "constitutional bureaucracy" in Canada.[68] While the CSC would for decades expend efforts to bring about an efficient public service, in the end it would be its role in maintaining the constitutional conventions of public service neutrality and non-partisanship that would provide it with its legitimacy and its longevity. Public servants were acquiring a similar constitutional position as the Crown, and based on the conventions of anonymity and ministerial responsibility, public servants would increasingly be like the Crown—unable to do any wrong!

By securing its new position of neutrality, anonymity and increasing autonomy within Canada's system of government, the CSC freed the public service from the burden of partisan politics. Yet, ironically, the CSC's gift of autonomy to the public service would also give it a role in the policy process. As Professor Kenneth Kernaghan has noted more recently, "While efficient staffing of the service required the separation of politics from administration, the need for effective development and execution of public policy drew administrative officials into the political maelstrom."[69] Thanks to the CSC, the public service was becoming less a trough at which the parties fed and more a source of policy advice and initiatives, a phenomenon that would end up creating, curiously, one of the main problems for public servants in the future: "A civil service free of detailed political control, trained in a purely instrumental science of administration, and insulated from the political life of the community will not be non-political: but it will be politically irresponsible."[70] In attempting to make the public service more responsible by freeing it from patronage, the CSC would give the public service the opportunity to be irresponsible. As many of the critics of merit-based reform noted, patronage may indeed have had its faults but it did have one political virtue: it brought the public service in touch with the political community. Ensuring that the public service remained responsive to the wishes of Cabinet, but also to the needs of the political community more broadly defined, would become one of many balancing acts that that new CSC would be asked to perform.

ENDNOTES

1   R. MacGregor Dawson (1929), *The Civil Service of Canada*, London, Oxford University Press.

2   R. MacGregor Dawson (1922), *The Principle of Official Independence*, London, P.S. King and Son.

3   Peter Gowan (1987), "The Origin of the Administrative Elite," *New Left Review*, vol. 162:2, 18.

4   Canada, House of Commons (1882), *Sessional Papers*, No. 32, 87.

5   J.E. Hodgetts, et al. (1972), *The Biography of an Institution,* Montreal, McGill Queen's University Press, 14.

6   Gordon T. Stewart (1986), *The Origins of Canadian Politics: A Comparative Approach*, Vancouver, University of British Columbia Press, 82

7   Gordon T. Stewart (1986), "The Origins of Canadian Politics and John A. Macdonald," in R. Kenneth Carty and W. Peter Ward (eds.), *National Politics and Community in Canada,* Vancouver, University of British Columbia Press,15–47, 22.

8   Ibid, 41.

9   Peter Smith (1987), "The Ideological Origins of Canadian Confederation," *Canadian Journal of Political Science*, vol. 20:2, 2–29.

10   See Alan Ryan (1972), "Utilitarianism and Bureaucracy: The Views of J. S. Mill," in Gillian Sutherland (ed.), *Studies in the Growth of Nineteenth Century Government*, London, Routledge and Kegan Paul; see also Bernard Schaffer (1973), *The Administrative Factor*, London, Frank Cass.

11   John A. Rohr (2002), *Civil Servants and Their Constitutions*, Kansas, University of Kansas Press, 36.

12   Henry Parris (1968), "The Origins of the Permanent Civil Service, 1780–1830," *Public Administration*, vol. 46, 164.

13   First and Second Reports of the Commission to Inquire into the Present State and Probable Requirements of the Civil Service, see Canada, House of Commons (1869) *Sessional Papers*, No. 19. For the Final Report see *Sessional Papers* (1870), No. 64.

14   *Sessional Papers* (1869), No. 19, 4.

15   *Sessional Papers* (1869), No. 19, 5.

16   *Sessional Papers* (1870), No. 64, 11.

17   *Sessional Papers* (1869), No. 19, 6.

18   Doug Owram (1986), *The Government Generation*, Toronto, University of Toronto Press, 46.

19   Dawson, *Civil Service of Canada*, 38.

20   For the report of the Select Committee, see Canada, House of Commons (1877) *Journals*, Appendix No. 7.

21   *Debates*, March 15, 1875, 708.

22   Ibid, 710.

23   *Journals* (1877), Appendix No. 7, 5.

24   Ibid, 5.

25   Ibid, 98.

26   Ibid, 6.

27   Ibid, 6.

28   Ibid, 8.

29   For the First Report of the Royal Commission to Consider the Needs and Conditions of the Civil Service of the Dominion, see *Sessional Papers* (1881) No. 113; Second Report, see *Sessional Papers* (1882), No. 32.

30   Dawson, *The Civil Service of Canada*, 44.

31   *Sessional Papers* (1881), No. 113, 12.

32   Ibid, 13.

33   Ibid, 13.
34   Ibid, 20.
35   Ibid, 17.
36   Ibid, 20.
37   *Debates*, March 15, 1889, 673.
38   For the Report of the Royal Commission Appointed to Enquire into Certain Matters Relating to the Civil Service of Canada, see *Sessional Papers* (1892), No. 16c.
39   Dawson, *The Civil Service of Canada*, 61.
40   *Sessional Papers* (1892), No. 16c, 22
41   Ibid, 23.
42   Ibid, 46.
43   Ibid, 59.
44   Ibid, xx.
45   Ibid, xx.
46   Ibid, 627.
47   Ibid, 630.
48   Ibid, xxi.
49   Ibid, xxviii.
50   Cindy Sondik-Aron (1987), *Ladies and Gentlemen of the Civil Service: Middle Class Workers in Victorian America*, New York, Oxford University Press, 115.
51   John S. Willison (1907–1908), "Civil Service Reform in Canada," in J. C. Hopkins (ed.), *Empire Club Speeches*, 128.
52   John Marshall (1906), "Civil Service Reform," *Queen's Quarterly*, vol. 14, 159.
53   House of Commons, *Debates*, June 25, 1908, 11341.
54   C. A. Magrath (1913), "The Civil Service," *University Magazine*, vol. 12, 248.
55   Reg Whitaker (1987), "Between Patronage and Bureaucracy: Democratic Politics in Transition," *Journal of Canadian Studies*, vol. 22, 55–71.
56   Owram, 41.
57   Robert Craig Brown (1975), *Robert Laird Borden: A Biography Volume 1: 1854–1914*, Toronto, Macmillan Canada, 120.
58   Canadian Annual Review (1908), 28.
59   Oscar Douglas Skelton (1921), *Life and Letters of Sir Wilfrid Laurier, Volume Two*, Oxford, Oxford University Press, 270.
60   Ibid, 270–271.
61   For the Report of the Royal Commission to Enquire into and Report upon the Civil Service Act and Kindred Legislation, see *Sessional Papers* (1908), No. 29a.
62   Ibid, 45.

63   Ibid, 16.

64   Ibid, 45.

65   House of Commons, *Debates*, June 25, 1908, 11331.

66   Hodgetts et al., *The Biography of an Institution,* 28.

67   Alasdair Roberts (1996), *So-Called Experts: How American Consultants Remade the Canadian Civil Service, 1918-21,* Toronto, IPAC, 35.

68   Henry Parris (1969), *Constitutional Bureaucracy*, London, George Allen and Unwin Ltd.

69   Kenneth Kernaghan (1976), "Politics, Policy and Public Servants: Political Neutrality Revisited," Canadian *Public Administration,* vol. 19:3, 435.

70   Herbert J. Storing (1961), "Political Parties and the Bureaucracy," in Robert A. Goldwin (ed.), *Political Parties, U.S.A.,* Chicago,Rand McNally & Co., 146.

CHAPTER

2

CREATING A MERIT SYSTEM: 1918–1944

We have studied with some care the Constitution and the duties of the Civil Service Commission in Britain. Both bodies exist for the fulfillment of the same purpose—to make impossible the admission of unfit persons to the Civil Service, as the result of private influence. As will presently be seen, however, the duties of the Civil Service Commissioners in Britain are much less extensive than those embodied in the Civil Service Act of Canada. We have been strongly impressed by the greater freedom of the British commissioners to concentrate upon the principal purpose for which they were appointed, *the selection of staff.* (emphasis added)

Royal Commission on Technical and Professional Services,
1930, p. 18

The context of the First World War and pressures associated with Canada's Union Government made conditions ideal for the passage of a new *Civil Service Act*. In 1918, a new act was enacted, and with amendments in 1919, it virtually eliminated patronage from the entire public service, not just the Ottawa-based or Inside Service.[1] The demands of reformers had been met and the rope of patronage that they felt was strangling the public service was finally severed. From this time forward, the ties that bound the public service to political parties were cut and the convention of neutral competence enjoyed some standing in law. This was an important first step in a process leading to a more interventionist state in Canada, which required a depoliticized public service capable of some self-direction. Yet at the same moment it seemed to be recognized that the public service could regulate itself only at the expense of external political control. The need for a neutrally competent public service and the need for political oversight of the public service would come into conflict over the next several decades.

The *Civil Service Act* of 1918 officially ended patronage appointment and as a result the Crown prerogative was reduced and there was now a formal separation of personnel administration from general management. While all these changes to the power structure within the institutions of government were substantial, it was the separation of personnel administration from general management that would have the biggest impact. This separation not only marked the end of an unambiguous executive authority over personnel management but also substantially increased the power of the Civil Service Commission, which guarded, protected and promoted its new authority. Hiving off personnel authority was a necessary step in bringing about merit-based recruitment and promotion. It, in turn, ensured that new public service values related to integrity, honesty, probity and impartiality could now flow from a process of merit appointment, allowing public servants to be dedicated but impartial servants of ministers. Public servants were now expected to be servants of the state.[2]

Creating a separate sphere for staffing authority in the CSC was a crucial reform for all concerned if genuine merit appointment was to be achieved. Anything less would have been susceptible, or would have appeared to be susceptible, to political influence. An independent commission was established because there was a consensus to do so; it was demanded by all parties. This separation of the administrative from the political became an important and durable feature of Canada's public service and resulted in a substantial shift of power in Ottawa. An independent commission resulted in a deliberate system of administrative pluralism that became a significant source of equality and greater freedom for Canadian citizens, and worked to ensure that the effective operation of government was achieved without too much authority accumulating in the hands of the executive branch. Separating the political from the bureaucratic also reinforced accountability, hierarchy and political control, while creating a separate neutral sphere in terms of the ethical conduct and behavioural norms expected from public servants.[3]

From the day it was given its expanded mandate through the *Civil Service Act* (1918) and took on its modern form, the CSC began to wrestle with the complexities and tensions associated with developing this separate sphere of personnel management. Much effort focused on creating a merit system for recruitment and promotion. Until 1908, the idea guiding reformers had always been that the most efficient and effective public workforce was to be identified through competitive examinations open to all Canadians. Those who achieved the highest results would have the first claim on jobs in the public service. Yet, by 1918, it was clear that appointment to the public service would never be based solely on examination results and that other assessments of a candidate's worth and suitability for a public service career would be part of the operational definition of merit.

This chapter will explore three themes that characterized the CSC's struggle to create a merit system that would find broad support among Canadians between the two world wars. During this very difficult twenty-five-year period, the CSC tried to ensure that appointment was based on fairness and equity in terms of access, that the public service was operationally efficient and that public servants were not subject to politicization in terms of appointment or influence. To achieve these goals, the merit system had to be fair; however, exceptions to a strict version of merit would quickly come to be accepted by the CSC and the broader community. First, the case of women and veterans illustrates how difficult it was for the CSC to live up to the ideal of merit in the face of social and political pressures. Second, merit and a career system were seen to be linked in the minds of many early reformers, but after 1918 it became obvious that strict adherence to merit appointment and promotion would limit the potential pool of candidates for senior positions to those recruited at the lowest ranks. The elements of what made up a career service would need to be redefined to include efficiency criteria that could only be achieved by recruiting professionals and 'superior' individuals into the senior ranks of the public service.

This was particularly important as the size of government and the scope of activities of the public service increased. Third, the responsibility and authority of the CSC was frequently questioned by MPs concerned about an organization with significant executive authority not subject to the traditional doctrine of ministerial responsibility and thus beyond parliamentary scrutiny. The dangers of the autonomy accorded to the CSC, and consequently, the public service, would be put on the agenda by MPs but would not be seriously heeded by the government, which continued to use new autonomous bodies with increasing regularity. Concerns of growing bureaucratic despotism were overcome through a variety of formal and informal control mechanisms centred on the Cabinet and particularly the Treasury Board.

THE FIRST REDEFINITION OF MERIT: WOMEN AND VETERANS

Despite looming challenges, by 1918 the CSC was in its modern form and would have no major reforms made to its structure or its authority until 1967. While the *Civil Service Act* passed in 1918 was not particularly new or original, it was nevertheless important because it extended the power of the CSC to the entire public service and gave it a number of new responsibilities regarding the organization and classification of the entire public service. The key activity of the CSC was the administration of competitive exams from which the CSC would compile an eligibility list that became the basis of appointment to all positions. Appointments were to be probationary for six months, during which time the deputy head could either accept or reject the appointment or extend it for another six months. Under this mandate, the CSC was receiving over 100,000 applications a year by 1921 and was conducting as many as 21,000 examinations in every region of Canada with the help of hundreds of examiners. The CSC had grown from a handful of people in 1908 to a large unit of more than 135 employees by 1920.

This organizational growth and activity was due to the new range of responsibilities assigned to the CSC under the 1918 *Civil Service Act*. Specifically, the CSC now had full authority to hold examination for transfers and promotions in the public service, investigate and report on the operation of the *Civil Service Act* and any violations, report on the organization of departments, make recommendations for the efficient administration of the service, make an annual report to Parliament, and compile an annual civil service list. The most important of these new responsibilities were organizing the Inside Service and the Outside Service, classifying all positions, defining the duties of each position, and determining suitable salaries. By 1920, the CSC was at the centre of personnel management in Canada.

However, with this new authority came new challenges. In particular, the CSC began to search for ways to establish a merit system to balance competitive examination with other important values. Interestingly, the *Civil Service Act* of 1918 did not explicitly define merit or the merit principle. It offered a description of the merit system that focused on recruiting those fit for the duties they would perform and ensuring that public servants would be prohibited from any involvement with political parties. With regard to the recruitment of qualified candidates, the *Civil Service Act* noted that

> the examinations held by the Commission to establish lists of persons eligible for appointment may be written or oral or in the form of a demonstration of skill or any combination of these and shall be of a character fairly to test and determine the relative fitness and ability of candidates actually to perform the duties of the class to which they seek to be appointed.[4]

With regard to the prohibition against partisan activity, the act noted that no public servant "shall engage in partisan work in connection with any such election, or contribute, receive or in any way deal with any money or any party funds."[5] It should be noted that nowhere in the act was neutrality defined in terms of anonymity, secrecy or providing loyal service; it was defined, rather, in terms of party political activity, in the sense that party affiliation should not influence the public service.[6] While these principles were straightforward, there were many exceptions to the rules and indeed the act listed a host of exemptions, including exemptions for language, locality, gender and age.

Two examples of the original balancing act performed by the CSC stand out. Women were actively discriminated against while veterans were given special privileges that ranked them ahead of more meritorious non-veterans on eligibility lists. Women and veterans represented two different claims on public service employment and had two different trajectories, but both groups would underscore the malleable meaning of merit and a willingness on the part of the CSC to respond to external social and political pressures. The CSC openly denied the obvious merit of women, acknowledging that its policies were based on sexual prejudice, while giving added privilege to veterans, many of whom had problems in securing public employment without the veterans' preference.

The issue of hiring women into the public service concerned the CSC from its inception in 1908 and it accepted that it would need to discriminate against women and restrict their role and eligibility for promotions so that it could make public service attractive to male candidates. In fact, the 1908 amendments to the *Civil Service Act* allowed the commission, on the recommendation of deputy heads, to specify the sex of candidates if it was felt that jobs clearly required a male candidate. The CSC noted that certain work involving carrying large files and books up and down ladders was not suitable for women, nor were those positions requiring travel alone from Ottawa, because "for obvious reasons, male clerks are required in positions involving such duties."[7] In its very first report to Parliament, the CSC observed that women were much more eager to work for government, in all of its divisions, for the salaries that the government was willing to pay. However, appointments, especially in the higher first and second divisions, were in fact limited almost entirely to men. The CSC observed in its report that "were these positions open to women, there would be no difficulty in securing candidates well qualified on the grounds of ability alone to fill the position."[8]

The CSC was quite honest about the problem and starkly noted, "It is freely admitted that there are women who have quite as good executive ability as men, and who might, on the mere grounds of personal qualification, fill the higher positions of the service."[9] Yet, the problem was that if these positions at the bottom of the hierarchy were open to women, this training ground for the male clerks would be lost, making the ideal of an internally recruited career public service harder to sustain. Women were restricted both in the sorts of clerical work they were permitted to do and in the sorts of promotions they were eligible for, so that junior male clerks would have the opportunity to move up the hierarchy.

While active discrimination against women would continue for decades in a variety of forms, women entered the civil service in large numbers during the First World War and, with the coming of position classification in 1919, they would begin to move in with even greater frequency. However, the movement of women into the civil service was part of the much larger social trend leading to the feminization of clerical work that ultimately revealed that the use of legislation and formal hiring policies was not meant to expand women's opportunities but rather severely restrict such opportunities.[10] In fact, the CSC did not see women as suitable for middle or senior positions and expressed concern that "the preponderance of women in the lower echelons of the service would eliminate these positions as a training ground for male officials."[11] The feminization of the lower ranks made the myth of a career in public service even harder to maintain because it created incentives for outside recruitment of men into the middle and senior ranks of the public service. While women were hired due to the labour shortages caused by the First World War, and then the Second World War, they were only permitted to occupy the lowest echelons of the hierarchy and after both wars women were expected to vacate their positions in favour of returning veterans. By 1921, the CSC implemented a rule that barred women from permanent positions within the public service.[12] Women also faced a notorious marriage bar, meaning that when a woman married, she was expected to resign her position. This particular regulation lasted past the Second World War.

While women felt the negative effects of this disregard for the merit principle, veterans reaped the benefits of an expanding and malleable definition of merit. Specifically, the government engaged in a policy of conscription during the First World War that was unpopular in many regions of the country and was reluctantly implemented towards the end of the war. Conscription inaugurated a period in which the country began to develop the notion of reciprocal obligations between the state and citizens. Prior to the war, the state "made few demands and imposed few obligations; but, in compensation, it performed few services and gave little assistance. There were no mothers' or children's allowances, and no pensions for the blind or the aged."[13] However, during the war, the state asked, and eventually legislated, that its citizens die for services. The more that was demanded of citizens, the more citizens could legitimately expect from the state. Thus, notions of veterans' benefits and widows' benefits created the beginnings of the modern welfare state.[14]

Topping the list of immediate obligations to veterans was the issue of pensions and employment in the public service. Prior to the First World War, veterans of conflicts involving Canadian soldiers, specifically the Northwest Rebellion of 1885 and the Boer War of 1899–1902, received grants of land and more generous rates of pay and allowances when they were employed by the Canadian government as a form of compensation. However, during the First World War, a more formal system of pensions was deemed necessary to attract soldiers, especially given the hostility of Canadians towards conscription. Indeed, the minister of militia and defence at the beginning of the First World War, Sir Sam Hughes, decided that it was necessary to take care of the veterans of previous conflicts to ensure that those who were now being encouraged to sign up would be assured of compensation in the event that they were maimed or killed.

Consequently, public service employment was seen not as the privilege of individuals involved in partisan politics but rather as the right of those who had served the state in battle and especially of those who had been injured in battle. As early as 1916, the various governments in Canada agreed to the following rule: "that all Dominion and Provincial Government and Municipal positions as they fall vacant be filled by partially disabled men if they are capable of doing the work required."[15] This was the beginning of the modern notion of employment equity, which altered the notion of merit as established through competitive examination and made characteristics such as gender, race, language and disability hiring considerations. Until the eve of the Second World War, the Amputations Association of the Great War felt that such actions on the part of Canadian governments "give expression to the wish of the people of Canada who felt at that time and still feel that the public services of this country would be enriched and rightly so by men who had rendered faithful service to the State in the time of war."[16]

Eventually, the *Civil Service Act* included preferences for three classes of individuals. These were pensioned veterans who were incapacitated because of the war and could not pursue their former employment, veterans who had been on active service and finally, widows of fallen soldiers. Disabled veterans were granted the first preference.[17] Preferences resulted in a higher placement on the eligibility lists from which public servants were hired when there was an opening. Veterans still had to write the general examinations for the class of employment they were seeking, but if a veteran received a minimum pass mark, this placed him above those who received better marks but were not veterans. Of course, this meant that the best qualified candidates were not appointed. Instead, only the best qualified veterans were hired, a practice that had the potential to negatively affect other groups.[18] Veterans were granted an absolute preference, as opposed to the American system, in which veterans were given bonus points on civil service examinations: 10 for disabled veterans and 5 for all other veterans.[19]

This willingness to engage in a broadening of the definition of merit reflected the needs of the nation, the demands of political constituencies and the preferences of political elites at the time. Nevertheless, it became clear that various exemptions to the principle of open competition would begin to collide. For example, an amendment to the *Civil Service Act* created the "locality preference" requiring that local positions, defined as any position outside Ottawa, be filled by an individual who had resided in that locality for at least one year. This provision took precedence over the veterans' preferences, but the rationale for giving priority to residency was not clear.[20] A language requirement was added in 1938 prohibiting the appointment of individuals unless they had knowledge of the language of the majority of the members of the public that they dealt with. Since departments were delegated the responsibility of specifying the nature of language requirements, in Quebec, for example, this meant that francophone non-veterans were higher on eligibility lists for most public service posts than Anglophone veterans. There were also a variety of age restrictions related to examinations and older applicants were discouraged, and in some cases, restricted from applying. While thirty-five was the age limit, it was generally accepted that the service was always looking for younger male employees. Merit was originally determined by competitive examinations, but this simple procedure quickly ran into problems and was subject to a large list of exemptions, some contained in the *Civil Service Act* of 1918 itself, related to languages, temporary appointments, layoffs, locations of employees, age restrictions and nationality. Women and veterans represent two groups of potential employees that exposed the contested nature of merit. Even with all its independence and freedom from the institutions of government, the CSC remained mindful of the needs of Cabinet and Parliament and the overall mood of the nation in crafting its policies and procedures as well as its definition of merit.

THE CLASSIC DILEMMA OF EFFICIENCY: POSITION CLASSIFICATION VS. PUBLIC SERVICE ELITISM

The CSC would never actually adopt a merit-based staffing philosophy based solely on success in national examinations. Early in its history, it also demonstrated due regard for other characteristics that would contribute to building an effective and responsive public service. Balancing the building blocks of merit was never easy. However, while merit needed to be broadened to accommodate new characteristics, the merit system, in the form of position classification, quickly became a source of controversy. Here, we witness the first echoes of the now familiar theme that rather than protecting public servants from inappropriate pressure from politicians, the CSC was creating a structure that was better at protecting mediocre public servants and limiting the ability of the public service to recruit the best and the brightest. The CSC was coming to be viewed not as an agent of increased efficiency but rather as one that reduced the effectiveness of the public service as an instrument of democracy. The problem for critics was that the CSC's system of position classification did not really allow for considerations such as "fitness" or "character" when selecting public servants. Thus, the public service that was being built was not that of the superior generalist; rather, it was becoming the preserve of the narrow specialist recruited to a particular job and not to public service as a career or vocation. Replacing patronage with merit was designed to rid the civil service of the plague of inefficiency for the last time, but the system that was used, based on the principles of scientific management, raised a number of serious concerns lacking easy resolution.

The problem that would never be satisfactorily resolved involved the desire to build a merit-based job classification system as well as a classic career civil service in which recruitment into the lower ranks would eventually be the source of civil service leadership. The problems with combining these two goals appeared quickly. In 1919–1920, the commission hired the noted American management consulting firm of Arthur Young and Company to investigate and classify every position in the civil service.[21] The result of their efforts was a 678-page volume with more than 1,700 separate classifications.[22] This system of classification would exist for decades and its impact still lingers in the public service. It also brought about a great deal of conflict with deputy ministers and probably represented the greatest threat to the very existence of the CSC during its early years.[23]

At the time, position classification was based on the theoretical principles of scientific management, which fit nicely with hierarchical ideals supported by the CSC as it worked to establish a viable merit system. As position classification was closely allied with scientific management, it contained much of its zeal and its faith in progress, reason and the ability of rational comprehensive planning to solve all personnel management problems in the public service. Within the classification movement itself, there was an emphasis on work as an "abstract phenomenon, analytically separated from the worker. To the practitioner of civil service classification this meant that what was to be classified was always the job, never the person."[24] This was its great promise but, to many critics, its great weakness as well.

Position classification would provide a foundation that would permit the equitable treatment of public employees through the accurate definition, orderly arrangement, and fair examination of all public service positions. Initially, this seemed like a blessing in that it substituted patronage with the more rational criteria of utility, achievement and performance. It was expected to advance the "principle of equal pay and fair pay for equal work."[25] Employees across the country would be hired and paid according to the work that they performed and the system would become fair, equitable and transparent.

Unfortunately, the enthusiasm and extravagant expectations for reform were not matched by the classification scheme that actually emerged and that inflicted long-term damage on the former ideal of what a merit-based career public service should in fact look like. It became apparent that this system created a rigid hierarchy that became the antithesis of the ideals of a merit-based public service committed to competence, character and a lifelong vocation of public service.[26] The classification scheme proved to be so damaging to the idea of an efficient, motivated public service that a Special Committee of the House of Commons was established to examine a private member's bill that advocated removing certain positions from the purview of the CSC entirely and placing them once again in the hands of ministers and deputy ministers.

The issue was to what extent the CSC should impose this rigid position classification system on the entire public service. This Special Committee accepted the necessity of eliminating patronage from the service, but conversely

> when the application of this principle seriously affects the prompt and efficient administration of public business the interest of the State and not the interest of the Civil Service is paramount.[27]

The merit system could not be allowed to become an impediment to the ideal of a merit-based public service designed to create an effective instrument of government. Thus, the position classification system could not trump all other values in building an effective public service based on criteria such as locality or language, or even less tangible criteria such as fitness for a public service career and character. The biggest fear was that the regulations and salary structure contained in the classification scheme would discourage qualified professionals and experts from a public service career. Most professionals would be attracted to the private sector, where they did not have to write exams, where their salaries were higher, and where their status was greater. The merit system had to build a structure that would attract and promote individuals with the skills and character needed to ensure that they spent their career in public service. Because of these arguments, a bill amending the *Civil Service Act* was passed, allowing both manual labour and professional categories to be removed from the control of the CSC and placed in the hands of deputies.[28]

Noteworthy is this amendment's underlying philosophy: keep the upper reaches of the public service free from excessive control by the CSC. If efficiency and effectiveness were the primary concerns, so the argument went, an excessive concern for fairness, equality and other aspects of the merit system should not interfere with the efficient implementation of the public will. Clearly, this was a new skirmish for the CSC in the more or less ongoing battle between the needs of fairness and the needs of efficiency. The CSC ended up defending both positions in an attempt to broaden its definition of merit.

Deputy heads, despite their overall acceptance of the CSC, were concerned about the new merit system because it threatened their ability to manage their departments. They were especially concerned about losing their power to appoint professional, technical and other senior personnel. Even Adam Shortt, former chair of the CSC, in his new role as head of the Historical Records Branch, complained about the practice, in which experts and professionals would no longer be selected by deputies but rather through a time-consuming national search. Yet, the CSC would not budge from its defence of this new system, always insisting that it was fair and just. The deputy community, not unreasonably, felt that promotions should be regulated departmentally rather than through the CSC, which was beginning to conduct, according to the deputies, useless and ineffective promotion examinations. Eventually, deputies argued for a complete repeal of the classification system, which they felt was "a positive hindrance to effective administration."[29] Ultimately, they hoped to return to a system "divided into a number of classes on lines similar to those established by the Civil Service Act of 1908 or 1918."[30] The aim was to divide the service into two or perhaps three classes, with one elite class that would be closed off to promotion from the others, with a few exceptions. Besides creating an administrative elite, deputies also desired the complete control of transfers, leave of absences, cost-of-living bonuses and other personnel authority that had been accumulated under the CSC. Additionally, and characteristically, they completely opposed any form of tripartitism in the negotiations of salaries within the public service.[31] What was constant in these complaints was the deputies' desire to ensure that their own ability to manage was not diminished.

It may not be surprising that deputy ministers would be comfortable with abandoning the idea of a unified career service based on job classification. More unusual was the eventual acceptance of this view by the CSC itself. Charles H. Bland had been with the commission since its inception in 1908, initially as a senior clerk, and he eventually became its highly regarded chairman in 1935. He had been an unceasing champion of examinations, probationary periods and a host of other reforms which he hoped would greatly improve the operations of the public service. Yet, as he came to see it, the greatest problem in the public service was the myth that it was a career system.

> [If] the entire service ... is to be recruited only from the lowest grades and the higher positions are to be continuously and completely filled by promotion, I think you are going to have a weakening in your structure, perhaps not for a few years, but in ten or fifteen years you will have a decided weakening.[32]

A key for a truly merit-based public service was the ability to recruit highly skilled individuals who would be better able to deal with the complex policy issues facing governments.

Bland was not a critic of merit, but rather he questioned the rigid merit system that was making it difficult to recruit experts and professionals. Of course, promotion to the highest positions always needed to be open to those in the system. However, Bland warned,

"If we are going to keep up the standard of the service, particularly for executive positions, we must not only promote from the lower grades, but bring in a modicum each year of material for executive and administrative positions."[33] Bland's idea was that "promotion will be carried on just as before, but instead of everybody coming in at the bottom some will come in a few steps further up."[34] This idea of a merit-based administrative elite was simply an acknowledgement of reality and came to be endorsed by most Canadian intellectuals of the day.

The emerging consensus, as articulated by W. L. Grant, president of the Civil Service Reform League of Canada, was that a rigid merit system might be justifiable at the bottom of the civil service more than at the top because the bottom was where the worst abuses of patronage had occurred.[35] The merit system was not necessary at the top of the hierarchy because merit was assured by the technical and intellectually demanding skills of the job. However, a merit system that would guarantee neutrality and non-partisanship was essential to ensure that the bottom of the hierarchy did not again become abused by political parties and politicians.

Throughout this period, there was growing popularity for some exclusions to the coverage of the CSC and a willingness to accept fragmentation in the operation of the merit system. This in itself is an important indicator of the changes that were taking place in the political and administrative culture of Canada during the interwar period. There were growing demands for positive action from government requiring quick responses by dedicated experts working in the public interest. One way of making sure this quick action was taken in the best interest of the nation was to ensure that a disinterested, but highly regarded, elite was at the helm of the public service. Some even argued that this form of elite rule was both inevitable and highly desirable in a liberal democracy; it was the only way a liberal democracy could be saved from its own mediocrity. An efficient bureaucracy would therefore require the sacrifice of some of the democratic procedures and safeguards that were coming to surround appointment to the public service in Canada. In place of these democratic procedures would stand a responsible public service elite conscious of the national interest.

However, despite some willingness on the part of Chairman Bland to consider modifying merit recruitment at the senior levels, the CSC would remain committed to ensuring that the merit system prevailed throughout the civil service from top to bottom, excluding of course deputy ministers. The consequences of this hard line would be felt in subsequent years, with managers engaging in phony promotions, grade escalations and temporary appointments to circumvent the established rules. Thus, the CSC, rather than building a professional, career-based public service instead entered the business of building a control structure that would come to frustrate public service managers for decades. Its emphasis was on control and reporting, not on professional autonomy and decentralized authority. Rather than being a personnel management agency supporting line managers, the CSC was coming to act as a management agency imposing control that would create conflict and disagreement and lead to an early example of the problems now associated with the so-called web of rules. [36]

Specifically, one of the problems attributed to this "web of rules" was the increased growth of non-departmental forms of organization staffed by professionals and experts from outside the purview of the CSC. The establishment of such forms of organization was symptomatic of the growing complexity of policy-making and the contentious environment in which policy was made, but also the desire to be free from the burden of control imposed by the CSC. It also reflected the growing conflict that existed between public service managers and the CSC over issues such as promotions, discipline and transfers when authority resided with the CSC and responsibility for results often resided with the public service manager. This problem relating to the division of responsibility between managers and the commission had been apparent from the time the CSC was created. Yet, an important tenet of public management within a democratic society was the new view that authority for personnel management and policy must remain somewhat aloof from executive authority despite the problems this might create for managers.

Despite the recognition of the need to keep personnel policy separate from political authority, problems with elite recruitment ultimately resulted in the appointment of the Royal Commission on Technical and Professional Services.[37] For Canada to prosper in this new era of positive government, it needed the active, energetic and creative use of the discretion that was accumulating in the hands of the increasingly professional and expert public service. According to the royal commission, the only limitation on state activity was

> the quality of the Civil Service, which is called upon to investigate many subjects of national importance demanding consideration by the Government, as well as to make governmental policies effective and governmental decisions operative.[38]

That these individuals could exercise such authority responsibly was not a concern in that they were part of the "fellowship of science" and capable of self-regulation in the public interest. That is,

> It must be remembered that the staff of the technical, scientific and professional services have fitted themselves for specialized duties by undergoing a specialized and preliminary training; and that in many cases the nature of their duties is such that no one who is not intimately acquainted with the field of knowledge in which their work lies is competent to form a judgment.[39]

In fact, many believed that being aloof from pure executive authority could help protect the public interest and enhance organizational efficiency. Not surprisingly, this view found less support among members of Parliament in Canada, who were beginning to express their alarm at the new power and lack of meaningful accountability of the CSC and the public service. MPs felt that they had lost power to the CSC and throughout the interwar years they became increasingly critical of it. Most parliamentarians recognized that the new *Civil Service Act* of 1918 was going to cause a "very considerable change" in the balance of power in Ottawa.[40] This powerful CSC was seen by some members of the House of Commons as the cause of a giant rift in the traditional doctrines of responsible government, particularly ministerial responsibility. In their view, eliminating patronage through the creation of the CSC meant weakening ministerial responsibility to Parliament. The significance of this change becomes apparent when we consider that for the first fifty years of Canada's existence the convention of ministerial responsibility and its corollary, ministerial nomination, had been synonymous with a responsible public service and had enjoyed the status of a constitutional convention in the minds of many. By their very nature, constitutional conventions do not change easily, quickly or quietly and the acceptance of public service independence has always been a contested concept.[41]

THE CIVIL SERVICE COMMISSION: PARLIAMENT AND PUBLIC SERVICE INDEPENDENCE

While the CSC continued to struggle with the notion of merit and the position classification system, it also had to justify its own constitutional legitimacy. For many critics, the CSC represented, in its fullest form, the constitutional danger associated with the growth of non-traditional governing instruments. While initially directed at the CSC, the fear was later aimed at the Canadian National Railway, the Canadian Broadcasting Corporation, the Canadian Wheat Board and other public boards and commissions that started to flourish in the 1920s and especially the 1930s. Ironically, some of these bodies emerged to dodge the controls imposed by the CSC. The fear of these new instruments was noted by one disgruntled MP, who warned that

> there has been a tendency in recent years in this Dominion, as in others countries, to urge that national affairs will be best administered by those who are not responsible to the people…. This tendency has increased considerably in recent years, and as a consequence we have had a perfect avalanche of boards, bureaux, and commissions all administering in some degree the affairs of the people, and many of them in no way whatsoever answerable to the nation.[42]

He went on to note that the attack on democratic government reached its "culmination in 1918, when our Parliament created the most irresponsible body which has ever been known in the history of

Canada."[43] He was referring to the CSC, "which has power of almost life and death, at any rate, power of influence or starvation, over thousands of our fellow citizens, and power to expend millions of public money, [but] is not directly or indirectly answerable to parliament."[44] Another MP concluded that the CSC was unconstitutional because it was in

> violation of section 53 of the *British North American Act*, because these rules and regulations, arrears in pay, new positions, are no more nor less than an appropriation of some portion of the public money and all this emanates outside of the House of Commons, which is prohibited by this section.[45]

Throughout the 1920s and 1930s, these anxieties were echoed by other MPs, who were grappling with this new institution and its exact place in Canada's scheme of responsible government. In their view, while the CSC might have some independence from Cabinet, it should not avoid responsibility to Parliament altogether.

Such anxieties were always due to the belief that the convention of ministerial responsibility had been damaged by the creation of the CSC. This view was even held by the deputy minister of justice at the time, E. L. Newcombe. He felt that under the old system of patronage, there "is a responsibility attached to that appointment, which is entirely lacking now because the Government is not responsible, the member is not responsible so far as I can see; nobody is responsible under the present conditions."[46] These views were vigorously supported by many MPs, both government and opposition, who saw the creation of the CSC as an assault not only on their own power but also on the essentials of responsible government (as many had come to define it at that time). Some public servants even shared these constitutional fears about the CSC.

Notable in this regard was Sir Joseph Pope, under secretary of state and Sir John A. Macdonald's first biographer, who was perhaps the last exponent in the civil service of the Macdonald-Laurier model of a constitutional civil service.[47] Pope expressed his criticism of the CSC and its practices in a number of ways. For example, he was of the opinion that individuals should be rewarded for the effort they made and not because of the position they held in the bureaucracy. "His natural abilities, usefulness, aptitudes, quality of suggestiveness, age, experience, and other personal factors should be taken into account in determining his remuneration."[48] Thus, Pope rejected the new system of position classification and the principle of secure tenure because they were rigid and inhibited the full and loyal performance of tasks due to the protection provided by the regulations. An even more decisive indication of his views is his defence of patronage as a proper component of responsible government:

> One reads nowadays the most appalling trash in the newspapers about the 'evils of patronage,' as though patronage was necessarily an evil to be shunned. I wonder if these sapient journalists ever reflect for a moment who is best fitted to exercise the patronage of Government—the Ministers, for the most part men trained in public affairs, responsible to the Crown and to Parliament for their every action, or an inexperienced, unrepresentative and irresponsible body such as the Civil Service Commission.[49]

These opinions led Pope to continue to regard the CSC as unconstitutional because it was a creature of Parliament and was not, as in the case of the British civil service, an executive agency created by an Order-in-Council. As a result, the convention of ministerial responsibility was damaged because the ministers' responsibility for appointments was taken over by Parliament. Pope acknowledged that while the CSC was unconstitutional because it destroyed the convention of ministerial responsibility to Parliament, it was nonetheless legal.[50] As future events would underscore, the CSC actually began to embody a series of new conventions related to enforcement of behaviour around neutrality, anonymity, non-partisanship and independence and would become a force in the creation of the new constitutional personality of the public service.

While there may have been some people during the interwar years who, like Pope, still felt that "patronage is the democratic way of appointing to the civil service,"[51] most party elites were glad that the CSC had rid them of the nuisance of the large-scale patronage system of the previous era, which had always produced many more dissatisfied patronage seekers than satisfied ones. There were also growing constituencies such as farmers, businesses and even provincial governments who were coming to depend on the services of the federal government and believed that having an efficiently run public service was more important than patronage. Especially delighted was Mackenzie King who, from the early 1920s onwards, pushed for an entirely new understanding of the position of the CSC and other independent bodies. King eagerly defended the use of such bodies on the grounds that they were all approved by Parliament, and "when parliament has enacted a law which prescribes certain conditions and lays down certain obligations, members of parliament, like the public generally, are obliged to respect the law as it stands."[52] If the House of Commons passed the legislation that empowered the CSC, it would have to respect its own decision. Indeed, during the debates that raged in 1907–1908, many parliamentarians were very eager to see this responsibility removed and handed over to an independent agency. They had been early proponents of independence and a new constitutional position for the public service as a neutral adviser to the Crown.

Subsequent generations of parliamentarians were less supportive. Eventually, however, most MPs came to accept the fact that party elites were not about to do away with the CSC; nor was Cabinet in any hurry to strengthen parliamentary oversight of the civil service. As a result, most MPs accepted the separation of administration from politics as well as the conventions that surrounded that separation, including neutrality, anonymity and non-partisanship. What they were less willing to accept was the notion that the public service should have autonomy from the executive; they were demanding a more efficiently managed public service with more direct executive leadership. In this way, the public service would be politically responsible to Parliament. An effectively managed public service with politically responsible ministers was the best that parliamentarians could hope for given the transformations occurring in the political and administrative institutions of the time.

These changes led to a reformulation of Canadian doctrines of responsible government in which the conventions of bureaucratic behaviour took on increasing importance. In particular, Professor Robert

MacGregor Dawson noted with irony that responsible government was no longer as responsible as it had been in the past.

> Democracy succeeds simply because democratic controls do not exist: The people think they govern through their representatives in Parliament, but in reality they are being ruled by a trained and skilled bureaucracy accountable to no one.[53]

According to Dawson, there were only two options: "efficient bureaucracy on the one hand, inefficient democracy on the other."[54] However, Dawson was not one of those who worried about bureaucratic despotism.[55] He went on to note, "Responsible government can be worked in such a way as to use the best and avoid the worst features of both alternatives."[56] Dawson did not dichotomize the two; rather he thought that administration and politics could be combined to compose an efficient whole. To do this, it was necessary to elevate the bureaucracy to a status equal to but different from that of government. There were simply those officers who were political and changed and those who were non-political and permanent. When it came to a decision between efficient bureaucracy and inefficient democracy, Dawson chose the former. The danger was that the merit system might come to be regarded as encouraging "inefficient democracy" at a time when the power of organizations and their managers, and people's faith in them, were gaining ground.

Similarly, while MPs criticized the CSC, its product, the professional public service, was coming to be seen as something that Canada needed to develop and prosper. This view was common on both the right and the left of the debate in Canada and many began to consider the civil service as superior to Parliament and even to Cabinet because of its ability to govern exclusively in the interest of the nation. Those on the right used the public service as a check on the excesses of popular democracy, while those on the left saw it as an ally in their attempts to move society toward more populist goals. Both groups saw the public service as more than a technical instrument responding to the will of the executive or even Parliament. In the end, most Canadians came to agree with the League for Social Reconstruction, which suggested that with "a well-trained and disinterested bureaucracy drawn from the best minds of the nation the state could safely be given power without threatening civil liberties."[57] In fact, this is testimony to the ability of the CSC to create a public service that not only had the support and respect of the nation, but also was seen as a body that could clearly function in the broad national interest in a way in which partisan politicians appeared incapable.

CONCLUSION: REPRESENTATIVENESS, EFFICIENCY AND NEUTRALITY

This chapter has examined the problems that the CSC experienced as it tried to find ways to create a public service that was at once representative, efficient and neutral. Between the two world wars, the CSC was struggling to find ways to balance its competing principles of social and procedural equity, managerial efficiency and independence from the partisan influence of both Cabinet and the House of Commons. It needed to remain sensitive to requirements in terms of geography, language and gender, strive for efficiency and ensure that it respected the principles of neutrality and non-partisanship. Furthermore, there was a steady growth of government activity, and with it came the acceptance that "it [was] necessary to bring more expert and dispassionate guidance to the Canadian democracy."[58] The motivation for establishing the CSC in the first place was a growing belief that the public service had to actively serve broader national interests as opposed to narrow partisan interests.

The public service was also witnessing a plurality of new institutions and evolving attitudes. This would continue to put pressure on the CSC to move beyond its narrow focus on merit recruitment and begin to take on responsibilities for the efficiency of the public service more generally in terms of building an organization capable of providing policy advice and delivering services. According to many critics, its procedures, aimed at enforcing a rigid adherence to merit, were coming into conflict with the need to organize the public service in a way that would bring about maximum efficiency in its core activities. The CSC was beginning to feel the heat from nascent unions, frustrated deputies and senior administrators, as well as aggressive parliamentarians about the paper burden created by the merit system that it was building.

The CSC clearly felt that it both could and should further the managerial aims of the executive while at the same time balancing the guardian aims of Parliament. This was indeed the hope of those who created the CSC with duelling functions, but inevitably the CSC would be pulled in one direction more than the other over its long history. The initial motivation for both the 1908 amendments to the *Civil Service Act* and the new act of 1918 was clearly to make the CSC the guardian of the principles of neutrality, merit and anonymity and to foster professionalism, competence and independence, all in the service of ministers. However, the CSC quickly came to take on important personnel management functions that linked it with the executive branch of government, including pay determination, promotion, organization development, personnel counselling and a host of related activities. Over its history it moved, both by intention as well as by circumstance, to become more of a central human resource agency than a parliamentary or constitutional overseer. The central tension between its duelling responsibilities was one of the reasons that the CSC survived, but it was also why it accumulated so many critics. At the end of the Second World War, some were still demanding a rethinking of its roles, and pressure would begin to grow to have the CSC become an agency with much less executive power, or none at all.

ENDNOTES

1   Revised Statues of Canada (1918), Chapter 12, Section 32, amended by 10 George V (1919), c.10.
2   John Swettenham and David Kealy (1970), *Serving the State: A History of the Professional Institute of the Public Service of Canada, 1920–1970*, Ottawa.
3   Paul du Gay (1994), "Making Up Managers: Bureaucracy, Enterprise and the Liberal Art of Separation," *The British Journal of Sociology*, vol. 45:4, 656–674.
4   10 George V, Chapter 10, Section 38.
5   10 George V, Chapter 10, Section 32.
6   Chris Williams (1985), "The Concept of Bureaucratic Neutrality," *Australian Journal of Public Administration*, vol. 44, 48.

7   *Sessional Papers*, No. 31 9–10, Edward VII A, 1910, 17.

8   Ibid, 18.

9   Ibid, 17.

10   Graham Lowe (1980), "Women, Work and the Office: The Feminization of Clerical Occupations in Canada, 1901–1931," *Canadian Journal of Sociology*, vol. 5, 361–381.

11   Ibid, 364.

12   Kathleen Archibald (1972), *Sex and the Public Service*, Ottawa, Queen's Printer.

13   Donald Creighton (1971), *Canada's First Century, 1867–1967*, Toronto, Macmillan of Canada, 135.

14   Theda Skocpol (1992), *Protecting Soldiers and Mothers: The Political Origins of Social Policy in the United States*, Cambridge, Harvard University Press.

15   Canada, House of Commons (1938), "Special Committee on the Operations of the Civil Service Act," *Minutes and Proceedings*, 1230.

16   Ibid.

17   Revised States of Canada (1927), Chapter 22.

18   Gregory B. Lewis and Mark A. Emmert (1984), "Who Pays for Veterans' Preference?", *Administration and Society*, vol. 16:4, 328–345.

19   Gordon H. Josie (1945), "Administration of the Veterans' Preference in the Canadian Civil Service," *Canadian Journal of Economics and Political Science*, vol. 11:4, 601–611.

20   Ibid, 604.

21   Canada, Civil Service Commission (1919), *The Classification of the Civil Service of Canada,* Arthur Young and Company, Ottawa, King's Printer; see also Hodgetts et al. (1972), *The Biography of an Institution,* Ch. 4.

22   V. Seymour Wilson (1982), "The Influence of Organization Theory in Canadian Public Administration," *Canadian Public Administration*, vol. 25:4, 545–564.

23   Hodgetts et al. (1972), The *Biography of an Institution*, 93–100.

24   V. Seymour Wilson (1973), "The Relationship between Scientific Management and Personnel Policy in North American Administrative Systems," *Public Administration*, vol. 51:2, 202.

25   Report of the Special Committee of the Operation of the *Civil Service Act*, *Minutes and Proceedings* (1938), 58.

26   Gerald Caiden (1991), "What Really Is Public Maladministration?" *Public Administration Review*, vol. 51:4, 486–493.

27   *Journals* (1921), Appendix No. 3, 369.

28   Revised Statutes of Canada (1918), *An Act to Amend the Civil Service Act*, Chapter 22, 1921.

29   For the Report of Committee of Deputy Ministers, see *Journals* (1923), Appendix No. 5, 1038–1042, 1039.

[30] Ibid, 1040.

[31] Ibid, 1041.

[32] For the Report of the Special Select Committee on the Civil Service and the *Civil Service Act*, see *Journals* (1932), Appendix No. 3, 865.

[33] Ibid, 866.

[34] Ibid, 867.

[35] W. L. Grant (1934), "The Civil Service of Canada," *University of Toronto Quarterly*, vol. 3:2, 437.

[36] Geneviève Lépine (2007), *The Web of Rules, A Study of the Relationship Between Regulations of Public Servants and Past Public Service Reform Initiatives*, Ottawa, Public Policy Forum.

[37] Canada (1930), Royal Commission on Technical and Professional Services, *Report*, Ottawa, King's Printer.

[38] Ibid, 9.

[39] Ibid, 20.

[40] For the Report of the Special Committee on the Working of the Inside Civil Service, see Canada, House of Commons (1919), *Journals*, Appendix No. 6, 20.

[41] Andrew Heard (1991), *Canadian Constitutional Conventions: The Marriage of Law and Politics*, Toronto, Oxford University Press.

[42] *Debates*, February 16, 1923, 346.

[43] Ibid.

[44] *Debates*, February 16, 1923, 346.

[45] *Debates*, February 13, 1923, 380.

[46] For the Report of the Special Committee on Bill no. 122, *An Act to Amend the Civil Service Act* (1918), see *Journals* (1921), Appendix No. 3.

[47] Maurice Pope (ed.) (1960), *Public Servant: The Memoirs of Sir Joseph Pope*, Toronto, Oxford University Press.

[48] For the Report of the Special Committee on the Civil Service of Canada see, *Journals* (1923), Appendix No. 5, 613.

[49] Ibid.

[50] Ibid, 618.

[51] Ibid, 624.

[52] *Debates*, June 16, 1924, 3252.

[53] Robert MacGregor Dawson (1929), *The Civil Service of Canada*, London, Oxford University Press, 110.

[54] Ibid, 110.

[55] Lord Hewart (1929), *The New Despotism*, London, Ernst Benn Ltd.

[56] Dawson, *The Civil Service of Canada*, 110.

[57] Quoted in Douglas Owram (1986), *The Government Generation*, Toronto, University of Toronto Press, 264.

[58] Alexander Brady (1932–33), "The State and Economic Life in Canada," *University of Toronto Quarterly*, vol. 2, 440.

RETHINKING THE CSC: GORDON, HEENEY AND GLASSCO: 1945-1967

> In the interests of good administration, it may frequently be desirable, and sometimes necessary, for the Commission to be empowered either to decentralize certain functions to a greater extent than hitherto, or to *delegate its authority* (emphasis added) in certain matters and under certain conditions to deputy heads.
>
> Arnold D. P. Heeney, 1958, 11

As a result of developments beginning directly after the Second World War, the Civil Service Commission eventually handed over a number of its key responsibilities to a more powerful Treasury Board while at the same time delegating more authority to operating departments. What brought about this simultaneous centralization and decentralization was a growing managerial orthodoxy based on the belief that the division of authority over personnel management hindered effective management. Departments had long been interested in acquiring more personnel authority, yet since the creation of the CSC they had been net losers of administrative authority to both the CSC and later the Treasury Board. From a departmental perspective, the result was an overly centralized system of negative control. After the Second World War, even those with a rudimentary understanding of the logic of management would conclude that it was essential that authority be commensurate with responsibility for a management system to be effective. This would mean at a minimum getting authority over personnel management into the hands of managers.

The CSC had seen a number of changes already, given that it had begun its life as a simple testing agency in 1882, progressed to a recruitment agency in 1908, and expanded to a full service staffing agency for the entire public service in 1918. During the post-war era the CSC would become, for all intents and purposes, a full-service personnel management agency. Throughout each of these phases, the CSC faced serious challenges to its authority, its responsibilities, and its legitimacy. Yet the CSC would continue to be given new authority and expand its program offerings and overall responsibilities during this period despite concerns that it was not the appropriate body to take on such functions because of its independent status. By the end of the 1950s, the CSC would recruit, classify and train; it would advise government on personnel policy; it would regulate and conduct research; it would investigate outside conditions and the efficiency of the public service, and it would exercise appeal functions regarding examination and promotion.

Simultaneous with this growth in responsibilities was the emergence of counter-pressure for the delegation of its newly acquired authority. In particular, three powerful post-war reports would make it clear that in the minds of many knowledgeable observers, the CSC had accumulated too many executive functions for a body with formal independence from government. This was to be the central critique aimed at the CSC until some resolution was reached in 1967. While the CSC had been designed to increase the efficiency of the public service by protecting public servants from political interference and by providing stable career structures, according to critics this system was becoming the main impediment to improved service delivery. The CSC's independence was becoming less central to the cause of reform and, if anything, its independence was now an obstacle in the path of further reform. The protections offered by the CSC were viewed as a hindrance to effective management, and the growing consensus was that these powers needed to be removed, decentralized and disaggregated if the goals of efficiency were to be met. The defence of merit was becoming a lonely pursuit in Canada in the face of some powerful forces of decentralization.

THE GORDON COMMISSION (1946): A NEW DEBATE BEGINS

The debate on the future direction of the CSC began with the establishment of the Gordon Commission[1] immediately after the Second World War. The inquiry, which would shed light on what influential Ottawa insiders were thinking about the direction of reform, was headed by Walter Gordon, a business consultant with very strong ties to the Liberal party. Given this connection one might expect that the inquiry would merely endorse the administrative preferences expressed by Mackenzie King and other leading Liberals. With hindsight we can see that Gordon had greater ambitions in that he was attempting, unsuccessfully as it would turn out, to create a new and sounder footing for the newly expanded post-war civil service. Gordon shared his task with two like-minded individuals: Major-General Edouard de B. Panet, a former senior officer with the Canadian Pacific Railway, and Sir Horace Hamilton, a former senior official in the British civil service.

The Gordon Commission report began by noting some of the defects of the public service caused by the Second World War. These included a lack of men of sufficiently high calibre in the senior and intermediary grades, a lack of clear-cut responsibility for the overall management and direction of the public service, a deficiency in the machinery to facilitate the changes that were essential in a large organization like the public service, and considerable delays in making appointments and promotions at all levels of the service.[2] These were not new complaints; they were part of a well-rehearsed litany about the failures of personnel management in Canada.

The one alleged defect that would have clear implications for the future of the CSC pertained to the blurring of responsibility for the overall management and direction of the service, a concern linked to the problems associated with the division of responsibilities between the CSC and the Treasury Board. Gordon, like most Canadian commentators who have reflected on the CSC, was not an advocate of divided authority and was uncomfortable with the ambiguous position of the CSC. The way to bring about a reduction in this division of authority was to move away from the growing division of responsibility over personnel administration that the *Civil Service Act* of 1918 had created. According to the Gordon Commission, "The Treasury Board has the authority in relation to all matters of establishment and organization but not the immediate responsibility; the Civil Service Commission has the responsibility but not the authority."[3] In order to have responsibility commensurate with authority this situation would have to change. In fact, this "division of duties is the outstanding weakness in the central direction and control of the service and [had to] be eliminated."[4] According to the growing managerial orthodoxy, administrative responsibility could not possibly be obtained in a situation in which authority and responsibility were divided.

The most suitable mechanism for overcoming the division of authority and responsibility would be to centralize both personnel and financial functions within the Treasury Board. In this argument the CSC could not be strengthened because it lacked ultimate financial control.[5] Even more, the Treasury Board was the natural place for this control to reside as it was a responsible body with a minister who reported to Parliament. Additionally, the requirements of an effective system of management as articulated by the emerging managerial theories demanded a centre of executive control. But exercising this new executive authority would "call for a positive approach rather than the negative one hitherto followed in the exercise of financial control."[6] The desire to develop a more positive or proactive approach to management would become a new theme and would require that public servants be given an environment in which they were encouraged to do good, rather than one that merely discouraged them from doing bad.

The Gordon Commission was really an attempt to rein in the CSC and have it function more or less exclusively as a recruiting/staffing agency. The Gordon Commission wanted to remove the CSC's duties with regard to the numbers and grades of personnel required and place this power in the hands of a new division of the Treasury Board under the leadership of a director general who would have the rank of a senior deputy minister. This person would become the director general of the civil service with responsibility to the government, and thus to Parliament, through the Treasury Board. The new agency would help facilitate transfers, examine candidates from outside the service for senior positions, act as chairman of the official side in the recently established National Joint Council and recommend policies concerning working conditions.[7] The Gordon Commission also recommended that a personnel officer in each department be responsible for personnel matters and assist and advise the deputy minister. It was also felt that deputy ministers should have control of promotions in the departments and that ministers and deputy ministers should have responsibility over all matters of discipline. Finally, it was recommended that the absolute veterans' preference be reviewed and amended in favour of a point system that was used effectively in both the United States and Britain.

While all these reforms appear sensible and indeed many would come to pass in the future, the Gordon Commission also identified something that would trouble a number of reformers over the years: the increasing accumulation of executive functions, central to the operations of government, within an independent agency like the CSC. The Gordon Commission's understanding of this duality was as follows:

> In order to remove the possibility of political interference the Commission has independent status and is responsible solely to Parliament. But, while the powers of the Commission as to who shall be appointed and who shall be promoted are decisive, its responsibilities regarding scales of remuneration, the organization of departments and branches and the number of positions to be established are restricted to the formulation of recommendations which are not effective until approved by the Governor in Council. In practice this has meant the approval by the Treasury Board.[8]

The CSC's activities fell into two categories: those relating to its primary responsibility for recruitment and staffing, over which it had complete control, and those for which its role was only to make recommendations to the Treasury Board. The Gordon Commission wanted to transfer to the Treasury Board all the CSC functions that the CSC had no authority over, such as departmental organization, scales for remuneration and so on. The Gordon Commission noted that "with the transfer to the Treasury Board of the functions referred to, the Civil Service Commission would be in a position to concentrate on the primary and all-important task of recruitment, in which regard there is need for considerable improvement."[9]

Therefore, right after the Second World War we were again hearing what was to become a refrain: the CSC should be restricted to a recruitment agency. The Gordon Commission also noted that recruitment needed to take place at various levels in the public service. Like previous critics, the Gordon Commission was dismissive of the notion that "the messenger boy who enters the Canadian civil service has a Deputy Minister's baton in his knapsack."[10] While the CSC could do more training and development, in the end it also needed to bring in the best products of universities as well as "outsiders" and train them for senior public service leadership. In a similar vein, the Gordon Commission criticized the CSC for not recruiting an appropriate number of French-speaking Canadians, "due in large measure to the existing system of classification and recruitment."[11]

Many of these recommendations and criticisms had to do with the structure created in 1908, which was deliberately designed to reduce the control of Parliament and Cabinet over recruitment and staffing decisions. Indeed it appears that what Gordon and other critics wanted to do was to end the paradoxical position of the CSC as a legislative and executive agency by having it become a recruitment agency with limited authority. Yet there was some recognition at the time that whatever success the CSC had achieved was due in no small measure to its overlapping responsibilities. As was noted by Professor J. E. Hodgetts, rather than being a hindrance, the division of responsibilities created a system that appeared to work well for all parties concerned:

> The Treasury Board, believing that the CSC's reputation for independence was in open question, maintained the CSC for routine labour and as legitimizing agent for its own power. The staff associations, believing that the CSC's reputation for independence was valid and that it was a bulwark against patronage, supported

the CSC's as their spokesman. The deputy ministers, believing that the CSC had some independence from the Board, but also believing it to be ineffectual, wished to maintain it as a means of fending off the Board, which they feared as being all too powerful. And finally, the government itself was thoughtfully guarding the guardians, by making certain that two control agencies should be in competition, rather than having one in command.[12]

A complex web of group conflicts and interests had emerged since the CSC had come into existence and was putting it at the centre of a growing system of administrative pluralism to create a balance of power within the executive branch. The CSC, by using its ambiguous position within the system of responsible government, found a way to survive by juggling its multiple responsibilities. During the late 1940s and most of the 1950s, the CSC was able to work with the Treasury Board to modernize personnel policy. Yet the CSC was aware of the criticism being levelled against it and

> sought to improve its image with its departmental clients by taking a more positive approach to recruitment and other services, while quietly experimenting with the devolution to selected departments of certain of its functions, such as control over promotions.[13]

The CSC continued to develop new methods of recruitment, but it struggled with the classification system, which had grown synonymous with the merit system. While adjustments were made to eliminate classification in the professional, scientific and technical grades, the CSC had a hard time attracting new recruits in many classes due to low levels of unemployment and its own cumbersome methods of appointment. There had always been a debate between those who held that public service recruitment should be based on the selection of people who would develop into career public servants and those who thought that they should be hired for a particular position. This desire to recruit for general ability had been expressed in the earlier Beatty Royal Commission in 1930 and was taken up in the Gordon Commission as well. Similarly, there was a fear that in the post-war period the various preferences for veterans, locality and so on were making merit less effective and meaningful and therefore making the public service less attractive to the most talented Canadians.

The push to build a public service that was efficient and responsive to executive leadership, while at the same time representative of Canadians and able to function independently, would remain at the core of the CSC's activities during the period of growth after the Second World War. However, this balancing act would finally begin to shift during the brief reign of Arnold D. P. Heeney as chairman of the CSC. His chairmanship resulted in an influential report out of which came a new *Civil Service Act* in 1961 and the beginning of a move toward a new balance of power in personnel management in Canada.

THE HEENEY COMMISSION (1959): PRELUDE TO A NEW BALANCE

Arnold D. P. Heeney was one of the best known and influential of the "Mandarins" and had the reputation of being a reformer. With these two qualifications in mind Prime Minister Louis St. Laurent lured him into the chairmanship of the CSC by offering him the opportunity to completely review the *Civil Service Act*. He was encouraged to continue with this task by the incoming Conservative government, even though the new government was planning its own inquiry into the public service. With a "bi-partisan" mandate, Heeney examined the *Civil Service Act* and the role of the Civil Service Commission, and his endeavours culminated in the passage of Canada's second *Civil Service Act* in 1961.

Heeney believed that the increasing demands on government were going to change the character of the public service. When the CSC was created in 1908 it was possible to classify almost all civil servants as clerks, but by the late 1950s this was no longer true. The CSC was struggling to keep up with many of the challenges of recruitment.

> Today the public servant may be scientist, medical doctor, meteorologist, film maker, airport attendant, forestry expert, canal operator; he may engage in any one of a host of occupations which include every known skill and calling.[14]

This growth in both the size and variety of specializations, as well as the expanding areas of government activity, meant that public servants were taking a more central role in the framing and administration of public policy.

With this understanding of the new civil service in mind, Heeney, though personally wed to the idea that the CSC should recruit the "superior" person, was willing to concede that there was "a good deal to learn from the specialist."[15] In essence Heeney was a progressive, not content with the traditions of the past. He wanted to continue to innovate and improve the quality of the public service. Not only did he want the bureaucracy free from patronage and maladministration, he also wanted it to become more independent, more efficient and capable of self-management. He wanted to encourage developments toward a better civil service in the future.[16] The trends he wanted to encourage were related to the "increased importance and influence of senior civil servants."[17] The one tradition that Heeney did hope to maintain was the British tradition of continual bureaucratic reform and self-improvement.

What Heeney was trying to do was find ways to move beyond the highly defensive nature of the CSC's operations, which he felt had become a hindrance to good government. Heeney was aware that recruitment by merit itself was not enough to build a successful public service and that it needed to be supplemented; he would supplement it with a philosophy of management that would envelop the entire public service, particularly the senior ranks. While he regarded the preservation of the merit system as his major task as Chairman of the CSC, he also wanted greater "speed, flexibility, and simplicity" in administration, leadership in developing sound and progressive administrative techniques, clear division of authority and responsibility and greater devolution of managerial authority to departments. A sound philosophy of management was essential if public servants were to develop the "capacity and sense of responsibility needed to maintain a high order of managerial efficiency in the increasingly complex business of government."[18]

The creation of a managerial philosophy was to be balanced with a "clarification and preservation of the rights and obligations of civil servants to a degree consistent with efficiency in management" and a "greater participation by employees in the processes leading to the determination of their conditions of employment."[19] At the time, public servants had only two rights: the right to certain statutory holidays and the right to a pension. Public servants' rights, like the rights of all citizens, were emerging as a subject of considerable interest in the country and would take on increasing importance in the practice of public administration in the near future.[20] Heeney felt that the CSC's future lay in its ability to develop strong managerial capacity in the senior service, and in the recognition of employee rights in the remainder of the service. Yet the managerial revolution that would soon sweep over the public service would always find the CSC somewhat awkward, and executive leadership would pull more of these functions toward the Treasury Board and later the Privy Council Office.

As always, the key to improved public service management and regularized employee relations was clear authority and responsibility. In this regard Heeney was willing to acknowledge something that for the most part eluded early critics of the CSC: the CSC had essentially been designed to be part of a system of checks and balances. As Heeney notes, "This 'grape-shot' distribution of authority and responsibility was deliberately designed as a system of checks and balances, and it is hardly surprising, therefore, that it inherits the weaknesses implicit in such a system."[21] Despite his awareness that this system had been created with the approval of the House of Commons, he was not in favour of it. Indeed, it appears that anyone looking at the Canadian administrative system sees a distribution of authority and responsibility that needs to be 'fixed' by centralizing authority in a single executive agency with a responsible minister. Yet this system of divided authority, the creative compromise reached between Parliament and the executive over the control of personnel policy in Canada, was important in shaping the character of the public service, particularly by allowing the service to function on more than the narrow value of managerial efficiency.

A realist, Heeney recognized that the needs of management were going to change this situation and create a dilemma for the CSC:

> The central issue is to resolve, so far as we are able, the conflict between
> the freedom and flexibility which the administrator must have to do

his job, and the control which Parliament, and the Executive must
retain in order to fulfill their responsibilities to the nation.[22]

Heeney went on to note with disappointment that the authors of the
previous *Civil Service Act* of 1918 "were not concerned to encourage but
to restrict executive initiative; administrative integrity and continuity,
not efficiency and dispatch, were their chief preoccupations."[23] For
Heeney the central tension at the core of the CSC was balancing the
requirements of effective executive action and the demands of democratic
responsibility.[24] Pressures to ensure effective executive management and
executive expediency were gaining ground over more traditional values
of equality of opportunity and the constitutional position of the public
service.

This growing tension could be resolved in only one way for those
in favour of a new managerial orientation. More authority would have
to be granted "to deputy heads, subject only to some form of post-facto
central control."[25] This would mean a long process of increasing the
managerial autonomy of ministerial departments and establishing
post-facto controls to be exercised by the CSC. In attempting to
shift the CSC in this direction, the Heeney Commission made
fifty recommendations. Most of the recommendations focused on
traditional topics concerning public service reform and the role of the
CSC, including the organization of the service, position classification,
compensation, recruitment, selection, appointment and promotion,
transfer, discipline, hours of work and the veterans' preference; they
also dealt with two relatively modern themes: staff relations and
language qualifications. In most of its recommendations, the Heeney
Commission displayed simultaneously a tremendous amount of
administrative orthodoxy and a willingness to be influenced by the
surrounding intellectual environment.

Heeney wanted to maintain the merit principle in recruitment,
but he hoped it could be made more flexible. He wanted to see the
act administered more efficiently and more promptly while ensuring
continued respect for the basic merit principle. By the late 1950s there
was a need to protect merit, not because there was a fear that political

parties would attempt to revert back to the old patronage system but rather because it was essential to ensure a solid career structure in which employees could be relatively sure of their advancement if they displayed the correct behaviour. Merit was needed, not because it helped keep political patronage at bay but because it represented a desire to protect the norms of bureaucratic behaviour, thereby ensuring loyalty and efficiency among civil servants.

Heeney felt that the rapidly developing economy and the multiplicity of technical skills required in government had made the traditional principle of open competition in determining merit impractical. The skills being demanded by the public service were now so far beyond those of a clerk that in most cases the meritorious were appointed by necessity. Administrative necessity and common sense were also needed to ensure that recruitment, selection and promotion were dealt with efficiently, while respecting the spirit of the merit system. Functions previously seen as central to the CSC could be transferred to departments while the CSC retained post-facto control and an appellate function. "The function of the Commission would become essentially that of advice and audit and there would be new emphasis on the primary responsibility of deputy ministers for the efficient organization of their departments."[26] Delegating personnel authority to departments was an idea whose time was clearly at hand, and with it came a strong desire to reduce the role of the CSC to that of an audit and appeals agency.

Despite its desire to delegate, the Heeney Commission accepted the fact that the CSC should be involved in the process of job classification because an "equitable classification plan, centrally controlled is an essential ingredient of a sound merit system."[27] It was also felt that the CSC, because of its independent position, should be involved in issues of compensation and that it should become an independent arbitrator in wage disputes.[28] The most significant aspect of the recommendation on pay determination is that it acknowledged that there should be employee participation "in the process by which their salaries and conditions of work are determined."[29] Heeney stopped short of suggesting the "simple and unqualified application to the civil service of the normal industrial pattern of collective bargaining."[30] However, it is interesting to note that this system was only ten years away from becoming the pattern of wage determination in the public sector and that it would be Heeney himself, as chairman of the Preparatory Committee on Collective Bargaining, who would recommend it, albeit in the face of political pressure from many quarters and the unanimous support of all political parties.

The Heeney report served as the basis for many of the changes that occurred in the civil service in the following decade. It was especially influential in the drafting of the new *Civil Service Act* of 1961, which incorporated many of its recommendations. As Heeney noted in his memoirs,

> Although governments did not choose to implement all our proposals, notably those regarding pay determination, the report nevertheless formed the basis for many, if not most, of the reforms effected in the administration of the service during the Diefenbaker and Pearson administrations.[31]

These reforms centred on a delegation of authority to operating departments, which were expected to use this new authority to increase their operational efficiency.

The future direction of reform became clear with the passage of the new *Civil Service Act* in 1961. Under the new act, the payment of public servants became a matter of right, consultation with public servants' associations on questions of remuneration and employment conditions became legally mandatory, vague requirements regarding bilingualism were introduced, promotional competitions were extended, interdepartmental transfers were facilitated, the grounds for civil servants' appeals were broadened and the power of the CSC over the organization of departments was restricted to an advisory one.[32] It is no wonder that this act came to be referred to as the "Magna Carta of the Clerk 2."[33] At the same time, the 1960s marked the beginning of a serious discussion of the right to strike, and the right of civil servants to engage in more and wider forms of political activity.[34]

Becoming evident by the late 1950s was the recognition that building an efficient and responsible civil service required more than the creation of a self-perpetuating and remote elite; the task required the adoption of the principles of modern management.[35] As CSC Commissioner Ruth Addison pointed out, "The time is now past for a defensive approach in the application of the merit system and the time has now come to move forward in the field of public administration in a more constructive fashion."[36] As we will see, this would mean the application of modern management techniques, the recognition of employee rights, organizational autonomy and increased delegated authority, as well as the increased use of all manner and variety of professional civil servants. The CSC was moving well down the road toward delegation of its authority after the 1961 act was passed. In 1963 the commission delegated full responsibility to deputy ministers to conduct promotion and transfer competitions up to the most senior levels. While standards were set by the CSC, departments were now in a position to conduct such competitions, open to their employees only, without referring these decisions to the CSC.

THE GLASSCO COMMISSION (1962): THE CIVIL SERVICE COMMISSION AS AN AUDIT AGENCY

The Royal Commission on Government Organization, known as the Glassco Commission, was established in 1960 by Prime Minister John Diefenbaker, who, with other prominent Conservatives, had been calling for a major inquiry into the public service long before the 1957 election.[37] Modeled on the second Hoover inquiry in the United States,[38] the Glassco Commission proved to be one of the most influential inquiries into the role of the public service in Canadian history. It accomplished what many reformers within the public service had been asking for since the establishment of the CSC in 1908: a greater centralization of administrative power over personnel in the Treasury Board, a reduction in the influence of the CSC, an intellectual division of labour between managers and non-managers and a decentralized system of financial and personnel management centred squarely on operating departments and agencies—in short, a stronger executive leadership focused on a strong senior civil service, with oversight from a new, powerful central agency.

The Glassco Commission recognized that to ensure better management it would need to examine the old conflict between the need for efficiency in the civil service and the need for political control. This conflict, as old as the CSC itself, was at the very core of many of the Glassco Commission's recommendations, which called simultaneously for decentralization and centralization, devolution and central control, and freedom for managers supplemented by central agency guidelines. Yet, as has often been pointed out by its critics, the Glassco Commission clearly favoured managerial elegance over the cluttered world of democratic politics.[39] As an agent established to ensure respect for democratic principles in public service recruitment, the CSC would not endear itself to this commission.

The Glassco Commission was aware that the "good management is good government" adage was unacceptable to many Canadians, particularly members of minority groups, civil libertarians and parliamentarians. Consequently, there was a recognition that the machinery of administration had to be made "responsive to the wants and needs the Canadian people."[40] The Glassco Commission also acknowledged that "because of the generally recognized influence enjoyed by the central public service, the confidence reposed in it throughout the country will depend, in large measure, on how representative it is of the public it serves."[41] Even so, the Glassco commissioners were unwilling to consider specific action such as quotas for any disadvantaged groups. They simply wanted to find "positive ways of tapping the best human resources in all parts of Canada."[42]

Changes in the political dynamic such as growing Quebec nationalism might have been making the Glassco Commission's task of modernizing the civil service along managerial lines more difficult, yet many in Ottawa, including the Glassco commissioners, believed the public service desperately needed modernization. Modernization had become essential because of the errors of past reforms, most of which could be characterized by an over-reliance on the traditional concept of negative control favoured by the hierarchical approach, which often supported the CSC's role in position classification. The problems all centred on a proliferation of controls imposed on the public service by the CSC. Even though these controls were imposed with the best of intentions inspired by the promotion and protection of merit, they had come to represent serious fetters on the administrative capacity of the public service, which weakened rather than strengthened the civil service's sense of responsibility.[43] According to Glassco, the only thing that had saved the public service from the disastrous effects of excessive control was its ability to create a very competent administrative elite over the previous twenty years.[44] And while building an elite might overcome many administrative obstacles, ultimately, as others had argued, it could not overcome the "burden of control." That would be achieved only through modern managerial techniques designed to set managers free.

A further consequence of the burden of control imposed by the CSC was the increasing use of non-departmental forms of administration. "The costly, frustrating and unproductive character of the existing system has been most strikingly acknowledged in the frequent resort to the use of semi-autonomous boards, commissions and corporations."[45] However, the lesson to be learned from the Crown corporation experiment was that meticulous control and overhead supervision were not necessary to ensure honesty and efficiency in government operations; nor were they needed for conformity to public policy, democratic responsibility or merit recruitment and promotion. For the Glassco commissioners, the very existence of so many autonomous agencies and Crown corporations demonstrated that managerial concepts developed in the private economy could provide responsible public administration that respected merit.[46] Departments should therefore be set free so that they could accomplish their mission, and if the example of the Crown corporations was reliable, there should be no fear that Canadian democracy would be imperilled by such devolution of authority to specialist/managerial senior civil servants.

While the CSC was responsible for some of the negative controls, the commissioners could not avoid the obvious fact that the Treasury Board was becoming an even bigger culprit. The Treasury Board's appetite for control had come to blur the lines of authority between departments, central agencies and Cabinet, and it had become a tremendous source of frustration, which discouraged "departmental managers from accepting responsibility for their plans, and [led] them to regard this responsibility as being shared with the Treasury Board staff."[47] It permitted senior bureaucrats to escape responsibility by claiming that they shared authority with the central control agencies, particularly the Treasury Board. Controls designed to create a system of democratic oversight were having just the opposite effect.[48] This led the Glassco commissioners to issue an ultimatum: either accept the precepts of managerialism, in particular the increased need for administrative discretion, or accept a continuation of the inefficiencies of overly centralized oversight with the CSC and the Treasury Board as the chief villains.

It is quite astounding how frequently the freedom/control dilemma was seen as the central tension faced by the modern public service and that the solution proposed was always greater freedom from the controls of the CSC. Glassco, like those before him, attempted to resolve this tension by creating more autonomy for departmental managers supplemented by democratic/bureaucratic restraint in the form of a reconstituted Treasury Board, complete with additional statutory powers and its own minister. In essence, the Glassco Commission was relying on ideas that had been percolating since at least the Gordon Commission in 1946, and that had become part of the dominant managerial orthodoxy.

Underlying the Glassco Commission's attempt to deal with the freedom/control dilemma in this manner was a belief that bureaucrats working cooperatively with each other in a managerial, goal-oriented environment would achieve a new form of administrative responsibility. This is clear from the commission's general plan of management, which described a version of administrative checks and balances featuring a structure of countervailing functions between departments, the Treasury Board and the Privy Council Office as well as a much reduced role for the CSC. While the commission wanted to strengthen the auditor general, it also wanted to streamline the CSC into an audit agency.[49] Beginning with the Glassco Commission, there would come to be a series of reform proposals to have the CSC limited to a recruitment and audit capacity and to put more authority in the hands of line managers. Of course the Glassco Commission recognized that these various agencies exerted a restraining influence on departmental ambitions and abilities, but it nevertheless hoped that, because central agencies served broader interests and were staffed with officers familiar with the needs of departmental administration, the agencies would be welcomed by the departments as a source of guidance when new and unfamiliar problems arose.[50] The commissioners did not anticipate the sometimes intense bureaucratic rivalry that was to emerge over the next decades between these agencies. What they had in mind, rather, was a more harmonious system of management based on rational objective setting, cooperative agendas and decentralized budget-centred management.

The Glassco Commission is of course known for its dictum "let the managers manage." It also recognized that it is inconsistent to delegate responsibility and then ask for a detailed accounting of how the responsibility was exercised. Its forthright views were motivated by the changes that the advance of the welfare state was having on the public service generally. The rapid growth of government signalled the replacement of the traditional concept of the public service as a neutral transmission belt with a new view that was coming to demand that the public service begin to set objective standards of performance, create long-range plans, make decisions and hold itself accountable to certain standards of financial and social behaviour.

For the Glassco Commission one of the key ways to build a more responsible public service was to unite it through a dynamic managerial philosophy that would make the public service increasingly autonomous from the control of executive agencies. The commission did acknowledge the importance of other values in achieving a more responsible public service, such as representative bureaucracy, suggesting, for example, that more effective recruitment of French Canadians would be required so that they would come to "share a proper feeling towards the federal public service."[51] But it also cautioned against adding more ministerial departments and held favourable views regarding the growth of independent organizational structures. While accepting that there was room for alternative political values, in the final analysis, it wanted to subsume all those values under the overwhelming need for better management and bring a new technocratic/managerial approach to the operation of the public service of Canada.

The Glassco Commission led the campaign to unfetter management, pursuing the trend toward more autonomy for departmental
administration. This movement would gain momentum shortly after
the release of the Glassco Commission report, when a new legislative
regime was established and the *Civil Service Act* was replaced by the *Public
Service Employment Act* (PSEA). The PSEA signalled a move toward
more employee and management rights, reflecting a much broader
recognition of rights, particularly minority rights, in Canada's political
culture. This recognition led to initiatives aimed at creating a more
representative bureaucracy. Such initiatives began in earnest in the late
1960s with the Royal Commission on Bilingualism and Biculturalism,
which argued passionately and persuasively for a linguistically balanced
public service. Language-related demands eventually led to other long
overdue demands by women, aboriginal peoples and people with
disabilities. Thus while the CSC was to help create a more managerial
public service, it would also be asked to take on a more formal role in
helping the public service increase its own democratic legitimacy, based
not only on efficiency and constitutional principles of neutrality but
also, increasingly, on its ability to represent Canadians.

Conclusion: The Public Servant as Public Manager

The CSC always had an important role to play in creating a public
service that was staffed efficiently and effectively, protected from
unwelcome political interference, and reflective of broader social,
regional and cultural values. The public service that emerged from the
CSC's efforts was therefore able to play a role in helping to ensure that
governments remained within the bounds of constitutional propriety.
The public service had the necessary, but circumscribed, independence
to help balance the executive's need for effective action and Parliament's
desire for constitutionally appropriate action. This view of the public
service would be challenged by initial thrusts in the post-war era toward
a stronger managerial approach that sought to subject the public service
to more explicit executive leadership in an increasingly goal-oriented

environment. That is, the self-denying gesture on the part of the House of Commons and the executive guaranteeing the independence of the CSC, and thus the public service itself, was unravelling in favour of the executive branch. The system of checks and balances that had been growing, in which an independent CSC played a critical role in helping to ensure that politicians understood and respected the boundaries between the political and the bureaucratic, was beginning to erode.

Pressures to bring about a more effective form of management had always been great, but the new management style that was coming to dominate discussions about public service reform would result in public servants playing a more functional role. Little concern was expressed about the appropriate balance between the legislature and the executive that the CSC had originally represented. The CSC was coming to be seen as a nuisance standing in the way of the unassailable logic of effective management. Bringing management consciousness to centre stage would mean the slow erosion of the one resource that was the product of a powerful CSC, and which is always in great demand in any well-governed state: public service independence. The pressures for a greater focus on management would almost by definition erode professional independence and try to turn the public service into a more goal-oriented organization, in which performance, not probity, was the overarching value.

As emphasis on management grew, Canada was beginning to see changes in the operations of the personnel policy regime that would stretch the notion of merit to the breaking point. As noted in the first two chapters, merit had always been based on more than open competition and had begun to incorporate notions of fair and orderly processes for purposes of pay, rewards, promotions and employee discipline, in addition to a number of positive and negative exclusions based on region, language, gender and veteran status. Merit, beginning in the 1960s and 1970s, would formally include language ability, gender, and other sociological characteristics. Merit-based practices would bring a variety of new procedures, including equity-based classification and pay structures, more due process and appeal mechanisms, while allowing employees the opportunity to form and join unions unless otherwise exempt by law. Far from being a simple linear concept, merit was set to become increasingly weighed down by procedural and legal definitions, and the notion that it represented the ideals at the core of career public service would become increasingly distant.

The public service itself was going through a series of changes that would see it all but abandon the image that it was merely a very dedicated but impartial servant of ministers. As governments took on more social and economic responsibilities, first during the Depression, then during the post-war expansion of the welfare state, there was a growing sense that this limited view could no longer be sustained. In its place was a more managerial public service, one whose main concern would become the efficient and effective use of scarce resources. If the public service was to be an effective institution, the reformers now wanted it to embody more than the classic principles of continuity between different governments and the roles that had traditionally been based on complex and ill-defined constitutional conventions.[52] While support for this more gentle view would never disappear entirely, the direction set by the post-war reforms would be unstoppable and a more technical view of the public service would come to dominate by the 1970s and 1980s. The CSC would be seen by many as an antiquated institution supporting an outdated view of the public service, which was rapidly acquiring a more technical role in the delivery of public services.

ENDNOTES

[1]   Canada (1946), Royal Commission on Administrative Classification in the Public Service, *Report*, Ottawa, King's Printer.
[2]   Ibid, 11.
[3]   Ibid, 17.
[4]   Ibid.
[5]   Ibid, 20.
[6]   Ibid.
[7]   Ibid, 24.
[8]   Ibid, 16-17.
[9]   Ibid, 17.
[10]   Ibid, 18.

11   Ibid.

12   Hodgetts et al (1972), *The Biography of an Institution*, 216–217.

13   J. E. Hodgetts (1973), *The Canadian Public Service: A Physiology of Government*, 1867–1970, Toronto, University of Toronto Press, 256.

14   Canada (1959), Civil Service Commission, *Personnel Administration in the Public Service: A Review of Civil Service Legislation*, Ottawa, Queen's Printer, 7–8.

15   A. D. P. Heeney (1957), "Permanence and Progress in the Civil Service," *Professional Public Service*, vol. 36:4, 8.

16   A. D. P. Heeney (1957–1958), "Traditions and Trends in Canada's Public Service," Toronto, The Empire Club of Canada, 173–179.

17   Ibid, 178.

18   Civil Service Commission, *Personnel Administration in the Public Service*, 9–10.

19   Ibid.

20   Paul Pelletier (1959), "The Heeney Report," *Proceedings*, Toronto: The Eleventh Annual Conference of the Institute of Public Administration of Canada, 21–24.

21   A. D. P. Heeney (1959), "Civil Service Reform: 1958," *Canadian Journal of Economic and Political Science*, vol. 25:1, 5.

22   Ibid, 4.

23   Ibid, 5.

24   Peter Self (1974), *Administrative Theories and Politics*, Toronto, University of Toronto Press, 277–278.

25   Heeney, "Civil Service Reform: 1958," 6.

26   Civil Service Commission, *Personnel Administration in the Public Service,* 24.

27   Ibid, 12.

28   See Saul J. Frankel (1959), "Staff Relations in the Civil Service: Who Represents the Government?" *Canadian Journal of Economics and Political Science*, vol. 25:1, 11–22

29   Civil Service Commission, *Personnel Administration in the Public Service*, 14.

30   Ibid, 15.

31   A. D. P. Heeney (1972), *The Things That Are Caesar's: Memoirs of a Canadian Public Servant*, Toronto, University of Toronto Press,151.

32   Taylor Cole (1965), *The Canadian Bureaucracy and Federalism: 1947–1965*, Denver, University of Denver, 7.

33   S. H. S. Hughes (1962), "A Comparison of the Old and New Civil Service Acts," in Paul Fox (ed.), in *Politics: Canada*, Toronto, McGraw Hill Canada, 164.

34   *Debates* (April 14, 1964), Mr. Reid Scott moved for second reading of Bill No. C-10, which argued that by denying civil servants their rights

as citizens their ability to develop into citizens would be affected and the quality of service rendered to the state would be lessened.

35   Peter C. Newman (June 4, 1960), "The Twenty Men Who Really Run Canada," *Macleans,* vol. 73, 2; see also Christina Newman (May 1968), "The Establishment That Governs Us," *Saturday Night.*

36   Ruth E. Addison (1959), "The Thinking Behind the Heeney Report," *Professional Public Service,* vol. 38:2, 3.

37   *Debates* (March 16, 1949), 1547; *Debates* (April 12, 1954), 3987.

38   See Herman Finer (1949), "The Hoover Commission Reports," *Political Science Quarterly,* vol. 64:3, 405–419; James W. Fesler (1957), "Administrative Literature and the Second Hoover Commission Reports," *American Political Science Review,* vol. 51, 135–157.

39   See T. H. McLeod (1963), "The Glassco Commission Report," *Canadian Public Administration,* vol. 6:4, 386–404.

40   Canada (1972), Royal Commission of Government Organization, *Report,* Ottawa, Queen's Printer, 25.

41   Ibid, 27.

42   Ibid, 28.

43   Fritz Morstein Marx (1949), "Administrative Ethics and the Rule of Law," *American Political Science Review,* vol. 43:4, 1134.

44   Royal Commission on Government Organization, *Report,* 44.

45   Ibid, 50.

46   Ibid, 51.

47   Ibid, 98.

48   Ronald S. Ritchie (1963), "Glassco Commission Report: Technical Aspects," *Public Personnel Review,* vol. 24, 213.

49   Canada, Royal Commission on Government Organization, *Report,* 62.

50   Ibid, 57.

51   Ibid, 265.

52   Nevil Johnson (1985), "Change in the Civil Service: Retrospect and Prospects," *Public Administration,* vol. 63:4, 415–433.

THE MANAGEMENT ASSAULT ON THE PUBLIC SERVICE COMMISSION: 1967-1979

Being both operator and guardian over staffing, we are a safety valve defusing an otherwise potentially explosive issue. It is an awkward role to be sure: it does violate some of the simpler tenets of conventional organizational wisdom. At the same time, the present PSC model to my mind is essentially an inspired creation, taking into account with considerable sensitivity the realities of the Parliamentary/public service environment.

PSC Commissioner John Edwards, May 1, 1979[1]

The decade immediately following the 1962 Glassco Commission report was perhaps the most active period of administrative reform in Canadian history. The Glassco Commission inspired a flurry of decentralizing reforms contained in a new legislative framework: the *Public Service Staff Relations Act*, the *Public Service Employment Act* (PSEA) and the *Official Languages Act*,[2] combined with several minor amendments to other statutes, redistributed responsibilities among the central agencies, departments and the new civil service unions. The reforms were so intensive that, by the early 1970s, public servants were feeling rather overwhelmed and were considered to be suffering from a "saturation psychosis."[3] In addition to the currents of reform washing over the public service, there was also rapid growth in the size of the public service, which added 74,000 new employees between 1970 and 1975, creating a generational shift and new expectations from the younger workforce.[4]

These legislative developments, in particular the enactment of the PSEA in 1967, were aimed at, among other things, making the renamed Public Service Commission efficient and effective within a more limited staffing role and thus a more valuable partner in the transformation of the public service into a more managerially competent organization. Improving the efficiency and effectiveness of staffing processes, while always a part of the PSC's mandate, crystallized with the report of the Glassco Commission and was a key goal of the PSEA; this agenda was given a further push with the appointment of J. J. Carson as chair of the PSC. Having authored the Glassco Commission volume on personnel management, Carson brought with him the zeal of a true believer in the Glassco-style management reforms.[5] Central to this new vision was delegating staffing authority to departments based on the provisions of the PSEA.

The new legislative framework was designed to allow the PSC to focus on its core responsibilities for the merit principle, staffing, appeals processes, and training and development services, as well as on its newly acquired responsibilities in the areas of language training and internal management consulting. With rhetoric of decentralization at a high pitch, the PSEA permitted the formal delegation to deputy heads of the authority needed to make appointments in their own departments.

The prevailing view now was that the path to a more managerially effective public service was to allow the PSC to delegate more of its authority to deputy ministers. The trend toward delegation of more authority, which had initially begun under the *Civil Service Act* of 1961, had received new impetus and urgency with the Glassco Commission report. The idea that managers needed the authority to make quick decisions regarding staffing was now central to the whole agenda of increasing the efficiency of the public service more generally. However, the PSC noted, at the time, that it "intends to delegate its appointing authority in accordance with a planned and controlled system which will ensure the preservation of the merit principle as well as permitting effective and economical staffing."[6] Such delegation of authority required that the PSC create selection standards that by law would be "not inconsistent with" classification standards. While it took a long time to get a classification revision, as required by the new 1967 PSEA, the selection standards were in place by 1969.

One thing the reforms of 1967 did not accomplish, however, was to simplify or streamline the whole personnel system in the Government of Canada. If anything the 1967 reforms made the system more complex by introducing the Public Service Staff Relations Board (PSSRB), which was assigned power to adjudicate grievances on issues of discipline arising out of collective agreements. This meant that the PSSRB and the PSC would both have systems of recourse and redress, with the PSSRB focusing on discipline and the PSC on allegations of incompetence, incapacity and improper selection. Confusion easily arose between the two roles. What's more, the new PSEA relieved the PSC of its responsibilities in matters of pay, classification and conditions of employment, and transferred them to the "employer" in the form of the Treasury Board Secretariat (TBS) which, post-Glassco, was now hived off from the Department of Finance with its own Cabinet minister called the president of the Treasury Board and a secretary who had the rank of senior deputy minister.

The establishment of public sector unions in the 1960s not only complicated the personnel system but also reflected the expansion of democratic rights in the public service. This was a step away from the view of the public service as a servant of the Crown toward a view of the public service as an institution with its own rights and responsibilities. Public servants were less a part of a great chain of responsibility leading to Parliament and instead were becoming possessors of rights and interests of their own, a development that would bring them into conflict with the other institutions of government. Naturally, considerable debate ensued with the advocates of a more traditional definition of responsible government, who felt that these changes would result in a withering away of administrative responsibility through the minister to Parliament. Yet, an emerging consensus held that democracy would be better served if public servants were treated as other citizens. This new consensus would be one factor in the slow erosion of the notion that public sector employment was a "privileged" vocation; increasingly, it would be regarded as just another line of work.

This chapter will examine the transformation of the PSC's conception of the public service between 1967 and 1979, the period in which it had to deal with issues concerning minority representation, emerging political rights of public servants that might threaten the neutrality of the public service and the persistent view that the PSC was frustrating the managerial ambitions of governments. In a sense, those challenges were typical of the balancing act that the PSC had always played as it reconciled competing imperatives around representativeness, constitutionality and efficiency. However, pressures had mounted, forcing it to accept the view that the public service needed to be a more managerial organization with goals, plans and responsibility for effective service delivery. In this environment, the PSC, unwilling as it was to abandon its other roles, came to be seen not only as a brake on reform but as an organization that was incapable of playing an effective role as a component of the executive government and needed to be relegated to the role of watchdog with audit powers and relieved of its executive authority. This was a view that found new advocates in two major commissions in the late 1970s but that was resisted by the PSC itself.

REPRESENTATIVE PUBLIC SERVICE IN CANADA: LANGUAGE, GENDER AND RACE

The definition of merit has always been flexible, and issues of representation have never been far from the PSC staffing equation. Nonetheless, pressures for greater linguistic and democratic representation reached a boiling point by the late 1960s and early 1970s. The idea that equality in public service employment could end with the issue of procedural fairness and the ability of all Canadians to apply for public employment was no longer adequate. More proactive approaches aimed at encouraging greater representation by francophones, women and aboriginal peoples eventually dominated the debate about staffing and became an issue on the PSC's permanent agenda. The PSC had long been targeted by criticism that it was the actual cause of underrepresentation in the public service and therefore an unsuitable body to address the issue of inequality in the public service. This argument had been expressed for decades and was based on a clear decline in the number of French-Canadian public servants overall, especially in the senior ranks, since 1918. According to this view, the PSC was responsible because it allowed the continuation of a position classification system in which deputy ministers and other managers set position requirements that often favoured incumbents. Underrepresentation of francophones was also blamed on the PSC because it had failed to use its power under the earlier *Civil Service Act* to report on the organization of departments. Critics in Parliament had long argued that the PSC did not use its power to ensure that the public service exemplified the democratic principle of representation by population, which needed to be a requirement just as it was for other political institutions such as the House of Commons and the judiciary, which had guaranteed French-Canadian representation.[7]

The argument for a more representative public service had existed at least since the publication of Donald Kingsley's *Representative Bureaucracy* in 1944.[8] However, it was not until the late 1960s and early 1970s that the idea shed its "socialist" roots and was embraced by all governments as a reform whose time had come. To be rejected now was the idea of the public service as a clan of "Mandarins" who would function as a caste existing apart from the society surrounding it.[9] The idea of a representative public service became a core concept of public service staffing despite the controversy it generated. While there was always a community that favoured a more elitist approach to recruitment, the idea of a more representative public service moved from the fringe of academia into the realm of major social reform, redefining the legitimacy of the public service. The idea that the public service should be reflective of the community it serves now in fact enjoys the status of a truism, even if it is still less than completely realized.

Representative bureaucracy had always been a central feature of arguments favouring a more democratic civil service.[10] It was a tacit admission that the public service had independent power and that, for this reason, the public service, especially the senior public service, had to become representative of the major social segments of Canadian society. Recognizing that it needed to rethink its understanding of

merit, the PSC came to the obvious conclusion in the early 1970s
that the existing merit system "[had] failed in one respect. It [had]
not given us a representative public service."[11] The senior public
service was dominated by English-speaking males, creating barriers for
many Canadians. While francophones had made some progress, both
francophone and female participation was nearly non-existent in the
higher ranks, and aboriginal people were almost completely absent at
every level. The PSC, well aware that it had been applying the concept
of merit too narrowly, began to develop a dynamic concept for creating
a public service that would more accurately represent the people it
served. The PSC came up with individual programs aimed at French
Canadians, women and aboriginals in its first major efforts to improve
democratic responsibility through representation. While the PSC took
the lead in the development of these programs, by the 1980s the issue
moved up the agenda and the Treasury Board began to challenge the
PSC's leadership in this area.[12]

The model the PSC pursued favoured a passive form of
representation easily adaptable to concepts of representative democracy.
Passive representation "concerns the source of origins of individuals
and the degree to which, collectively, they mirror the total society,"
whereas active representation occurs when the individual public servant
is "expected to press for the interests and desires of those whom he
is presumed to represent, whether they be the whole people or some
segment of the people."[13] While there was some feeling that passive
representation would lead to active representation, it is clear that the
PSC was only ever interested in passive representation, which meant
ensuring that the number of designated group members reflected
their numbers in society.[14] The PSC has, in fact, never conceived of
public servants from minority groups as being representatives of the
social groups from which they emerge, nor have those public servants
been encouraged to think that representing their respective groups is
or should be part of their role in the public service. Such a concept
would be inconsistent with responsible government and would mean
conceding the notion of the public service as an independent player in
public administration.

The issue of language representation received its first impetus with the *Civil Service Act* of 1961, which created an expectation about the language qualifications of public servants based on the needs of the population being served in a given region.[15] The next significant push came in the aftermath of the Royal Commission on Bilingualism and Biculturalism,[16] when Prime Minister Lester B. Pearson announced that "the linguistic and cultural values of the English-speaking and French-Speaking Canadians will be reflected through civil service recruitment and training."[17] Thus, merit came to be redefined in such a way as to include the ability to speak French, an idea endorsed by Prime Minster Pierre Elliott Trudeau when he noted in 1970 that "Canadians whose mother tongue is French should be adequately represented in the public service—both in terms of numbers and in levels of responsibility."[18] As a result of these clear directions from political leaders, the PSC began a concerted effort to recruit more francophones. The PSC also became the home of an expanded language training effort that it would manage for the next forty years.

While pursuing its language programs and goals, the PSC also began to respond to the long simmering issue of women's representation in the public service and opened its Office of Equal Opportunity for Women on the heels of its own report entitled "Sex and the Public Service."[19] Its efforts also received a significant boost from the Royal Commission on the Status of Women.[20] The PSC committed itself to increasing the number of women in the public service and particularly in the senior ranks of the public service. It began by involving more women in the Career Assistance Program (CAP), which had begun in the 1950s; it made sure that women's volunteer experiences were rated in the same manner as other relevant experience; it developed new small courses for women and it removed any male-only restrictions from career areas. While the *Civil Service Acts* of 1919 and 1961 had never actually endorsed discrimination, they had remained silent on the matter, and the PSC had tacitly approved of deputies designating certain occupations as being suitable for men only. The 1967 PSEA, on the other hand, clearly stated that discrimination on the basis of gender would no longer be allowed. By 1978, the PSC felt that it needed to devote a chapter of its annual report to the issue, noting that it "[did] not see itself as having a mandate from Parliament to extend preferential treatment, and hence its strategy in this field has been one of actively promoting equality of opportunity."[21] It wanted to avoid the experience with the French language, in which the establishment of quotas had led to criticisms of "reverse discrimination". Maintaining that it had no parliamentary mandate concerning women as it did with the French language, it wanted to avoid anything that had the feel of affirmative action. It was the view of the PSC at the time that the existing merit system, with no restrictions on women, was adequate to increase the representation of women.

The issue of aboriginal representation centred on education qualifications, as had the decades-long debate on francophone participation. There were almost no aboriginal public servants in the 1970s. In response, the PSC developed programs to help increase aboriginal representation throughout the public service. These included programs that waived merit requirements for aboriginal people working in the north and replaced education criteria with requirements such as knowledge of native customs, ways and languages. While these modifications proved of some benefit, they were clearly not having a significant impact. Treasury Board President Donald Johnson suggested, as a result, that the performance of deputy ministers be evaluated on the basis, at least in part, of the number of aboriginal people they hired into their departments. Yet, even here the government was never willing to go so far as to legislate quotas, maintaining instead its notions of targets, guidelines and encouragement.

From these early beginnings emerged programs that required all departments to develop strategies to promote targets for all three groups of employees; people with disabilities would later form a fourth group. An *Employment Equity Act*[22] eventually was passed and revised in 1995.[23] But prior to these legislative changes, the PSC, as lead agency, developed an anti-discrimination branch to investigate complaints of discrimination in the public service based on sex, race, national origin, colour or religion. By the mid-1970s, 67% of the PSC's budget was spent on its many and varied training and development activities, while another 27% was spent on statutory functions related to staffing and representational career development activities. The remaining 6% was spent on activities related directly to the merit principle, including the development of selection and language standards and of merit specifications of positions, which now included notions of representation. While the PSC would share these responsibilities with other agencies over the years, by 2004 full responsibility for ensuring the implementation of the *Employment Equity Act* was transferred to the Public Service Agency of Canada, which is now responsible for the role of employer with respect to employment equity and the related planning and accountability frameworks.[24] Today, while there remain critics of the pace of movement towards representativeness, a great deal of progress has been made. French Canadians throughout the public service have achieved representational equality, and it is only the Executive Group that still requires new efforts toward this goal for women and aboriginal Canadians.

The PSC moved on the issue of creating a representative public service for two reasons that had evolved over time. First, it was a matter of human rights. Second, one way to ensure that the power of public servants was used responsibly was to make the public service broadly representative of the citizens it served. By convention, public servants were anonymous and could not be blamed or identified to the public. Thus, a representative public service would serve as a means of making sure that the public service was passively responsible. The true test of a representative public service then was not that it had the same values as the public it served but that it reflected Canadian society in terms of education, social status, employment, gender and ethnicity.[25] This notion of statistical representation would remain central to the ideal of a representative public service.

THE POLITICAL RIGHTS OF PUBLIC SERVANTS: NEUTRALITY REDEFINED

While questions of representation were rising to the top of the agenda and demanding an evolving and ongoing response, the constitutional rights of public servants began to evolve fundamentally. In the past, neutrality had been linked exclusively to political party activity; the *Civil Service Acts* of 1919 and 1961 had limited all engagement of public servants with political parties so as to maintain the perception that the public service was not in any sense subject to pressure by politicians. Indeed, the PSC tended to regard any political activity as part of a process of politicization. However, the outright ban on party activity eventually gave way to the idea that public servants needed to be considered as citizens and should not be banned from all political activity. Political activity came to be viewed less as an indication of politicization and more as a basic right that all citizens should be able to exercise.[26] Again, this change in attitude did not take place in a revolutionary manner. It was a slow, piecemeal process of expanding the political and constitutional rights of public servants in terms of partisan political activity and free speech, and of balancing those rights against the requirement that public servants be supportive and be seen to be supportive of the government of the day. The issue of non-partisan appointment and public service neutrality may have become widely accepted by the 1960s, but it was seen to have been achieved at the expense of the rights of public servants.

Since 1908, the notion that the PSC would ensure a neutral and competent public service had been central to its credibility and mandate. Part of its success in creating a space of political neutrality for the public service had been its ability to limit the political activity of public servants to voting in elections. The goal had always been to reassure the public at large that the public service was operating in an impartial manner, but also to reassure Canadians that access to employment in the public service was open to all Canadians, regardless of their political affiliation. However, even before the *Public Service Employment Act*, a variety of exceptions had begun to appear, and with the PSEA, boundaries of permissible political activity were opened up. The arrival of the *Canadian Charter of Rights and Freedoms* in 1982, which expanded the free speech rights of public servants, advanced the push for new rights even further.[27]

At the core of the challenges faced by the PSC in the redefining of political activity was a consensus in the PSC that no public servant should be involved in politics or be vested with power to influence the political judgment of the community. It was also recognized, however, that public servants needed to be responsive to the public will as expressed by politicians.[28] This meant that public servants needed also to be alert and submissive to changes in the public will as expressed in political decisions. Hugh Heclo captured this notion well when he noted,

> Neutral competence does not mean the possession of a direct-dial line to an overarching, non-partisan conception of the public interest. Rather it consists of giving one's cooperation and best independent judgment of the issues to partisan bosses—and of being sufficiently uncommitted to do so for a succession of partisan leaders. The independence entailed in neutral competence … exists precisely in order to serve the aims of partisan leadership.[29]

In order to do their job effectively, public servants in Canada were expected to identify with the political leadership and not simply provide the same sort of advice no matter who was in power. That is, not only did public servants need to provide impartial policy advice, but they also had to suggest what the likely political consequences of that advice might be. As collaborators with ministers, public servants needed to anticipate both political and policy consequences.

For decades, the PSC had maintained that the key value of staffing the public service on merit principles lay in the fact that it politically sterilized public servants (and therefore supposedly made them impartial), and that this outweighed other values that might be attractive to politicians, such as staff enthusiasm for policies, contributions by public servants to the life of politics, or the right of public employees to influence their employer through political means.[30] Yet, pressure built within the system and this concept of shielding the public service from politicians by limiting their ability to participate in politics gave way to a new view that public servants were less valuable if they were denied an ability to engage in political activity. At one point, Canadians may have desired a public service that was free from any taint of partisanship, thereby justifying a limitation on political rights, but opinion had slowly shifted in favour of the idea that public servants should function as complete citizens with complete political rights and privileges.

The political rights of public servants are closely related to constitutional conventions surrounding neutrality, and changes in one invariably lead to changes in the others. As Professor Kenneth Kernaghan has noted, the elements of the doctrine of neutrality are interdependent and

> a substantial expansion of the political partisanship of public servants may erode the reality and appearance of a politically neutral public service by such means as increasing patronage appointments, expanding public comment by public servants, reducing public service anonymity and diminishing job security.[31]

The PSC had always been concerned with maintaining the confidence of the public and the administrative efficiency of the public service. Nevertheless, the *Public Service Employment Act* gave the PSC the authority to determine whether public servants could seek election on the basis of how their candidacy would affect their usefulness to the public service. Even so, the PSC in its role as the guardian of political neutrality felt that participation in politics was a clear threat to this core value of neutrality.

The PSC had consistently argued that the public service had to be neutral relative to the minister, the public and other public servants. Of paramount concern had always been the notion that public servants were required not only to be neutral but also to have the appearance of neutrality. This became even more crucial as the public service became more active in public policy as well as the various quasi-judicial functions that it was acquiring as a result of the growth of government. Also, for the doctrine of neutrality and anonymity to be effective, it had to be clear that promoting or giving advantages to certain public servants who had exercised their political rights would destroy the morale of the public service and taint public service professionalism.

Thus, political rights were often cast as something that would lead to a new form of patronage.

For the PSC, the understanding that public servants needed protection from political interference was crucial to finding balance. However, public servants also needed to be able to exercise their right as citizens to engage in political activity. This dilemma found some resolution only after the arrival of the *Charter of Rights and Freedoms* in 1982 and after public servants took their individual cases to the Supreme Court. Yet, in the meantime, what constituted acceptable political activity remained a moving target and, in individual cases, the PSC often had to exercise a great deal of judgment. The PSC was shifting its focus from an exclusive concern with ensuring public service impartiality by policing merit to a new concern about appropriate limitations on the political activity of public servants, particularly those without access to sensitive information or without any obvious conflicts of interest. Pressures mounted in the 1970s to both define these rights and protect public servants while ensuring that the decision-making process was protected from public servants with declared political bias. During the 1970s, federal employees began to participate in politics, and disapproval of this participation led to the suspension of those seeking political nomination. At the time, the PSC was accused of acting in a high-handed manner in suspending individuals and not allowing them an avenue of appeal.[32] But this issue had struck at one the PSC's core values.

By the end of the 1970s, it was clear that the political rights of public servants would get a boost with the coming of the *Charter of Rights and Freedoms*. In addition, the PSC was also becoming adept at managing political rights on a case-by-case basis. The public service was now so large, divided, classified and organized that it proved possible to grant expanded political rights to large classes of employees who did not come into contact with the decision-making apparatus of the government and therefore in no way threatened to bring the public service's neutrality into disrepute. It should be noted that demands for improved political rights were coming not only from staff associations and unions but also from those interested in expanding the idea of human rights. This situation was typical of the way the PSC responded to pressure for change. Its actions were incremental and ad hoc and suggested little in the way of overarching conceptions; they were related to an immediate need to find a solution to a pressing issue.

THE LAMBERT COMMISSION: PERSONNEL MANAGEMENT UNDER THE MICROSCOPE

The mid-1970s saw a number of substantial changes at the PSC, including the departure of Chairman John Carson, who had been a staunch advocate of the new managerial orthodoxy, his replacement by Edgar Gallant and the appointment of John Edwards and Anita Szlazak as commissioners. The new commissioners supported the PSC's traditional guardian role, more so than Mr. Carson, but they also recognized that change was inevitable once the Liberal government established two commissions to. help clarify the PSC's role. These major inquiries were the Royal Commission of Inquiry on Financial Management (Lambert Commission) and the Special Committee on the Review of Personnel Management and the Merit Principle (D'Avignon Committee). While the PSC had not yet become an audit agency as the Glassco Commission had called for in 1962, it had begun to lose responsibility for personnel policy with the growing strength of the Treasury Board Secretariat.

The Lambert Commission famously emerged out of the 1975–1976 report of Auditor General J. J. Macdonnell, who noted, "I am deeply concerned that Parliament and indeed the government – has lost, or is losing, effective control of the public purse."[33] To rectify this situation, the Lambert Commission, even more so than the Glassco Commission, reaffirmed the need for more effective management and put pressure on the PSC to vacate its last remaining positions within the executive management framework and become responsible only for preserving and monitoring the merit principle.[34] In particular, the Lambert Commission did not care for the PSC's original, far-reaching executive role in personnel management because it felt that this role gave the public service too much autonomy from government. While the report was mostly concerned with financial control, it contained many recommendations about personnel policy, many of which, if implemented, would have fundamentally altered the PSC. In the end, this report had little impact due to the political turmoil in Canada in the 1979–1980 period, but it heralded a direction of change for the future.

The Lambert Commission followed the Glassco Commission's lead in trying to increase the managerial role of the Treasury Board, which ultimately assumed heavy new responsibilities for overseeing the management of all aspects of government.[35] The Lambert Commission's recommendations for changes to the Treasury Board were

> designed to clarify its role as the central agency responsible for effective management in government of both personnel and financial resources, and also as the primary instrument through which the Cabinet calls departments and agencies to account for how they have fulfilled their managerial responsibilities.[36]

The recommendations further strengthened the managerial orthodoxy by imposing more Cabinet direction and overhead control over the public service, which, as usual, meant a diminished role for the PSC.

For the Lambert Commission, this recommendation for more executive control of personnel management had the advantage of ending the old problem in which the PSC had executive authority but was at the same time required to audit itself to ensure that its activities were carried out within rules approved by Parliament. Lambert disliked this process because he felt that accountability suffered

> when the Public Service Commission, in effect, monitors itself through its review systems. Consolidation of personnel management responsibilities in the Board of Management would clarify the lines of accountability for staffing on the one hand and monitoring staffing procedures on the other.[37]

The Lambert Commission also pointed out the problem of the lack of clear parliamentary oversight. In its view, the problem was not being adequately addressed and had become obscured in the obsession to facilitate both merit and efficiency. For example, there were no parliamentary reviews of personnel management similar to the review of financial management that took place in the Public Accounts Committee. Once again, underlying the problem was the PSC's ambiguous position. "It is unclear whether the PSC should appear before a parliamentary committee to account for the exercise of its staffing authority, as well as to provide an independent assurance that staffing had been carried out on the basis of merit."[38] While Parliament needed an accounting of both, it was not clear that it should be provided by the PSC alone. Rather, personnel management activities needed to become the responsibility of the new secretary of personnel management and deputy heads, and the PSC "should report directly to parliament on its responsibility for ensuring that appointments within the public service are based on merit and not subject to political or administrative patronage."[39]

The Lambert Commission is perhaps the most dramatic example of an attempt to turn the PSC into a classic parliamentary watchdog agency. It argued that the independence of the commissioners had to be guaranteed by having both Houses of Parliament ratify appointments of commissioners for a period of ten years, by having salaries established by statute and by ensuring that salaries were not subject to appraisal procedures applicable to Governor-in-Council appointments. The PSC had to be given enhanced power to request documents and be able to require responses and explanations from the public service whenever it deemed necessary. In essence, the Lambert Commission wanted to ensure that the PSC would be capable of fulfilling three core responsibilities. First, the PSC needed to examine the personnel policies established by central agencies and deputy heads and make sure that they were protecting merit principles. Second, the PSC needed to hear appeals against staffing decisions that contended that the merit principle had been violated, and provide statistical data on the number of appeals heard and the number of appeals pending. Third, the PSC needed to report to Parliament on instances where personnel policies were not protecting merit principles and where departmental internal audits revealed non-compliance with the merit principle.

This was the most radical vision of the PSC yet put forward. The PSC would have the capacity to audit, but would be stripped of all its executive authority for staffing; it would become an appeal body and an audit body and move into a new category of parliamentary agent like the auditor general. Yet, as radical as it may seem, it was this vision that was implemented by the civil service commissions of the USA in 1978 and the UK in 1991.

There were two decisive directions set out in the proposals put forward by the Lambert Commission. On the one hand, it wanted to increase overhead control by Parliament and Cabinet by expanding the mandate of various watchdog agencies, one of which would be the PSC. On the other hand, it considered that the current weakness of financial management in the civil service stemmed from a failure to delegate sufficient authority to enable the public service to manage its affairs in the pursuit of clearly defined objectives. In its view, if these two directions were simultaneously pursued, a more accountable government and administration would develop. In actual practice, this would mean that the proposed board of management could ensure that departments made realistic program proposals and carried them out with economy, efficiency and effectiveness. Parliament would receive clear comprehensive and consistent information on spending proposals and achievements.

For the Lambert Commission, as well as for nearly every other public service inquiry, in the final analysis the senior public service, and deputy heads in particular, were the fulcrums of reform. Senior officials represented the most important link in the entire chain of responsibility. This meant that deputy heads needed to be accountable directly to Parliament. At the root of the problem, according to Lambert and others, was a fatal flaw in the doctrine of ministerial responsibility. As Lambert argued, "Any defence of ministerial responsibility that did not take into account the real and independent role of the deputy in the administration of government would ultimately prove destructive to the doctrine itself."[40] This warning would be echoed over the years, but it would be disregarded in Ottawa. The notion that the deputy should be made formally responsible for the administration of departmental activities based on goals and objectives agreed with the ministers was somehow considered a reform that would divert too much power away from Cabinet. The Lambert Commission was not the first group to note that the constitutional conventions governing the Canadian public service were weak and required strengthening. If those conventions were not strengthened, the public service would continue to be subsumed under more direct political control.

However, the bulk of Lambert's recommendations focused on making the senior civil service more managerial; this required giving it more discretion, more autonomy and more power and assigning a number of overhead agencies responsibility for providing the necessary administrative checks and balances. The PSC would be but one of those agencies. In attempting to create a bridge between a modern and traditional approach to public administration, the Lambert Commission emphasized the need to respect traditional parliamentary authority as exercised through various watchdogs, including a PSC that would audit merit and neutrality while accepting the expressed desire for managerial autonomy. One critic, however, complained,

> Commissioners have been childlike in their innocence, painfully lacking in modesty where they had much to be modest about, and inadequately informed about a number of crucial matters where ignorance could have been readily dispelled.[41]

Most troubling in this critique was the implication that the recommendations would actually lead to a massive centralization of authority in the proposed board of management, which would accumulate all of the PSC's operational functions along with more financial control, tilting the balance of power to the centre and undermining not only the authority of deputy ministers but that of individual ministers as well.[42]

D'AVIGNON COMMITTEE AND MERIT IN DECLINE?

Despite its own willingness to accept the need for more effective management in the Government of Canada and to help bring about this goal, the PSC faced persistent concerns about the scope and clarity of the legislative framework that had emerged in 1967. The legislative framework was still viewed as an impediment to effective management and, in particular, there was dissatisfaction with the confusion caused by the reforms affecting the PSSRB and the PSC, each of which exercised appeal functions. The confusion stemmed from the fact that individuals who appealed down one avenue were deprived of access to the other appeal process. The growing perception was that people were being unjustly treated through no fault of their own. To help remedy the situation, the government established the Special Committee on the Review of Personnel Management and the Merit Principle to examine the problems arising from the *Public Service Employment Act*, particularly as it related to merit, promotion and procedures for redress and appeals in regard to appointment, promotion and demotion and access to employee training. This inquiry, headed by Guy D'Avignon and consisting of both government and union representatives, was instructed to inquire into the operation of personnel management and the merit principle, two activities at the core of the PSC's mandate.[43] While some of the D'Avignon Committee's recommendations were helpful in resolving the jurisdictional disputes over appeals procedures, the committee was no champion of the merit system. Rather, it came to view merit much like many critics of the PSC had since as early as the 1920s: merit was a secondary consideration in the face of the overwhelming need for effective personnel management in the public service and the more pressing need for effective executive leadership from Cabinet. Merit, rather than being a substantive value at the heart of personnel policy in a democracy, was now commonly viewed as a series of instrumental procedures centred on ensuring fairness, equality and transparency but not on ensuring that new public servants had the character and values associated with being a responsible public servant.

According to the D'Avignon Committee, the problems of personnel management and merit could be traced, yet again, to the absence of any philosophy of management or sense of organizational leadership. In these circumstances, managers were poorly equipped to manage, suffered from excessive and inflexible regulation governing merit and slavishly adhered to universally applied merit rules at the expense of efficiency and effectiveness. Many believed that the PSC should concentrate on activities construed to "establish high standards of managerial competence, to identify managerial jobs and develop managers."[44] This meant moving from a preoccupation with protecting the merit system toward a greater focus on developing a philosophy of management and developing managers.

But what would that philosophy of management look like? The D'Avignon Committee suggested that a philosophy of management needed to occupy itself with the relationship between managers and their employees, state the areas where high achievement was expected, and specify appropriate performance criteria. Employees were more productive if they knew what was expected of them. For this reason, it was vital that the management philosophy be goal oriented. It was probably impossible, and certainly unreasonable, to hold employees accountable for failing to achieve goals that were not clearly specified at the outset. According to the D'Avignon Committee, the greatest problem with the public service was that it "simply lacks a system that defines goals, secures the commitment of managers to their achievement, and feeds progress reports to provide the mechanism for accountability."[45]

The D'Avignon Committee reflected the accumulated wisdom of the two previous royal commissions, plus the new intellectual orientation in the field of management studies, all of which urged that managers be given the opportunity to manage while being subject to a series of checks and balances provided by central agencies and oversight bodies like the PSC, which would establish policies and procedures. Nevertheless, as with the past two decades of reform, changes to the PSC were difficult to implement. The committee pointed out that since 1920 there had been an ever-increasing burden of rules, regulations, guidelines, directives and controls, which managers claimed were sapping the system of its energy and limiting their ability to manage.[46] This rigid system was "the very antithesis of modern management philosophy" and while it could, in certain instances, prevent the worst abuses associated with older management philosophies (that is, patronage and corruption), it would never create the "results-oriented" management that was needed.

As part of its desire to modernize the personnel management system, the D'Avignon Committee, echoing a loud chorus of critics, wanted to modernize the concept of merit. It had been repeatedly pointed out that when merit was introduced in the 1920s, the vogue in managerial thinking was scientific management. But academic and professional understanding of management and organizational behaviour had evolved substantially over the years. D'Avignon noted,

> Among the organizations that comprise the public service are found structures, managerial styles and systems that reflect the entire range of organizational theory. Yet our merit system is firmly rooted in the school of scientific management and no other.[47]

What is striking about this statement is its lack of regard for merit as a key value associated with the constitutional convention of a non-partisan public service. There was no sense that merit was a value that had to be maintained if the public service were to retain its status as an important and independent institution of Canadian democracy. Indeed, by the end of the 1970s, the notion of a constitutional public service based on the core principles of merit and non-partisanship appeared to be rather romantic. It was an era in which the public service was expected to be responsive to politicians, citizens and managers, and there was little acknowledgment of its broader role.

What emerged from the D'Avignon Committee was a desire to create a more flexible merit system without returning to a patronage system. The concern was not a return to political patronage; rather, it was the old, ever-enduring concern that managers would create a form of bureaucratic patronage. There was also a concern about the rise of a closed career service that would be hostile to outsiders, particularly regional minorities, racial minorities and women. As a partial remedy, the committee proposed the old view that the PSC should continue to promote a closed career service in the unionized or lower public service but be much more open to talented outsiders in the more senior ranks. The senior civil service should be open to outside recruitment whereas the unionized parts of the public service should operate according to the principle of entry-level recruitment and internal promotion.[48]

The D'Avignon Committee report is not, strictly speaking, a report on the merit system at all, as the discussion of merit takes up only a small portion of the entire text. In addition, the committee's views regarding merit are generally unhelpful. The committee saw merit as something that bound the hands of management and was in need of reform so that the government could "adapt the merit system to management's needs."[49] It also stressed the idea that merit should not be paramount among administrative principles in the public service but rather should reside alongside efficiency, effectiveness, sensitivity, equity and equality of opportunity. Merit should "be designed to allow managerial flexibility to deploy staff according to changing program demands and fluctuating workloads."[50] The message is clear: if merit interferes with management, then the needs of management should prevail.

The D'Avignon Committee's only praise for the merit system came in its approval of the distinctly Canadian practice of applying merit to a particular job and not to the fitness of the candidate for a lifelong career that would typically involve different kinds of work. This practice had been in place since the 1919 classification plan and had ensured that recruitment to the Canadian public service was never confined to the entry levels but occurred at all levels.[51] Its main advantage had always been that it allowed elite recruitment into the senior public service, and it was seen as something that was encouraged in the existing legislation.[52] The committee's only suggestion regarding this practice was to amend the *Public Service Employment Act* to allow more direct recruitment when it was in the public interest, as opposed to the interest of the public service. This meant that the PSC needed to make sure that outside appointments to the senior ranks were more representative of Canadian society than before.

Conclusion: The Rise of the Performance Paradigm

New views about the changing role of the public service generally involved restricting the role of the PSC. Michael Kirby, principal secretary to Prime Minister Trudeau, expressed a growing trend in his call for a decentralized and disaggregated public service in which service delivery was brought closer to citizens. He envisioned establishing revenue dependency for units that offered services with market potential, private-public competition and full costing of public services. The goal was to

> make government managers subject to the strong economic incentives that now exist only in the competitive business world, and this would

> make at least part of government decision making subject to the
> same kind of discipline which governs decision making processes in
> the competitive private sector.[53]

Clearly, Kirby's ideas were part of the movement toward what would soon be referred to as "entrepreneurial government," and the PSC was seen to be a major obstacle on the road to that goal.

There was growing pressure to see the PSC restricted to a recruitment service at best or an audit agency at worst. It was supposed to focus on the lower levels where it could provide efficient service while becoming an audit or certifying agent to ensure that proper procedures were fulfilled in the case of higher-level appointments. One commentator noted that such a "slimming down would create a new role for the PSC, more akin, on the personnel front, to that of the auditor general on the financial front."[54] The PSC as an audit agency with all appointment powers transferred to executive control would remain a reform that was very popular with external reviewers but one that could never find a sponsor within government. No politician in Canada was willing to remove the PSC's executive responsibility and, in so doing, renege on the original 1908 bargain with Parliament.

Despite the reluctance to follow through on measures to downsize the PSC, there was nonetheless a slow but growing acceptance that the public service was an organization that had to modernize; it had to transform itself from a servant of vague principles associated with constitutional conventions into a more instrumental organization in the service of the executive. Slowly, the public service was being stripped of any moral content; the notion of merit as a substantive value was being replaced instead by the view that merit amounted to a series of instrumental procedures.[55] This chapter has focused on how the PSC was caught up in various attempts to play down the role of merit and was increasingly asked to see its role as helping to elevate the importance of management in the creation of a professional public service. To some extent, the PSC was forced into this role. It appears that merit had few friends and that everyone was calling for greater direct executive leadership over management functions in order to make the public service more accountable, more efficient and more responsive to political direction.[56] While this was not the only trend during this period, it does stand out as a key development in the post-1967 reforms leading up to the 1980s, the decade in which politicians around the world began to express great interest in public management reforms, which collectively, if somewhat vaguely, would come to be called the New Public Management (NPM). This managerial worldview arose from a desire to overcome the constraining influence of the merit system in the name of better management. Consequently, any agency that represented an attachment to the old view of public service was seen to be standing in the way of progress. It was at this time that the PSC's counterparts around the world were put on the chopping block.

Yet, the complaints were not new. The PSC was, from the outset, viewed as counterproductive to modernization. It was too slow, it deprived managers of their rightful authority and its emphasis on fairness and process meant that meaningful reforms were difficult to implement. What those examining the role of the PSC in the 1970s were suggesting was that if the Government of Canada followed the requirements of managerial reform, the result would be a better performing public service for Canadians. Public service reform was coming to be seen as a technical activity that could be made to work through clear lines of authority and concentrated executive power.[57] There was little willingness to defend any other considerations beyond those that would help improve performance. Emphasis was on the nature of the work and its ability to achieve results, and no longer on the earlier ideas of public service as a vocation that was part of a well-ordered and well-governed society. As well, there was a growing lack of interest in, and respect for, the professionalism and neutrality of the public service, which the PSC had been responsible for maintaining.

ENDNOTES

1   John Edwards, Confidential Memo (1979), "Some Initial Reactions to the Lambert Commission Report," Public Service Commission Archives, May 1, 1979.

2   Revised Statutes of Canada (1969), Chapter 54.

3   L. Laframboise (1971), "Administrative Reform in the Federal Public Service: Signs of a Saturation Psychosis," *Canadian Public Administration*, vol. 14, 303–325.

4   Public Service Commission (1979), *Annual Report 1979*, Volume 1, Ottawa, Supply and Service Canada, 9.

5   J. J. Carson (1968), "The Changing Scope of the Public Servant," *Canadian Public Administration*, vol. 11:4, 407–413.

6   Annual Report, 1967, 6.

7   House of Commons of Canada, *Debates* (July 7, 1947), 5183.

8   J. Donald Kingsley (1944), *Representative Bureaucracy*, Yellow Springs, Ohio.

9   V. Subramaniam (1967), "Representative Bureaucracy: A Reassessment," *American Political Science Review*, vol.61:4, 1010–1019; see also Fredrick Mosher (1968), *Democracy and the Public Service*, New York, Oxford University Press, 1968.

10 Frederick C. Mosher (1968), *Democracy and the Public Service*, New York, Oxford University Press; see also Kingsley (1944), *Representative Bureaucracy*.

11 PSC (1971), *Annual Report*, 1.

12 Carole Agocs (1986), "Affirmative Action, Canadian Style: A Reconnaissance," *Canadian Public Policy*, vol. 12, 152.

13 Mosher, *Democracy and the Public Service*, 11–13.

14 David Nachmais and David Rosenbloom (1973), "Measuring Bureaucratic Representation and Integration," *Public Administration Review*, vol. 33:4, 590–597.

15 Sylvain Cloutier (1968), "Senior Public Service Officials in a Bicultural Society," *Canadian Public Administration*, vol. 11:4, 368–406.

16 Canada (1968), Royal Commission on Bilingualism and Biculturalism, Ottawa, Queen's Printer.

17 House of Commons of Canada, *Debates* (April 6, 1966), 3915.

18 House of Commons of Canada, *Debates* (June 23,1970), 8487.

19 Kathleen Archibald (1970), *Sex and the Public Service*, Ottawa, Public Service Commission.

20 Canada (1970), *Report of the Royal Commission on the Status of Women*, Ottawa, Queen's Printer.

21 Public Service Commission (1978), *Annual Report 1978*, 17.

22 Revised Statutes of Canada (1985), c. 23 (2nd Supp).

23 Employment Equity Act, S.C. 1995, c. 44.

24 Canada (2007), Senate Standing Committee on Human Rights, Preliminary Findings, *Employment Equity in the Federal Public Service – Not There Yet*.

25 Pan S. Kim (1994), "A Theoretical Overview of Representative Bureaucracy: Synthesis," *International Review of Administrative Sciences*, vol. 60 (1994), 392.

26   Patrick Weller (1989), "Politicisation and the Australian Public Service," *Australian Journal of Public Administration*, vol. 48:4, 370.

27   Lorne Sossin (2006), "Defining Boundaries: The Constitutional Argument for Bureaucratic Independence and Its Implications for the Accountability of the Public Service," in *Commission of Inquiry into the Sponsorship Program and Advertising Activities, Restoring Accountability*, vol. 2, Ottawa, Public Works and Government Services, 25–71.

28   William F. West (2005), "Neutral Competence and Political Responsiveness: An Uneasy Relationship," *The Policy Studies Journal* vol. 33, 147–160.

29   Hugh Heclo (1975), "OMB and the Presidency: The Problem of Neutral Competence," *The Public Interest*, vol. 38, 83.

30   James B. Christoph (1957), "Political Rights and Administrative Impartiality in the British Civil Service," *American Political Science Review*, vol. 51, 68.

31   Kenneth Kernaghan (1986), "Political Rights and Political Neutrality: Finding the Balance Point," *Canadian Public Administration*, vol. 29:4, 650.

32   "Review Urged on Politics Rule in Civil Service," *The Globe and Mail*, Tuesday, March 28, 1972, 4.

33   Auditor General Report, 1975–76, 9.

34   Canada (1979), Royal Commission on Financial Management and Accountability, Final Report, Hull, Supply and Services Canada, 114.

35   Ibid, 36.

36   Ibid, 37.

37   Ibid, 121.

38   Ibid, 123.

39   Ibid, 124.

40   Ibid, 42.

41   Douglas Hartle (1979), "The Report of the Royal Commission on Financial Management and Accountability (The Lambert Report): A Review," *Canadian Public Policy*, vol. 3:2, 366–382, 367.

42   Ibid, 372.

43   Canada (1979), Special Committee on the Review of Personnel Management and the Merit Principle in the Public Service. *Report*, Hull, Supply and Services.

44   Ibid, 37.

45   Ibid, 43.

46   Ibid, 51.

47   Ibid, 78.

48   Ibid, 85–86.

49   Ibid, 91.

50   Ibid.

51   Ibid, 194.

52   Revised Statutes of Canada (1967), Chapter 71, Section 10 and 11.

53   Michael J. Kirby (2004), "Reflections on the Management of Government in the 1980s," in Bernard Ostry and Janice Yalden (eds.), *Visions of Canada: The Alan B. Plaunt Memorial Lectures*, 1958–1992, Montreal, McGill-Queen's University Press, 443.

54   Gilles Paquet (1985), "An Agenda for Change in the Federal Public Service," *Canadian Public Administration*, vol. 28: 3, 455–461, 61.

55   James. R. Thompson (2006), "The Federal Civil Service: The Demise of an Institution," *Public Administration Review* 66:4, 496.

56   Flora Macdonald (1980), "The Minister and the Mandarins: How a New Minister Copes With the Entrapment Devices of Bureaucracy," *Policy Options*, vol. 50:3, 3.

57   Jack H. Knott and Gary J. Miller (1987), *Reforming Bureaucracy: The Politics of Institutional Choice*, Englewood Cliffs, Prentice-Hall, 2.

STRUGGLING TO DEFEND POLITICAL NEUTRALITY: 1979-2006

> The existence of a convention of political neutrality, central to the principle of responsible government ... is not seriously disputed.
>
> The Supreme Court of Canada, Osborne decision, 1991

After two decades of virtually uninterrupted Liberal governments, the arrival in power of the Progressive Conservative Party in 1984 marked an important turning point in Canadian politics. The new prime minister, Brian Mulroney, had few good words to say about the public service throughout his campaign, going so far as to promise that, once in office, he would hand out "pink slips and running shoes to bureaucrats."[1] Beyond concerns for efficiency and economy, the responsiveness of the public service to the political executive was an important concern of the new government, leading to debates about the appropriate level of political influence over the staffing of the senior ranks of the public service. As a result, in addition to the return of the perennial debate about the need for greater managerial flexibility in staffing, the Mulroney years also saw the emergence of new concerns about the politicization of the public service, concerns that did not disappear after the Liberal government returned to power in 1993. In fact, the debate on the politicization of the public service acquired a new dimension in the 1990s when some of the prohibitions against political activities by public servants were found to be incompatible with the *Charter of Rights and Freedoms* adopted in 1982, creating concerns that politicization might occur in the lower ranks of the bureaucracy.

This chapter will recount the debates of the last few decades about the principle of the political neutrality of the public service and the events that challenged the traditional norms and policies associated with this principle. We will see that, in the period from 1979 to 2006, there was considerable disagreement about the meaning and value of the political neutrality of the bureaucracy in a liberal democracy and, more importantly, about the appropriate safeguards that should flow from the desire to apply this principle to the staffing of Canada's public service. Throughout these debates and events, the Public Service Commission (PSC) played a key role in defending a strong version of political neutrality, reminding critics of its value to democratic government. But, as legitimate concerns about responsiveness to democratic control and the protection of the fundamental political rights of public servants gained in prominence, the PSC and its traditional conception of political neutrality suffered some setbacks. As it had done when facing other issues in the past, the PSC had to adapt and strive to find a new balance among these competing values, all of which were integral to Canadian democracy.

CONTROLLING A DISTRUSTED BUREAUCRACY: POLITICIZATION FROM THE TOP?

As already noted, the election of the Mulroney government in 1984 represented a historical shift in power for Canada. After decades of Liberal governments that had presided over the development of the welfare state, the arrival of a Progressive Conservative government committed to fiscal restraint and smaller government was somewhat of a worrisome prospect for the federal bureaucracy. The feeling of apprehension was mutual: several ministers and advisers of the incoming government distrusted the public service and saw it as a potential impediment to the implementation of its agenda.

While the new government might have harboured some prejudice about the competence of public servants,[2] the broader issue was their responsiveness to political control. In the government's view, public servants were invested in the status quo and excessively loyal to the social programs which they had built up over the preceding decades under Liberal leadership and which they were now paid to administer. As Peter White, a senior adviser in the Prime Minister's Office, put it in a memorandum to the Prime Minister in 1985,

> The Liberal Party, in office for 20 years out of 21 up to 1984, built the public service that we have inherited…. These appointments were made in a conscious and perfectly proper effort to fashion a senior public service that would be compatible with Trudeau's style and approach—the very style and approach that Canadian voters so emphatically rejected in September 1984. It is idle to think that these men and women, who have spent most of their public service careers designing and implementing the Trudeau/Pitfield approach to government, could suddenly become strongly committed to radically altering their own creation.[3]

In his note, White went so far as to say that more than half of Mulroney's Cabinet ministers appeared to be "dominated" by the "bureaucrats inherited from the Trudeau years" and that these senior officials were hindering the government's ability to implement the changes desired by the electorate.[4]

This view of the senior bureaucracy, in which the loyalty and responsiveness of senior officials was believed to be clouded by a combination of self-interest, past loyalties and ideological affinity with previous governments, undoubtedly coloured how the Mulroney government initially approached the issue of staffing the senior public service. Establishing greater political control of the bureaucracy became an important objective, and the government took a number of steps in this regard.

First, there is no doubt that the government looked carefully at the Order-in-Council appointments that were legitimately under its control. For example, Peter White, who served as the Prime Minister's special assistant for Governor-in-Council appointments at the time, explicitly argued that the Prime Minister's Office needed to get involved more intimately in the appointment and supervision of senior officials, especially deputy ministers, in order to ensure that the public service did not become an obstacle to implementing the government's agenda. As he put it,

> To reassure [Canadians], [the government] must make an early start on gaining control of the bureaucracy by identifying and installing some of our own chief operating officers as outlined above. This should not be done with fanfare and only at long intervals, but routinely and continuously over the government's mandate. We must also bear in mind that a handful of positions, in the PCO, the PSC, the Treasury Board, DRIE, etc., are the key to effective control of the bureaucracy.[5]

To gain political control of the public service, a new team of senior executives needed to be progressively put in place. The Mulroney government did move forward on this agenda, at least to some extent. About a year after taking office, it had already made forty-five new appointments at the deputy minister level.[6] Within two years, "virtually all the deputy ministers" had been changed and a new senior management team was in place, a level of transfers that Peter Aucoin, in his study of the new public management in this period, called "unprecedented".[7] However, while these appointments were seen "as a way of quickly establishing political control of the bureaucracy,"[8] they brought few political appointees from outside the public service into the senior executive rank. The difficulty of the work, coupled with a relatively poor compensation package, made it difficult to attract appropriate candidates from the private sector. In the end, the Prime Minister turned largely to experienced public servants to build his new team. As a result, while a measure of personal and ideological affinity might have been sought in making these senior bureaucratic appointments, it certainly did not lead to a major, American-style "politicization from the outside".[9]

A second approach to gaining greater political control of the bureaucracy was to exert political pressure for certain appointments to be made to positions covered by the *Public Service Employment*

Act (PSEA). This tack was more worrisome from the Public Service Commission's point of view. As Jack Manion, a former senior public servant, would later recall, many Progressive Conservative politicians were advocating for a more American approach to staffing, including "by extending political appointments down into the hierarchy."[10] For example, in interviews for this book, a number of former executives who worked for the PSC and for the senior personnel division of the Privy Council Office in the mid-1980s remembered that several new ministers had wanted to appoint their own senior officials at the assistant deputy minister level. The interviewees recounted having had multiple meetings with new ministers and their staff to explain why they could not simply hire the people they wanted. Some senior ministers, such as Deputy Prime Minister Erik Nielsen, who was well known for his aversion to the bureaucracy, were said to have particularly strong feelings about the need for more extensive ministerial input into the selection of senior departmental staff. While appointment requests were not unheard of under previous governments, the distrust of many ministers in the Mulroney government resulted in greater pressures on the PSC to yield to ministerial preferences. In the end, PSC officials were able to resist such pressures by pointing to the PSC's clear statutory authority in the area of staffing as well as to its institutional independence from the political executive.

A final, more innovative step taken by the Mulroney government to reassert political control over the bureaucracy was the strengthening of ministerial offices through, in particular, the creation of a new chief of staff position in every ministerial office. In fact, for some key ministers and advisers, such as Don Mazankowski and Tom d'Aquino, strengthening the political staff working with ministers seemed to provide the best means to counteract the power of the bureaucracy.[11] While ministerial offices obviously preceded the Mulroney government, they were smaller in size and rarely constituted a significant challenge to the bureaucracy. However, under the new government, ministerial advisers would be expected to play a larger role in the policy-making process and to help ensure that the ministers' decisions were understood and diligently implemented by their departments.[12] To clearly signal this new status, the most senior policy adviser was given the title of chief of staff, and the position's rank (and salary) was elevated to the equivalent of an Assistant Deputy Minister (i.e. EX-04).

From the point of view of staffing and the merit principle, the growth of ministerial offices presented a dual challenge. The first challenge was that ministerial staffers were political appointees who were exempted from the normal requirements associated with the merit system. In this regard, the *Public Service Employment Act* simply stipulated that ministers had the authority to hire their own staff, including their chief of staff; their appointments consequently fell outside the authority of the PSC.[13] However, as Liane Benoît has argued in a study done for the Gomery Commission, while the formal authority of ministerial staffers may be very limited, their access to the minister, their role in the policy process and their ability to speak "on behalf" of ministers in the operations of departments provides them with considerable influence.[14] As a result, ministerial staffers represent a set of actors who can often insert themselves into the operation of the public service without having been elected or selected on the basis of merit. In the long-standing tension between necessary bureaucratic responsiveness and undue politicization, growth in the number and influence of ministerial staffers would pose a danger of tilting the balance in favour of the latter.

The second challenge concerned the priority rights granted to political staffers who wanted to enter the public service after having spent at least three years in a minister's office. Under the provisions of the PSEA, senior exempt staff, such as chiefs of staff, legislative assistants and policy advisers, had the right to be appointed, in priority, to a position at an equivalent level in the public service. In effect, this meant that these former political appointees could enter the public service, at a fairly senior level, without being subject to the examinations and competitions normally required by the merit system.

The virtues of this kind of system have long been debated.[15] By providing a measure of security to political staffers, it can help attract people of high quality to important but short-lived jobs in politics. And there is no doubt that many former political staffers who have entered the public service in this way have turned out to be outstanding public servants and served loyally under governments of different partisan stripes. However, the potential for abuse also remains real, and a few instances of abuse can inflict considerable damage on the public trust.[16] In recent years, the "sponsorship scandal," involving the misuse of public funds for the benefit of the Liberal Party of Canada and a series of advertising firms,[17] certainly brought this fact into focus. In this case, the abuse of the government program was linked in part to the priority appointment of a minister's former chief of staff to a director general's position within the same department. In a matter of weeks, a political staffer who had been involved in the bureaucratic decision-making process for the attribution of funds to outside groups came to directly head the same program as a public servant.[18] While this priority appointment remained a small aspect of the controversy, it was a vivid example of the potential for abuse of the exempt staff provisions of the PSEA, and it was no doubt the reason why the new Conservative government repealed these controversial provisions in December 2006,[19] as had been recommended by the Gomery Commission.[20]

Ultimately, the attempts by the Mulroney government to gain greater political control of the bureaucracy do not seem to have resulted in significant change, the presence of chiefs of staff and the stronger ministerial offices having largely been described as "ineffective" and "unsuccessful".[21] The desire to make more political appointments to the senior bureaucracy did not yield much result either: there was no influx of outside political appointees into the ranks of deputy ministers and the anecdotal efforts to gain a greater say in the appointment of senior executives below the deputy ministerial rank were quashed by the PSC. After the initial period of distrust, like its predecessors, the Mulroney government turned to the professional bureaucracy to help run the government, and the Prime Minister began to urge his ministers to rely on the professional public service to manage their departments and to focus instead on their own ministerial and political duties. As Paul Tellier, clerk of the Privy Council at the time put it, "The Prime Minister started to realize after six months in power that he needed the public service perhaps more than they needed him."[22]

From the point of view of merit and the staffing system, this period can nevertheless be seen as characterized by the re-emergence of debates and concerns about the politicization of the public service. While it would be prudent not to exaggerate the importance of the political pressures placed on the staffing process at the time, one former PSC executive believed these pressures to be sufficiently strong to describe this period as "a crucial period for the PSC,"[23] in that it found itself having to fend off unusual pressures and affirm its independence. While the events of the period do not seem to have seriously threatened the integrity of the staffing process or the application of the merit principle, they do remind us of the ongoing need for safeguards against the politicization of the staffing process in a liberal democracy.

Moreover, as the particular case of the Mulroney government also reminds us, in a representative democracy, there are always legitimate concerns about the responsiveness of the bureaucracy to the direction of the elected government. Security of tenure, political neutrality and merit-based appointments are the foundations of a professional public service that can best serve the country's long-term interests, but care must always be taken to ensure that the implementation of a merit system does not inadvertently result in an unresponsive bureaucracy, unwilling to bend to the elected government's legitimate preferences. Staffing a professional bureaucracy is thus always a challenging balancing act, and the Mulroney government's efforts to exert greater control over the senior public service at least serve as a reminder that the desired point of equilibrium between political neutrality and responsiveness remains a matter of debate.

THE POLITICAL RIGHTS OF PUBLIC SERVANTS: POLITICIZATION FROM THE BOTTOM?

While the concerns and behaviour of the Mulroney government brought to the fore the difficult balance between neutrality and responsiveness in the senior ranks of the public service, over the same period, some key court decisions also forced the PSC to deal with concerns about the appropriate balance between the political neutrality of the bureaucracy and the political rights of public servants in the lower ranks of the public service. It has been a long established principle that, in order to preserve the political neutrality of the public service, it is necessary to curtail the rights of public servants to engage in partisan political activities. As we have seen, the protection of the political neutrality of the public service has been a central function of the PSC since its inception in the early 20th century. However, the exact norms and prohibitions that must flow from this general principle have been a more contentious matter. In the late 1980s and early 1990s, the PSC was forced to change its policies on this central issue.

The ideal of a neutral and professional public service able to independently provide policy advice and implement government policy without political consideration requires that public servants be non-partisan, and be seen as non-partisan by both the government of the day and the citizens who interact with them. If, because of their visible political engagement, public servants were to be known as partisan, their loyalty to the government of the day might be cast in doubt. But, equally problematic, their impartiality in the conduct of their duties might also be questioned by the citizens who are forced to interact with them and who do not share their politics. For example, a businessman with a well-known political affiliation might come to doubt the impartiality and motivation of a tax official making a determination about tax matters if it were well known that the official was extensively involved with a different party. Many public servants hold positions that grant them a measure of discretion in the implementation of the law or in the distribution of public funds and to sow doubts about potential political bias in the exercise of such discretion would undoubtedly be injurious to Canadian democracy and public trust in the public service.

For these reasons, the *Public Service Employment Act* has long contained provisions constraining the right of public servants to participate in political activities. More specifically, before the PSEA's reform in 2003, section 33 forbade deputy heads and other employees of the public service to "engage in work for or against a candidate" in an election, "engage in work for or against a political party," or "be a candidate." However, the act also made exceptions to this blanket prohibition. It stipulated clearly that making financial donations to a candidate or a political party and attending a political meeting were not prohibited.[24] Obviously, public servants also had the right to vote. Moreover, employees, unlike deputy heads, could also seek nomination and run for office, but only if they obtained permission from the PSC. In order to grant such permission, and consequently a leave of absence, the PSC had to determine that "the usefulness to the Public Service of the employee in the position the employee then occupies would not be impaired by reason of that employee having been a candidate."[25]

Over the years, these provisions had been the object of some contention, but as the language of rights became more prevalent in Canadian society, the issue of the political rights of public servants became more salient in Ottawa. As the Special Committee on the Review of Personnel Policy and the Merit Principle (the D'Avignon Committee) observed in 1979,

> The views of intervenors on the question of whether public servants should be free to participate in partisan political activity ran the gamut. Some clearly believed passionately in their right to unfettered involvement and declared that no public service legislation would extinguish that right. At the other extreme was the view that partisan activity by any public servant was sufficient to cast a shadow on the political neutrality of the entire public service. Our experience is that the younger public servants are the most insistent on having the freedom to participate in the political process.[26]

Perceiving a growing desire among public servants for political involvement, the D'Avignon Committee believed that the widespread prohibition against political activities was "out of step with reality" and ultimately "unenforceable".[27] Consequently, already in the late 1970s, the committee was recommending that the PSEA be amended to grant public servants a greater measure of freedom to engage in political activities.

The scheme proposed by the D'Avignon Committee was inspired largely by the British system and it followed from the principle, which would become important in Canadian law as well, that the rights of employees to participate in politics should vary based on their rank and functions. The committee did not dispute the importance of the political neutrality of the public service or the fact that it enhanced the value of the public service to the government and citizens, but it believed that many public servants, due to the nature of their work, could fully participate in the political process without comprising the bureaucracy's impartiality. As the Supreme Court of Canada would later put it, the consequences of having known partisan ties are hardly the same for a deputy minister and a cafeteria employee.[28] The higher the level of responsibility, the level of discretion and the potential influence on government decisions, the more important political neutrality becomes. The widespread prohibitions contained in the PSEA, which, for the most part, applied in the same manner to all employee categories and levels, were therefore considered to be excessive.

As a remedy, the D'Avignon Committee recommended in 1979 that the public service be divided into three groups for the purpose of determining employees' rights to political participation. A first group, comprising senior executives and senior managers, would be denied the right to participate actively in the political process, but such individuals would be allowed to make financial donations, attend political meetings and vote. A second group, which would include employees who performed duties that could be tainted by their political engagement, such as those involved in personnel administration or the awarding of contracts and grants, would see their right to political involvement made conditional on the PSC's approval. Finally, a third group, comprising all remaining occupational categories, would be granted "full freedom of political action," including the automatic right to seek nominations and run for office.[29]

At the time, the PSC strongly opposed such reforms. In its opinion, the expansion of the political rights of public servants would necessarily threaten the principle of political neutrality of the public service. In interview, Edgar Gallant, PSC president at the time, recalled that he did not see eye to eye with most deputy ministers on this issue and that resisting these proposals was very important to him. He held a strong view that public servants were professionals who should not engage, or be seen to be engaged, in electoral politics and partisan activities. In protecting the professional reputation of the public service, the perception of neutrality was as important as neutrality itself. To allow greater, more visible political participation by employees in its lower ranks would run the risk of breeding distrust in the entire public service.

While it seemed to be part of a minority that was resisting an expansion of political rights for public servants, the PSC was not alone. Indeed, Gallant's adherence to a strong version of political neutrality was later echoed by Supreme Court Justice William Stevenson, who issued a dissenting opinion in a landmark court case on the subject:

> The [PSEA] could distinguish between various levels of employees, but, in my view, the case against partisan activities is a strong one…. Once allegiances are known, the principles of neutrality, impartiality and integrity are endangered. There is a danger within the service that those seeking appointments and promotions will feel some incentive to cut their cloth to the known partisan interests of those who have influence over appointments and promotions. Visible partisanship by civil servants displays a lack of neutrality, and a betrayal of that convention of neutrality. The public perception of neutrality is thus severely impaired, if not destroyed…. I must say that to permit overt partisan political activity is to come perilously close to abandoning the principle of neutrality.[30]

It was this kind of strong version of political neutrality that underpinned the PSC's opposition to changes to the PSEA.

However, while it was able to block these reforms in the late 1970s, the PSC would be unable to prevent changes from being made to the law in the years that followed. Two court cases proved particularly significant in redefining the substance of political rights for public servants between 1985 and 1992: the Fraser decision of 1985 and the Osborne decision of 1991.[31]

The Fraser case involved a challenge by a Revenue Canada employee who was fired after expressing strong public criticism of government policies on the adoption of the metric system and on the constitutional entrenchment of a charter of rights and freedoms. In newspapers and on radio shows, Neil Fraser, the regional head of the Business Tax Division in Kingston, had repeatedly criticized the Trudeau government's policies and the government itself, going so far as to compare the government to the dictatorial government of Poland and to the regime of Nazi Germany.[32] He even wrote to the Leader of the Government in the British House of Commons, criticizing the Canadian government and pleading with the British government not to grant Canada's request to adopt a new constitution.[33] After several warnings, Fraser was dismissed from the public service. He then appealed to the Public Service Staff Relations Board and ultimately to the Supreme Court of Canada, arguing that the government was placing undue constraints on his freedom of speech in order to allegedly preserve the public service's impartiality and effectiveness.

In the end, the Supreme Court upheld Fraser's dismissal. As the Chief Justice put it, while not a constitutional case per se, the Fraser case turned on the issue of the

> proper legal balance between (i) the right of an individual, as a member of the Canadian democratic community, to speak freely and without inhibition on important public issues and (ii) the duty of an individual, *qua* federal public servant, to fulfil properly his or her functions as an employee of the Government of Canada.[34]

In rendering its decision in the case, the court provided some guidance on how such balance should be approached. It made it clear that, while the curtailment of public servants' freedom of speech was warranted by the objective of maintaining an impartial and loyal public service, public servants could not be "silent members of society" and had "some freedom to criticize the Government."[35] In the court's view, it was also incumbent upon civil servants to ensure that the substance, context and form of their public criticism were such that it would not impair their ability to perform their job as loyal and impartial government employees.[36] In Neil Fraser's case, the adjudicator quite reasonably inferred that the extensive and vitriolic nature of his criticism of major government policies had indeed impaired his ability to perform his duties.

In itself, the Fraser case did not represent a major blow to the political rights provisions of the PSEA, which remained intact. But it was nevertheless significant for two reasons. First, it confirmed the need to strike a new balance between preserving the impartiality of the public service and protecting the political rights of civil servants. While Fraser himself had clearly gone beyond the permissible limits, it was by no means clear that the PSC's stronger version of political neutrality struck the proper balance. As a former official of the PSC recalled in an interview, "The Fraser decision encouraged people seeking changes to the status quo, including union officials and some of their political allies in Parliament."[37] Second, in its reasons, the Supreme Court clearly endorsed the view that "the degree of restraint which must be exercised [on the right of political expression] is relative to the position and visibility of the civil servant."[38] In this way, the court indirectly endorsed the general logic previously expressed by the D'Avignon Committee, a view that clashed with the broader prohibitions favoured by the PSC. It was a clear signal that a new balance, one that acknowledged the political rights of civil servants to a greater extent, would need to be found in the coming years.

The second court decision, which altered the definition of the political rights of public servants more fundamentally, was handed down by the Supreme Court in 1991 in the Osborne case. The decision actually involved a series of cases relating to public servants whose right to participate in various political activities had been denied by the PSC. Osborne and Millar, two of the respondents in the case, had been elected as delegates to the 1984 Liberal party leadership convention, but they were then forced to resign as delegates after being advised by their department that they would suffer disciplinary actions if they failed to do so. Other respondents wanted to work, on their own time, for various candidates in the 1984 election campaign. One wanted simply to stuff envelopes from her home or the campaign office of the party she supported. Another employee, who felt strongly about the place of women in Canadian society, wanted to speak publicly in her community about which party she believed had the best electoral platform for advancing the status of women. In all cases, the central issue was whether the freedom of expression guaranteed by Section 2 of the *Charter of Rights and Freedoms* was unduly restricted by Section 33 of the PSEA. The courts considered the cases together. Having lost their trial in first instance, the public servants won their appeal in the Federal Court of Appeal in 1988. Seeking to protect the integrity of the PSEA, the PSC then appealed the decision to the Supreme Court.

The Supreme Court's Osborne decision dealt a significant blow to the political rights provisions of the *Public Service Employment Act*, invalidating subsections 33(1)(a) and (b). These two subsections prohibited public servants from engaging in "work for or against" a candidate or a political party, prohibitions that the PSC had strongly defended over the years. In its reasons, the Supreme Court again emphasized the importance of striking an appropriate balance between the freedom of expression of civil servants and the legitimate constraints placed upon this freedom for the sake of protecting the political neutrality of the public service. It specifically found the prohibitions on working for or against a party or a candidate to be excessively broad. While the legitimacy of Parliament's objective—ensuring an impartial public service—was never disputed, the means of doing so were found to fail the "minimal impairment" and "proportionality" tests imposed by the charter. The prohibitions of the PSEA went beyond what was necessary to preserve the political neutrality of the bureaucracy, thereby unnecessarily trampling a fundamental freedom of civil servants.

Again, in reaching its decision, the Supreme Court argued for a more differentiated set of prohibitions, based on the level and type of jobs. Pointing out that "a great number of public servants who in modern government are employed in carrying out clerical, technical or industrial duties that are completely divorced from the exercise of any discretion that could be in any manner affected by political considerations," the court stated that "the need for impartiality and indeed the appearance thereof does not remain constant throughout the civil service hierarchy."[39] It thus built upon the Fraser decision, similarly lending indirect support for the D'Avignon Committee's original proposal to adopt the British approach to the regulation of civil servants' political rights.

In the end, the Osborne decision left the PSC in a difficult position. While the provisions forbidding public servants to seek nomination and run for office, except with the explicit permission of the PSC, were left intact, other limits on political participation were not as clear. Refusing to read new provisions into the act, the Supreme Court had simply struck out the unconstitutional provisions, explicitly inviting Parliament to redraft the impugned provisions and amend the PSEA. But such parliamentary guidance would not be forthcoming, certainly not in the near future, and the commission needed to clarify the nature of the constraints remaining on public servants.

A few weeks after the Osborne decision was made public in June 1991, the PSC issued a statement announcing its new position. Signed by the three commissioners, the commission's statement said that while the statutory prohibition against working for or against a candidate or a political party no longer had any force,

> at the same time, employees should be aware that the principle of a politically neutral Public Service remains intact. Therefore, in engaging in political activities, they should exercise judgment and consider their specific circumstances, particularly with due regard to the loyalty they owe to the Government and to their obligation to act, and be seen to act, impartially when dealing with the public.[40]

With respect to their right to criticize the government in public, employees were simply referred to the 1985 Fraser decision.

The exact meaning of this statement of policy is unclear and it certainly provided little guidance on what was actually permissible and what was not. More of an exhortation to act responsibly than a statement of rules, it no doubt reflected the absence of a clear legal foundation to regulate the political behaviour of civil servants. Following the Osborne decision, with the exception of the prohibition on running for office, the commission seemed to have little legal recourse to prevent other forms of partisan engagement by public servants. As a former official of the commission put it, "The PSC, TBS and deputy heads are not in a position to do much when an employee engages in political activity which is not acceptable."[41]

A few years later, at the time of the 1993 general election, the Treasury Board Secretariat issued a set of principles and guidelines, drafted in close collaboration with the Public Service Commission.[42] The *Guidelines on Employee Rights and Responsibilities during an Election* remained equally vague. After informing employees that they could engage in "activities of a political nature," the guidelines exhorted them to remain loyal to their employer, the Government of Canada, and exercise some restraint in their political involvement so as to avoid jeopardizing the tradition of the public service as a politically neutral institution. Employees were encouraged to consult senior management if they had doubts about the political activities that they were contemplating. Again, with respect to the public criticism of government, employees were simply reminded that the Fraser decision had held that a balance had to be struck between an employee's freedom of expression and the public interest in preserving an impartial public service.[43] The exact nature of that balance, and how it could be struck, was not explained.

This ambiguous situation, where the principle of political neutrality continued to be deemed important but failed to be supported by clear statutory provisions, did not sit easily with the PSC. Internally, the commission, which was already wishing for more detailed statutory provisions in the 1980s, discussed the rationale and potential outline of a new law that would enshrine the principle of political neutrality. In an internal document developed to consider new legislative measures, it argued,

> The integrity of the Public Service is at some risk: the TBS, deputy heads and employees themselves do not know with sufficient certainty where they stand…. The PSC's role as guardian of the non-partisanship of the Public Service had stood for years. Ever since *Osborne, Millar* its leadership role has become blurred. Yet federal, provincial and territorial general elections and by-elections are held on an on-going basis and employees and managers continue to look to the PSC (as well as TBS, now) for advice with respect to candidacy as well as other political activity. The PSC stands to gain from its role being clarified.[44]

A new law could bring the necessary clarity. In particular, in considering the potential content of such legislation, the commission's staff was proposing that the new legislation create a restricted class of employees and specify the activities that would be permitted, and those that would not, for this class of persons. Then, those employees who did not fall into that restricted class would enjoy broad freedom to engage in all activities, with the potential exception of some specified activities that would be universally prohibited. The restricted class would include the entire executive group, employees having substantial management duties or input in policy formulation as well as those exercising significant discretion in implementing government programs, such as making decisions on giving grants, imposing penalties or negotiating contracts.[45] Unfortunately, in the wake of the Osborne judgment, there seemed to be little interest among politicians in tackling this issue in Parliament.

In fact, the only attempt to amend the political provisions of the PSEA in the early 1990s was an attempt to further weaken the law by striking out the only part of Section 33 that was left unscathed by the Osborne decision: the prohibition on seeking nomination and running for office. In the early 1990s, concerns about electoral participation and democratic practices led the Mulroney government to establish a Royal Commission on Electoral Reform and Party Financing, also known as the Lortie Commission. The Lortie Commission tabled its report at the end of 1991, making a wide range of recommendations to reform the electoral process, and, somewhat surprisingly, it recommended that all federal employees be granted an automatic right to a leave of absence to seek nomination and to be a candidate in a federal election.[46]

The Lortie Commission's rationale for the proposed changes rested largely on perceived contradictions in the current federal policy on the political activities of civil servants. It pointed out that, under the existing system, the government could always appoint individuals from outside the public service, even people who had obvious partisan ties, to deputy minister positions. Moreover, the priority rights granted to ministerial staffers under the PSEA meant that a number of people with very recent, high-level partisan ties were entering the higher echelons of the public service on a regular basis. It was also a common practice for some senior civil servants to join ministerial offices for a while, before returning to their public service jobs, in order to provide ministers with needed expertise in policy and public administration.[47] All these movements in personnel, the Lortie Commission pointed out, amounted to an acknowledgment by the federal government that professional public servants can have partisan, political experience and still adhere to the norms of a neutral and non-partisan bureaucracy once they are appointed, or return, to a public service job. If we believe that partisan political activities, even recent ones, are compatible with maintaining a neutral public service in the higher ranks of the public service, the Lortie Commission asked, why would it not be the same throughout the entire public service? This view also seemed supported by the fact that several provinces already considered a leave of absence to run for election to be the right of public servants, as opposed to a privilege to be granted on a case-by-case basis.[48]

When it considered the Royal Commission's recommendation, the Special Committee of the House of Commons on Electoral Reform initially looked favourably upon the recommendation and considered it as part of a package of legislative changes. Needless to say, the PSC took a different view. Its president at the time, Robert Giroux, mounted a strong defence against the proposal. Giroux and his two commissioners wrote to Jim Hawke, chairman of the Special Committee, to express their "serious concerns with respect to the proposal," arguing that it could have "serious and potentially far-reaching effects on the political neutrality of the Public Service."[49] The commission also submitted a brief to the parliamentary committee arguing strongly against the amendment.

In these documents, the PSC pointed out that the impartiality of the public service had been considered by the courts as an important constitutional convention, even "an essential prerequisite of responsible government."[50] It also reminded the parliamentarians that the Mulroney government itself, in the context of its administrative reform initiative called "Public Service 2000," had recently reiterated its commitment to the "scrupulously non-partisan character" of the public service, stating that this non-partisan character was needed for it "to be professional and effective in supporting the Government of the day and providing service to Canadians."[51] By granting all public servants the automatic right to run for office, Parliament would threaten this desired political neutrality and could impair the usefulness of the bureaucracy.

In defence of this viewpoint, the commission relied on two key arguments. First, it pointed out that the Supreme Court, in the Fraser and Osborne decisions, had explicitly stated that, despite the need to allow civil servants a greater degree of political expression, political neutrality remained an important constitutional principle and that some balance had to be struck between these two competing objectives. Moreover, the court clearly thought that a public servant's level in the hierarchy, and his or her public visibility, degree of discretion in distributing sanctions or benefits and degree of influence on government policy were all factors that should be considered before permitting the public servant to fully engage in political activities. By granting an automatic right to seek nominations and run for office to **all** public servants, and taking away the Public Service Commission's discretion, the proposed legislative measures would clearly run counter to this approach. In the commission's words, it would "run contrary to the spirit of the Supreme Court judgment."[52] Without an authority like the PSC to judge each case on its particular merits, no proper balance could be struck.

Second, the commission argued that there was no convincing evidence that the Section 33 provisions created a significant barrier for public servants who wanted to run for office. In fact, these permissions were seldom denied. From 1967 to 1992, the PSC granted 230 permissions out of 256 requests, an approval rate of ninety percent.[53] Moreover, none of the twenty-eight employees who, over that period of twenty-five years, saw their application denied challenged the commission's decision in court.[54] In sum, the commission's discretion both allowed it to prevent cases where excessive political engagement by a public servant could have compromised the neutrality, or perception of neutrality, of the bureaucracy and allowed the vast majority of those who wanted to run for office to do so in perfect legality. From the point of view of encouraging electoral participation, Section 33 of the PSEA hardly seemed to be a significant barrier.

It is not clear whether the commission's position would have ultimately prevailed, as there appeared to be a fair degree of consensus across parties on most of the proposed reforms. But the dissolution of Parliament put a stop to the legislative process and, consequently, Section 33 of the PSEA was left untouched. A few years later, in the fall of 1998, Jean Chrétien's Liberal government considered reintroducing the same legislative proposal. In its internal debates, the PSC reached the same conclusion as in 1992 and intended to strongly oppose the measure, inside the public service but also in a more public way, using its independence as an agent of Parliament. As an internal memo stated at the time,

> [Privy Council Office] officials need to be informed that the Commission would not support a move to reduce the Commission's authority in this area. The Commission reserves the right to make this view known to any parliamentary committee that may subsequently study this matter.[55]

In the end, again, the PSEA was not amended, the provisions on running for office were left untouched and another attempt at undercutting the commission's remaining authority was pushed back.

Changes in the political rights provisions of the PSEA were finally made in 2003, when Parliament adopted the *Public Service Modernization Act* (PSMA) in an effort to overhaul the entire human resources system of the federal public service. Since the PSMA represented such a comprehensive legislative change, it presented an obvious opportunity to clarify the government's policy on the political rights of civil servants. However, it is interesting to note that the approach adopted at this time varied significantly from the one considered by Parliament in 1991 and 1998. Largely driven by the senior public service, in the context of a major initiative focused on improving the public service as opposed to a specific measure to improve electoral participation, the 2003 legislative reform did not seek to introduce an automatic right to a leave of absence to run for office, but rather to inscribe directly in law the state of policy resulting from the Supreme Court decisions of the previous decades and to restore the ability of the Public Service Commission to enforce this policy.

Part 7 of the new PSEA explicitly recognizes, for the first time, the need to reconcile the right of employees to engage in political activities with the need to preserve the political neutrality of the public service, and it allows employees to engage in such activities as long as they do not impair their ability to do their job in a politically impartial manner. Employees who wish to seek a party's nomination and run for office must obtain the Public Service Commission's approval, and, for the first time, this obligation extends to participation in municipal elections. These measures apply to all employees of the federal public service, with the exception of deputy heads, who are explicitly prohibited from participating in any political activity with the exception of voting. This new wording concerning deputy heads appears to further limit the scope of their political participation since, under the older version of the statute, they were also allowed to make donations to political parties and individual candidates. Finally, the new PSEA clearly established the Public Service Commission's authority to investigate any allegation that an employee has violated these provisions on the political activities of public servants. The PSC can even investigate alleged violations of the ban on political activities by deputy heads, reporting its conclusion to the Governor-in-Council, provided that the allegation is made by a person who is or has been a candidate in an election.[56]

By restoring some of the PSC's authority to limit the political activities of civil servants while taking into account the new legal landscape brought about by the Osborne decision, the new legislative measures tried to strike a new balance between the competing objectives of neutrality, political participation and freedom of expression. But they were found lacking by some observers and stakeholders. For example, Gordon Robertson, former clerk of the Privy Council, thought that they were "completely in conflict with the principle of neutrality" and he expressed great concern about their impact.[57] Similarly, Donald Savoie, a noted scholar of public administration, argued that the new act should have simply outlawed political involvement by all senior managers: "Every single executive or manager in the public service

should have no interest whatsoever in partisan politics," he said. "If
they do, then they should do the honourable thing and leave the public
service."[58] In contrast to these advocates of greater restrictions, Nycole
Turmel, president of the Public Service Alliance of Canada, argued that
the new provisions would amount to taking back "the right of federal
government workers to engage freely in political activities."[59]

However, despite these criticisms, the new provisions on the
political activities of civil servants attracted relatively limited attention
in the overall debate about the *Public Service Modernization Act*, which
focused to a greater extent on changes to the definition of merit and
on labour relations. As a result of the work of the parliamentary
committee that studied the bill, its original version was amended to
provide somewhat more flexibility for the PSC to grant leaves of varied
lengths for employees seeking to become candidates in elections. Other
amendments resulted in the strengthened authority of the commission to
investigate allegations of breaches of the political activities provisions.[60]
But, on the whole, these amendments subscribed to the overall approach
that now characterized the federal government's policy on the political
activities of public servants, and the proposed measures were adopted
with little change or resistance.

As a result, by the end of 2003, Parliament had brought back a
measure of clarity on how the federal public service should approach the
difficult balance between the political impartiality of the bureaucracy
and the rights of public servants to participate in the democratic
process. While the new law clearly represented a shift in policy from
the position historically preferred by Public Service Commission, it
nevertheless continued to rely on the commission, as an independent
authority, to guard the fundamental principle of the political neutrality
of the public service.

Conclusion: Balancing Neutrality, Responsiveness and Political Rights

Between 1979 and 2006, as its political and legal context changed,
the PSC had to find ways to continue to protect the fundamental

value of the political neutrality of the public service while ensuring an appropriate level of responsiveness to political leadership and respect for the fundamental rights of civil servants. As the events recounted in this chapter have illustrated, finding a new balance among these competing values and objectives was not easy. There is no doubt that events, especially court decisions, pushed the commission to rethink its definition of political neutrality, and how to best preserve it, to a greater extent than it would have done otherwise. Ultimately, a new compromise between the political rights of civil servants and their neutrality in service of the state, originally resisted by the PSC, came to redefine Canadian policy on the political activities of civil servants.

While blatant politicization at the top was resisted, this period saw developments in this regard that became worrisome for some observers of public administration. While ministerial offices were somewhat reduced in size as a result of the Mulroney years, they were now permanent and important fixtures of Canadian government, entrenching a cohort of potentially influential staffers at the higher levels of the Canadian government who were exempt from the merit system and whose role in government decision-making and operations was not always well defined. Also of concern was the appointment of political staffers through the use of priority rights under the PSEA, but that pathway into the public service was closed in 2006.[61]

However, while these developments could be regarded in some ways as setbacks, this chapter has also shown how the PSC contributed to ensuring that the fundamental value of political neutrality was not simply sacrificed on the altars of political responsiveness and participation over this period. It repeatedly reminded the courts of the fundamental importance of preserving a politically neutral public service, and it succeeded in pushing back attempts to automatically grant leaves of absence to public servants wishing to run for office. The commission also saw its role in preserving the political neutrality of the bureaucracy reaffirmed with the 2003 legislative reform, in particular with the entrenchment of new and clearer provisions in the *Public Service Employment Act*. In fact, as we have seen, these legislative changes even extended somewhat the coverage of the restrictions on political activities.

Clearly, then, the struggle over political neutrality in this period cannot be seen as a simple story of politicization. In fact, not only did political neutrality remain part of the set of fundamental principles meant to be protected by the staffing system, but it was even clearly and explicitly recognized by the Supreme Court as a constitutional convention, most notably in the Osborne decision. It is worth remembering that, in this case, the court stated that "the existence of a convention of political neutrality, central to the principle of responsible government ... is not seriously disputed" and that "while they are not laws, some conventions may be more important than some laws. Their importance depends on that of the value or principle which they are meant to safeguard. Also they form an integral part of the constitution and the constitutional system."[62] In sum, despite the transformations and setbacks over this period, the value of a politically neutral public service remained an important part of the Canadian model of public administration, and the Public Service Commission remained a central actor in promoting and protecting this fundamental principle.

ENDNOTES

[1]   Quoted in David Zussman (1986), "Walking the Tightrope: The Mulroney Government and the Public Service," in Michael J. Prince, (ed.), *How Ottawa Spends 1986–87*, Toronto, Methuen, 255.

[2]   Donald J. Savoie (1994), *Thatcher, Reagan, Mulroney: In Search of a New Bureaucracy*, University of Toronto Press, Toronto, 94.

[3]   The memorandum is reproduced in full in appendix of Peter C. Newman (2005), *The Secret Mulroney Tapes: Unguarded Confessions of a Prime Minister*, Toronto, Random House Canada, 453–456. The quote is on page 456.

[4]   Newman (2005), *Secret Mulroney Tapes*, 456.

[5]   The memorandum is fully reproduced in appendix of Newman (2005), *Secret Mulroney Tapes*, 456.

[6]   The number comes from a "patronage tally" done by the government at the time and reprinted in an Appendix to Newman's *Secret Mulroney Tapes*, 450.

[7]   Peter Aucoin (1995), *The New Public Management: Canada in Comparative Perspective*, Montreal, IRPP, 59.

8   Jacques Bourgault and Stéphane Dion (1989), "Governments Come and Go, but What of Senior Civil Servants? Canadian Deputy Ministers and Transitions in Power (1867–1987)," *Governance*, 2:2, 144.

9   Peter Aucoin (1995), *The New Public Management: Canada in Comparative Perspective*, Montreal, IRPP.

10   John L. Manion (1991), "Career Public Service in Canada: Reflections and Predictions," *International Review of Administrative Sciences*, 57:3, 362.

11   Liane E. Benoît (2006), "Ministerial Staff: The Life and Times of Parliament's Statutory Orphans," in *Commission of Inquiry into the Sponsorship Program and Advertising Activities, Restoring Accountability – Research Studies, Volume 1: Parliament, Ministers and Deputy Ministers*, Ottawa, Public Works and Government Services Canada, 160–161.

12   Loretta J. O'Connor (1991), "Chief of Staff," *Policy Options*, 12:3, 24.

13   The relevant provisions are contained in Article 39 of the *Public Service Employment Act*, 1985.

14   Benoît (2006), "Ministerial Staff," 190–204.

15   Ibid.

16   Obviously, the danger of politicization is not simply a matter of the number of employees who are appointed to the senior public service in this way. On this score, the number of ministerial staffers choosing to enter the public service through this method has always remained relatively small. Liane Benoît calculated that only about 8% of the exempt staff, or 26 persons per year on average, entered the public service in this way between 1998 and 2005. See (2006), "Ministerial Staff," 219.

17   For a detailed account of these events, see Gilles Toupin (2006), *Le déshonneur des libéraux: Le scandale des commandites*, Montréal, VLB éditeur.

18   The employee in question, Pierre Tremblay, resigned his position in November 2001.

19   The *Federal Accountability Act* repealed the Minister's staff priority provision of the *Public Service Employment Act*, effective December 2006. It should be noted that, while the exempt staff priority provision of the PSEA was repealed in 2006, public servants may still take a leave of absence from their job to work in a minister's office and benefit from a "leave of absence priority" to return to their job or an equivalent position if their job has been filled on an indeterminate basis, when they leave the minister's office. But, in these cases, the returning public servant's initial appointment to the public service has at least already been authorized by the PSC under the normal procedures associated with the merit system.

20   *Commission of Inquiry into the Sponsorship Program and Advertising Activities* (2006), *Restoring Accountability: Recommendations*, Ottawa, Public Works and Government Services Canada, 138.

21   Aucoin (1995), *New Public Management*, 52–53; and Donald J. Savoie (1994), *Thatcher, Reagan, Mulroney: In Search of a New Bureaucracy*, University of Toronto Press, Toronto, 225.

22   Tellier is quoted in Newman (2005), *Secret Mulroney Tapes*, 197.

23   Interview with a former senior official of the PSC.

24   *Public Service Employment Act*, section 33(2), *1985*.

25   *Public Service Employment Act*, section 33(3), *1985*.

26   *Report of the Special Committee on the Review of Personnel Management and the Merit Principle*, Ottawa, Ministry of Supply and Services Canada, 1979, 175.

27   Ibid.

28   *Osborne v. Canada (Treasury Board)*, [1991] 2 S.C.R. 69, 39.

29   *Report of the Special Committee on the Review of Personnel Management and the Merit Principle*, Ottawa, Ministry of Supply and Services Canada, 1979, 172–174.

30   *Osborne v. Canada (Treasury Board)*, [1991] 2 S.C.R. 69, 49–50.

31   *Fraser v. P.S.S.R.B.*, [1985] 2 S.C.R. 455; and *Osborne v. Canada (Treasury Board)*, [1991] 2 S.C.R. 69.

32   *Fraser v. P.S.S.R.B.*, [1985] 2 S.C.R. 455, par. 6 and 8.

33   Ibid, par. 49.

34   Ibid, par. 1.

35   Ibid, par. 31 and 36.

36   Ibid, par. 50.

37   Interview with a former senior official of the PSC.

38   *Fraser v. P.S.S.R.B.*, [1985] 2 S.C.R. 455, par. 30.

39   *Osborne v. Canada (Treasury Board)*, [1991] 2 S.C.R. 69, 38–39.

40   Public Service Commission of Canada (1991), *Political Activities of Public Servants: Judgment of the Supreme Court of Canada Public Service Commission v. Millar, Osborne and others – Section 33 of the Public Service Employment Act*, Ottawa.

41   Interview with a former senior official of the PSC.

42   Interview with a former senior official of the PSC.

43   Treasury Board (1993), *Guidelines on Employee Rights and Responsibilities during an Election*, Ottawa, September 1993.

44   *The Political Activities of Public Servants – Rationale for and Outline of a Legislative Proposal*, dated June 16, 1994, 1.

45   Public Service Commission, *Detailed Outline of a Legislative Proposal regarding the Political Activities of Public Servants*, dated November 12, 1993.

46   Royal Commission on Electoral Reform and Party Financing (1991), *Reforming Electoral Democracy*, volume 1, Ottawa, Minister of Supply

and Services Canada, 80–83. It can be noted that the royal commission actually proposed that federal employees receive an automatic leave of absence to run in federal elections only and that the parliamentary committee that studied its report and proposed changes did not extend these recommendations to provincial elections. For provincial elections, the PSC would have continued to weigh the consequences of granting such a leave for the impartiality of the public service. In its representation to the parliamentary committee that studied these recommendations, the PSC made the point that this distinction between federal and provincial elections seemed largely unfounded.

[47]   Ibid, 81.

[48]   Ibid.

[49]   Letter from Robert Giroux to Jim Hawke, chairperson of the Special Committee of the House of Commons on Electoral Reform, dated April 9, 1992.

[50]   Public Service Commission of Canada (1992), *Brief to the Special Committee of the House of Commons on Electoral Reform*, Ottawa, 2.

[51]   Ibid.

[52]   Ibid, 5.

[53]   Ibid, 3.

[54]   Ibid, 4.

[55]   Memorandum from Judith Moses, executive director, Policy, Research and Communication, to the Secretary General of the Commission, entitled "Political Activities of the Public Servants," dated November 4, 1998, 4.

[56]   All of these provisions are contained in sections 111 to 119 of the new *Public Service Employment Act*, 2003.

[57]   Quoted in Bill Curry (2003), "Letting Public Servants Become Politically Active a 'Mistake': Former Advisors to PMs," *National Post*, March 5, 2003, A7.

[58]   Ibid.

[59]   Public Service Alliance of Canada (2003), "Bill C-25: A Worrisome Piece of Legislation," Press release dated June 5, 2003.

[60]   See the speeches by Lucienne Robillard (president of the Treasury Board) and Paul Forseth, MP for New Westminster-Coquitlam-Burnaby (Canadian Alliance), in *Debates of the House of Commons (Hansard)*, No. 107, 37th Parliament, 2nd session, May 28, 2003, for a description of the amendments adopted in response to the parliamentary committee's work.

[61]   For example, see Donald Savoie (2004), "The Search for a Responsive Bureaucracy in Canada," in B. Guy Peters and Jon Pierre (eds.), *Politicization of the Civil Service in Comparative Perspective: The Quest for Control*, London and New York, Routledge, 152–153.

[62]   *Osborne v. Canada (Treasury Board)*, [1991] 2 S.C.R. 69, 24–25.

THE PSC AS A CAUTIOUS REFORMER: STAFFING REFORMS DURING THE MULRONEY YEARS: 1984-1993

"In summary, [the *Public Service Reform Act*], as I see it, represents very much a balancing act—balancing the very real need for a more effective Public Service with the equally compelling need to preserve merit, and protect employees."

– Robert Giroux, PSC president,
speaking before a parliamentary committee on March 11, 1992

When Brian Mulroney's government came to power in the mid-1980s, concerns about recurring federal deficits and the fast-growing national debt occupied an important place in public discourse. Government downsizing and cutbacks were prominent issues in policy discussions and the Progressive Conservative Party had made them significant electoral issues in the lead-up to the 1984 election. Moreover, the oil shocks of the 1970s, economic downturns, the ensuing crisis of the welfare state, and the rise of a new, or revivified, conservative movement in many countries also meant that the retrenchment of the state was popular well beyond Canada's borders. In fact, as Professor Peter Aucoin observed,

Mulroney's attacks on government generally, and the public service in particular, obviously struck a responsive chord; four years of international attention to Thatcherism, coupled with the rise of neo-conservatism and extensive government and bureaucracy bashing south of the border in two successive American presidential elections, had more than conditioned the Canadian polity to these new forces.[1]

Seen as a conservative in the mould of Margaret Thatcher and Ronald Reagan, Mulroney himself had long been critical of the public service, considering it "unresponsive, costly and largely ineffective" and wanting to transform it so that it would operate more like the private sector.[2] His views of the public service at the time were probably most vividly captured in his oft-quoted remark that he would dismiss public servants "with a pink slip and a pair of running shoes."[3] Clearly, in 1984, public servants had legitimate reasons to feel apprehensive about the new government.

The formation of the Mulroney government seemed to herald difficult times for the Public Service Commission (PSC) as well. In some ways, the cumbersome and rule-heavy staffing system that it was operating and overseeing seemed to be the antithesis of results-focused, private-sector-style management. At a time when the new government was resuscitating the Glassco Commission's mantra of "let the managers manage,"[4] the PSC appeared to embody an ineffective split in the human resource function of the public service and it seemed synonymous with excessive constraints on departmental managers. Moreover, the prospect of budget cuts and layoffs suggested that the PSC could anticipate both a decline in its own resources and a spike in the number of staffing transactions that it would have to handle as public servants lost their jobs or were displaced through governmental reorganization. The PSC could very well end up having to deal with significant downsizing at the same time as it would be fighting for its own integrity or survival.

As it turned out, while the downsizing and cutbacks were real and represented a challenge for the commission in the late 1980s, their size and effect were not as dramatic as might have been expected from the government's initial rhetoric. The announcement of the first downsizing program in 1985 certainly had an immediate impact on the level of appointments to the public service: the number of appointments dropped from 11,046 in 1985 to 7,627 in 1986, a stunning decline of 33.1%, and the PSC had to turn its attention to dealing with the priority status of laid-off and surplus employees. But this effect quickly subsided and normalcy returned: by 1990, new appointments had reached 11,609, a slightly higher number than in 1985.[5] Moreover, at the end of the Mulroney government's tenure, the size of the public service had remained essentially the same. The federal bureaucracy numbered 223,598 employees in 1992, only a slight decrease from the 224,026 employees that it had when the Progressive Conservatives took office in 1984.[6]

The reality was that the Mulroney government's eight years in power amounted to much more for the PSC than budget cuts and layoffs: those years were marked by successive attempts at reforming the staffing process, first through policy changes and then through the first changes to staffing legislation since the late 1960s. Throughout this period, the commission had to answer renewed calls for greater flexibility, economy and efficiency in staffing, while fighting for the preservation of sufficient safeguards for protecting the merit principle. It also had to fight off reforms that would have significantly curtailed its own authority in the staffing system, reducing it to little more than a parliamentary oversight body. The object of much criticism, it nevertheless continued to act as an important counterweight in the management system of the bureaucracy, trying to change its policies and practices to meet government expectations for greater efficiency while at the same time tempering the zeal of reformers by adhering to the more traditional values and principles of the Canadian public service.

RESPONDING TO CUTBACKS AND THE RHETORIC OF THE NEW PUBLIC MANAGEMENT

The Mulroney government did not lose any time in setting the agenda for the public service. On his very first day in office, the Prime Minister appointed a ministerial-level task force to look at potential reforms, with the purpose of decreasing the cost of the bureaucracy and improving its efficiency by shedding some functions, but mostly by streamlining its procedures. The Task Force on Program Review, the Prime Minister announced, would find ways to simplify government programs, make them more accessible for citizens and delegate decision-making about their operation closer to the frontlines of service delivery.[7] As a sign of its intended importance, as well as its orientation, Deputy Prime Minister Erik Nielsen, a well-known critic of the public service, was appointed as its chairman.

Indicative of the new government's philosophy, the Nielsen Task Force operated under the guidance of an advisory committee composed of private sector executives. A series of study teams made up of civil servants and business representatives examined government programs, and their recommendations were discussed with the private sector advisory committee before being submitted to ministers. It was thought that the heavy involvement of the private sector would help to bring in new ideas to improve public management.[8] In this way, much like the Grace Commission that advised President Reagan on administrative reforms in the United States in the same period, the Nielsen Task Force was largely premised on the superiority of private sector management and on the belief that the public service could not reform itself. It constituted an external challenge to the public service and a signal that private sector practices were deemed to be promising models for the public sector.

At the same time as the Nielsen Task Force got under way, the government's strong desire to bring significant changes to the public service was equally underscored by the announcement of significant cutbacks in personnel. In its first budget, tabled in May 1985, the Mulroney government decreed a net reduction of 15,000 person-years in the size of the federal bureaucracy, a target to be achieved by fiscal year 1990–1991.[9] The PSC itself faced significant cutbacks in personnel that were proportionally greater than those faced by the public service as a whole. As a result of the 1985 announcement, the PSC had to eliminate 276 positions; at the same time, changes to language training policy introduced by the Treasury Board meant that an additional 325 positions had to be eliminated in this program.[10] As a result, the number of employees at the Commission progressively declined, falling from 2,563 employees in 1985 to 2,017 employees in 1992.[11] This twenty-one percent reduction in personnel, at a time when staffing actions were on the rise due to layoffs and reorganization, not only created capacity problems for the commission, but it also affected the morale of its employees.[12]

These government decisions significantly affected the commission's operations. The immediate impacts were related to the staffing actions needed to deliver on the government's commitment to reduce the size of the workforce. Working with the Treasury Board Secretariat, the commission tried to limit the effects of the downsizing by using attrition as opposed to layoffs whenever possible and by retraining and redeploying employees. It also put in place a Priority Administration System to try to ensure that employees would be treated with fairness and that the public service would retain as much of its talent as possible through the efficient reallocation of personnel across the system. In sum, the commission sought to implement the government's decision to reduce the workforce of the public service, while seeking to ensure that the use of remaining personnel would be optimized and that the system would not lose sight of the public service's commitment to fairness in the treatment of employees.

However, beyond imposing these more immediate impacts on operations, the public discourse of the incoming government, the creation of the Nielsen Task Force and the announcement of the first wave of cutbacks also sent a clear message to the PSC: the new government was serious about an agenda of greater efficiency, streamlined procedures and economy. While staffing had not been publicly singled out as a specific target of managerial reform by the Progressive Conservatives, it seemed clear to the commission's leadership that the well-known and persistent dissatisfaction of managers with the rigidity and slowness of the staffing process would eventually make it a prime target for reform.[13] As recently as 1983, the Office of the Auditor General had identified staffing as an area of particular concern for public executives, citing excessive staffing rules as a key constraint to productive management in the public service. Having interviewed about 170 senior executives, the Auditor General reported,

> Of all the constraints mentioned by public service executives, staffing problems were viewed as the most persistent and frustrating.

> According to the majority of executives we interviewed, the number
> of months it takes to staff a position is seen as an unreasonable length
> of time, in view of pressing operational requirements.[14]

The Auditor General's report had already generated some reaction within the commission, and work had begun on a new administrative review of the staffing process. However, the arrival of the new government, and its embrace of the new public management philosophy, brought a new sense of urgency to these concerns.

With the appointment of a new president, Huguette Labelle, in 1985, the PSC decided to embrace the need for change by setting its own agenda. A former senior official working with the Treasury Board Secretariat at the time remembers how Labelle's appointment was seen as a sign that significant reforms would be made to the commission. Highly respected within the senior ranks of the public service, the new president was presumed by many observers to hold views largely favourable to managerial interests.[15] But under her leadership, the commission would proceed with caution in charting a course for reform, mindful that, despite calls for more radical changes from advocates of the new public management philosophy, the commission played a unique role in defending some of the fundamental principles and values of the Canadian public service.

Under Labelle's leadership, the PSC developed a new strategic plan, published in 1985, which acknowledged the need for greater efficiency but also carefully staked out its role as the guardian of merit and political neutrality. In describing its mandate, the commission clearly stressed its unique status as "a politically independent agency, accountable to Parliament for the administration of the *Public Service Employment Act*."[16] Moreover, as if to warn the government against possible encroachment on its territory, the plan asserted that "the resolve of commission strategy is dependent on the category of responsibility to which an issue relates,"[17] While it would respond as much as possible to the guidance of the Governor-in-Council and the Treasury Board in areas of shared responsibility (for example, training or the Management Category), it would remain independent and set its own direction in its areas of statutory responsibilities. In these areas, the document stated, "The Commission is secure in its authority to establish strategy and lead the administration of the *Public Service Employment Act*."[18]

It is only after clearly reaffirming the commission's independence in the area of staffing that the strategic plan outlined the need for change to adapt to the new management environment. But even then, it made it clear that change would be made incrementally, with caution. For example, as if to dampen reformers' expectations, the plan stipulated from the outset,

> *Major change is not likely to occur* as it pertains to the appointment of public servants on the basis of their professional and personal qualifications as opposed to political affiliation or for services rendered. But *refinements to the effectiveness* of the PSC's programs and activities both as a department and as a central agency are a continuing requirement within the context of the current public service restraint environment.[19] (emphasis added)

In other words, despite pressures for more radical changes, the commission would mostly set out to alter its practices at the margins, seeking improvements in the operation of the merit system without fundamentally altering its nature. The need for greater efficiency was acknowledged, but the commission remained committed to the protection of other values also served by the merit system.

However, despite this cautious approach to reform, the commission did promise some changes. As an organization, it exhorted its managers to "internalize and personalize the habits of restraint, management planning and creativity" needed to increase productivity "within a static or shrinking resource base."[20] But more significantly, as a central agency impacting the entire public service, it committed itself to a comprehensive review of the bureaucracy's staffing procedures, even raising the possibility of pursuing legislative changes for the first time since 1967.

At the administrative level, the commission was determined to engage departmental managers to a greater extent. The *1983 Report of the Office of the Auditor General* had clearly pointed to a significant degree of departmental dissatisfaction that needed to be overcome. To address this weakness, the commission's strategy would focus on closer collaboration with departmental managers in order to facilitate staffing decisions at the departmental level and ultimately improve productivity. A series of administrative reviews conducted with departmental managers would serve to identify changes in rules and practices that might improve performance. This collaborative strategy would guide its efforts in the area of non-legislative renewal.

But to improve efficiency in the use of personnel, the commission also proposed to amend the *Public Service Employment Act* (PSEA) to facilitate the transfer of employees across positions. Observing that Canadians expected more efficient services, the commission announced,

> The process of redeploying human resources must be accelerated and be made more effective if it is to keep up with changing government priorities and social needs. In this light, legislative changes will be considered while retaining the fundamental principles of respecting the public interest and the impartiality of the Public Service as defined in the *Public Service Employment Act* of 1967.[21]

This legislative change—the introduction of the concept of deployments into the PSEA—would eventually be made in 1992 with the adoption of the *Public Service Reform Act*. But it is interesting to note that, well before the launch of the system-wide reform process that resulted in the new law, the commission itself was considering adopting this change. In fact, having seen its efforts in this regard quashed by the courts over the years, the commission long desired to see such flexibility reconciled with the legal framework.[22]

Generally speaking, then, following the arrival of the Mulroney government in 1984, the PSC embraced a modest agenda for reform. Certainly, it did not commit itself to the kind of new public management thinking that eventually undermined its counterparts in the United Kingdom, New Zealand or Australia; but neither did it simply stand

as a barrier to change. It opened up its policies and practices for critical
review, including by departmental managers, and it worked on defining
legislative changes that would be needed to bring greater flexibility to
the staffing system.

THE QUEST FOR NON-LEGISLATIVE RENEWAL

As they sought ways to improve the efficiency of the staffing process,
reformers in the 1980s could hardly seek further delegation of the
Public Service Commission's staffing authority: in 1985, the PSC
could proudly state that approximately ninety-eight percent of staffing
activities governed by the *Public Service Employment Act* had already
been delegated to departments, a result of the efforts deployed since the
1967 reforms.[23] The commission itself focused essentially on making
policies and auditing departments to ensure compliance with delegation
agreements and related policies. It also spent considerable energies on
recruiting new employees from outside the public service, staffing the
Management Category and handling appeals and investigations.

However, despite this extensive level of delegation, many
departmental managers remained dissatisfied with the insufficient
flexibility of the instruments of delegation, which were believed to result
in a slow, cumbersome staffing process. Moreover, the constraints placed
on the exercise of this delegated authority were seen to be excessive and
to be partly negating the gains in efficiency that were expected to result
from delegation. Even before the Auditor General's 1983 report and the
arrival of the Mulroney government, the commission was well aware of
these criticisms.[24] Already in 1979, the commission had begun some
work on new instruments of delegation that would be better suited
to the specific needs of different departments.[25] But, evidently, for
departmental managers, progress still appeared insufficient.

It is in this context that the commission launched a more
comprehensive review of staffing policies and practices in 1985.[26]
The so-called administrative reform exercise sought to find ways to
expedite the staffing process, eliminate unnecessary documentation
and procedures and allow the subdelegation of staffing authority to line

managers whenever possible, without compromising on the protection of merit and while ensuring the overall quality of appointments.[27] The initiative first took the form of a series of six departmental-level studies meant to identify various factors that might be affecting the efficiency of the staffing process.[28] The commission then launched an internal review of its regulations and administrative procedures in order to identify elements of the staffing process that might not be required by a strict reading of the *Public Service Employment Act* and related decisions of the courts and appeal boards. This internal review was assisted by special panels of senior departmental managers, the Joint Consultation Committee and the Advisory Committee on Personnel Policy. The hope was that, through these reviews, superfluous procedures would be identified and the administration of staffing would be streamlined by their elimination.

The departmental studies yielded some interesting results. They found that, on average, it took 143 calendar days, or about five months, to staff a position through a closed competition (excluding the appeal process). Half that time was spent on preparatory work, such as writing the Statement of Qualifications and the guide used to rate candidates. Open competitions, which in about eighty-five percent of cases involved term appointments, were completed in forty-six calendar days. It took twenty-five days on average to appoint someone already on an eligibility list. Not surprisingly, the larger the area of competition, the longer it took to complete the staffing process. For example, competitions that were open to other departments took about a month longer to conclude than those restricted to the hiring department.[29] Clearly, there was room for some improvement. But, for many executives at the commission, these studies seemed to confirm that departmental managers, not the commission, exercised the greatest control over the speed of staffing, and that the commission's role in engendering delays was exaggerated.[30]

The commission used the results of the studies to launch an innovative, departmental-based process of staffing reforms. Between 1985 and 1988, seventeen departments collaborated with the commission in reviewing their internal staffing practices and worked on resolving the problems they experienced in receiving staffing services from the commission. In each case, a working group composed of an equal number of departmental managers and staffing experts from the commission worked on resolving the problems identified by the departments themselves.

The overall administrative reform exercise, combined with the commission's internal review of staffing policies, yielded a lengthy list of proposed modifications to the staffing process. But, in the end, it did not yield profound changes. In some cases, more discretion was granted to departmental managers in setting qualifications standards and using assessment instruments. The commission also agreed in principle to delegate the authority to appoint people from outside the public service to term positions, without competition, in cases of emergency. This new delegated authority was to be included, on a case-by-case basis, in the delegation agreements of departments that would request it.[31] These policy changes, coupled with modifications to departmental practices, generated some improvements. A study conducted in 1988 of three of the participating departments showed a fifteen percent improvement in the speed of staffing.[32]

However, on some more thorny issues, the commission clearly resisted the erosion, or further delegation, of its staffing authority. For example, despite departmental proposals to delegate and facilitate the conversion of term employees into indeterminate employees, the PSC defended the status quo. It argued,

> In keeping with the merit principle, it would be theoretically ideal if changes in tenure could only occur as a result of closed competitions. The Commission considered the benefits and liabilities of this idea and concluded that the status quo should be maintained. The Commission will retain its authority to change the tenure of employees from term to indeterminate without competition and will exercise this authority in those circumstances that it considers appropriate (e.g. skill shortages).[33]

Similarly, the delegation of authority to make certain types of appointments without competition (for example, the reappointment of a term employee to the same job after the term is over or the appointment of a surplus employee to a new position with a slightly higher maximum rate of pay) under Section 5(c)(v) of the *Public Service Employment Regulations* was considered but deemed to be legally impossible, barring a legislative amendment. The PSC rejected the delegation of authority to terminate the layoff status of employees (a status that comes with some priority rights), to appoint coop students or even to approve personality, interest and intelligence tests.[34]

While these are only some examples in a long list of issues considered, they nevertheless illustrate the overall outcome of the administrative reform exercise: while some additional flexibility was introduced at the margins and some processes streamlined, the division of responsibilities and the general constraints imposed by the merit system were not significantly altered.

These meagre results may not be surprising, given the overall lack of success of the early administrative reform initiatives pursued by the Mulroney government. For example, around the same time, the government's most high-profile reform initiative, the Nielsen Task Force, essentially unravelled: out of the $7 billion in cuts it recommended, only about $500 million were actually made and its report was soon abandoned as a blueprint for reforming the bureaucracy.[35] Similarly, another process aimed at cutting down on central controls in the same period, the Increased Ministerial Authority and Accountability (IMAA) project led by the Treasury Board Secretariat, also generated few significant and lasting results.[36] In this context, the results of the administrative reform exercise do not appear out of step with the times.

However, at the same time, those results clearly did not quench the system's thirst for greater flexibility and efficiency in staffing. Only a few years later, the Mulroney government would launch a new public service–wide reform initiative, Public Service 2000, to seek further changes in the area of staffing. Even the commission itself had explicitly acknowledged the need to make more fundamental changes. In fact, in order to build more flexibility and efficiency into the staffing regime, the commission was now inviting the government to seriously consider amending the *Public Service Employment Act*, going even further than it had in its 1985 strategy document.

The commission's position on legislative reform at the time is captured in a speech given at the end of 1986 by Commissioner Trefflé Lacombe.[37] Lacombe argued that, in the twenty years that had elapsed since the adoption of the *Public Service Employment Act*, Canadian society had changed and had come to demand greater efficiency in the delivery of public services. To answer those demands, the public service needed more flexibility in the use of its personnel, and since the statutory framework governing staffing offered little flexibility, especially following a number of court decisions on the definition of merit, legislative amendments were needed.

In retrospect, it is surprising to see the list of legislative changes that were being proposed by the commission back in 1986; many of them would in fact come to pass in the following years. For example, legislative changes needed to make it easier to transfer employees across the public service as well as the inscription of the concept of "appointment to level" (as opposed to appointments to specific positions) in the *Public Service Employment Act* would become reality with the adoption of the *Public Service Reform Act* in 1992.[38] Moreover, Lacombe was also advocating, on behalf of the commission, to inscribe into law, for the first time, a definition of merit that would restore some of the flexibility in hiring that he felt had been lost as a result of court decisions over the years. Under the new definition, hiring the "best qualified" candidate would still be required for initial appointments and promotions, but in the case of transfers it would only be necessary to establish that the candidate was qualified, given that the principle of merit had already been applied when the transferred employee was last appointed to the public service.[39]

These proposed changes demonstrate that the commission was actively searching for ways to improve the efficiency of the staffing regime. However, it was careful to do so while ensuring that it would remain institutionally able to act as the guardian of the merit principle, ensuring equitable access to the public service and preventing patronage. As Lacombe stated,

In order to ensure respect for the merit principle, equality of access to the public service, and fair and equitable treatment of public servants, we believe that the staffing regime must continue to be managed by a central agency that answers to Parliament. This agency, while maintaining complete and full responsibility for staffing in the public service, should delegate or transfer some of its powers to deputy heads in the interests of achieving greater efficiency and effectiveness [translation].[40]

As we can see, the commission itself was advocating greater flexibility in staffing procedures and supporting the delegation of staffing authority to deputy ministers, but only in the context of a legislative framework that preserved its independence and ultimately kept it fully in charge of staffing. However, it is on this issue that it would soon enter into conflict with the central leadership of the public service as it tried to further reform the staffing regime in the early 1990s.

PUBLIC SERVICE 2000 AND THE DEBATE OVER INSTITUTIONAL REFORM

Upon its return to office after the 1988 general election, the Mulroney government sought to revive its administrative reform agenda by announcing the launch of a major initiative: Public Service 2000. In contrast to the Nielsen Task Force, PS 2000, as it was commonly called, was driven by the senior public service and looked less to the private sector for answers to public-sector problems. Under the leadership of Paul Tellier, clerk of the Privy Council, the reform process relied on a series of ten task forces, each consisting of deputy ministers and assistant deputy ministers. As Tellier himself asserted at the time, "The primary focus of Public Service 2000 is on changing how people are managed" and, with the objective of motivating employees, the key to success would be "to move away from a philosophy of control to a philosophy of empowerment."[41] Given this objective, it is not surprising that the work of PS 2000 largely focused on human resources issues, including staffing.

Even before the Task Force on Staffing had had time to do much of its work, Tellier had made it clear that PS 2000 would be the occasion to seriously re-examine the role of the Public Service Commission. In a speech given at the University of Ottawa in March 1990, only three months after the initiative was launched, he explained that a key objective of PS 2000 was to clarify the distribution of responsibilities in the area of personnel management. As he stated at the time,

> Under existing structures, responsibilities are confused and, consequently, public service managers have taken refuge in systems of control. The personnel management system does not encourage initiative in the way that it should, and it is not always clear who is responsible for achieving results. A principal thrust of Public Service 2000, therefore, is to ensure that individuals have the authority to get the job done and that we are able to hold them accountable for their actions.[42]

To clarify the distribution of responsibilities, the Clerk believed, it would be necessary to rethink the respective roles of departmental managers, the Treasury Board Secretariat, and the Public Service Commission.

The PSC, in particular, was seen as a source of difficulty, its activities having created some ambiguity in the central personnel function of the public service. In order to end patronage, the 1918 *Civil Service Act* had given powers to the commission that went well beyond the protection of merit to embrace the entire personnel function. And, "under changing economic and political circumstances, this mixture of watchdog and executive functions within the Civil Service Commission [had become] a source of recurrent problems."[43] Notwithstanding the reforms of the 1960s as well as the work of Gordon, Heeney, Glassco, Lambert, D'Avignon and others over the years, this undesirable ambiguity remained at the heart of the personnel management system. It was now time to resolve it. In fact, Tellier asserted, PS 2000 would take as a *starting point* that "established as the guardian of the merit principle, the Public Service Commission [had] retained and acquired responsibilities for personnel management functions that do not sit comfortably with its role as Parliament's agent."[44] The anticipated result of the reform process was clear: "For the Public Service Commission, the changes will mean getting out of the management business and focusing on its role as Parliament's agent in protecting the integrity of the personnel system."[45]

However, despite this early statement of preferences by the most senior leader of the public service, the outcome of the PS 2000 exercise would in fact be quite different. When the *White Paper on Public Service 2000* was finally released in December 1990, it did recommend that the respective roles of the Treasury Board and the PSC be better defined to achieve greater accountability for the management of personnel and, overall, it did favour a stronger recognition of the primary responsibility of the Treasury Board and departmental managers for managing public servants. But the white paper fell short of recommending that the PSC be strictly relegated to the narrower role of a parliamentary watchdog. In fact, under the proposed scheme, the PSC would remain vested with the powers of recruitment, appointment, appeal and audit. The Treasury Board would be responsible for other personnel management issues, including career development, training, the allocation of resources to meet the personnel needs of departments and the setting of personnel policy in support of deputy heads. Despite the Clerk's original intentions, the white paper essentially proposed to keep the central functions of personnel management divided. And, while internal debates about the need for a more radical institutional reform continued for some time after the white paper was released, the idea had been abandoned by the time the government sought legislative changes in 1992.

The main reason for this outcome seems to have been the absence of sufficient support in the senior ranks of the public service. The commission argued strenuously in favour of retaining its executive authority over staffing, and many deputy ministers were actually sympathetic to that view. According to the people interviewed for this book, while there was widespread support for bringing an additional measure of flexibility into the staffing process and finding ways to accelerate making appointments, many senior executives in the public service were more apprehensive about significantly curtailing the authority of the Public Service Commission.[46] For one thing, its authority over appointments was still seen as an important shield against potential pressures by ministers to hire specific individuals. As a former senior official with the Privy Council Office (PCO) told us in explaining the lack of enthusiasm of many senior executives, "Deputy Ministers often found the PSC to be convenient, and it certainly was a useful tool to resist political interference in managing the public service."[47] For many executives, turning the commission purely into a parliamentary watchdog seemed to carry an element of risk that could endanger the principle of non-partisanship.

Furthermore, according to officials involved in the events at the time, there was also considerable aversion to taking on an agent of Parliament on an issue that could prove to be politically damaging to the government.[48] Over the course of 1991, as the government was finalizing its legislative proposal resulting from the PS 2000 initiative, the possibility of stripping the PSC of much of its executive authority was still being debated in the higher echelons of the bureaucracy. As tensions mounted between PCO and the commission, now under the leadership of its new president Robert Giroux, the prospect of having to defend such a reduction in the commission's authority before Parliament raised some concerns. As a former senior official with PCO recalled,

> The Clerk did not want to take on a public battle with the PSC and run the risk of losing the other parts of the reform. The PSC has its act and, to change it, you would have to go to Parliament and run the risk of being seen as weakening merit and democracy. Moreover, the Clerk doesn't want the Prime Minister to spend political capital on a battle that has no importance outside Ottawa.[49]

So, in the end, no fundamental institutional reform was put forward. As summarized by the former PCO official, "It was a case of 'achieving what you can achieve': making some legislative changes but leaving the PSC's role untouched so as not to lose everything."[50] Another observer, who worked on personnel policy at the Treasury Board Secretariat at the time, put it more bluntly: "The way I see it: the system was ultimately unwilling to tackle the PSC."[51]

Whether it was a fear of external opposition or insufficient internal support, the outcome of these internal struggles was the decision to shelve the idea of a more fundamental institutional reform that would have profoundly altered the commission's mandate. However, despite this decision, the *White Paper on Public Service 2000* nevertheless succeeded in significantly reforming the staffing process. According to an internal report, the white paper made eighty-eight recommendations that fell under the PSC's mandate, and the commission implemented most of them through changes to its policies and practices.[52] Moreover, even if most proposed changes involved relatively minor improvements, the white paper did propose some more significant innovations requiring amendments to the statutory framework. These amendments, supported by the commission, eventually made up part of the *Public Service Reform Act*, which was tabled in Parliament in June 1991.

THE *PUBLIC SERVICE REFORM ACT* OF 1992

Even if the content of the bill undoubtedly disappointed the advocates of radical institutional and legal changes in the area of staffing, the tabling of Bill C-26, the *Public Service Reform Act*, in June of 1991 still represented a significant step forward in staffing reform. The new bill constituted the first attempt to make important changes to the *Public Service Employment Act* since its adoption in 1967, more than twenty years earlier. The bill actually touched on a wider range of issues, including labour relations and leadership in the public service,[53] but it is the introduction of new concepts in staffing and the promise of a new measure of flexibility for managers that had the most significance for the commission.

On the staffing front, the bill contained five sets of measures of particular importance. First, with regard to appointments, the bill added a new section to the PSEA, which would allow a candidate's merit, in circumstances to be prescribed in regulations by the commission, to be measured by an "absolute" standard of competence, established by the commission, rather than through a process comparing him or her against the competence of other candidates. The bill also amended the PSEA to allow the commission to prescribe the standards to be used in the assessment of merit, a power to be held in addition to its existing authority to set the standards used in the traditional selection process. Moreover, in addition to the usual criteria used in setting such standards, such as knowledge, experience or language, the bill introduced the possibility of considering the future needs of the public service as an appropriate criterion.

Although meant to be used only in a limited set of circumstances, this second method of determining merit, based on an absolute standard rather than a relative one, represented a significant shift in how selection based on merit was viewed by the commission and the federal public service. Following a 1972 decision by the courts, merit had come to be defined as finding "the best persons possible" for each position to be filled.[54] While the PSC had originally continued to insist that merit could still be defined in absolute terms, another decision by the federal court, issued in 1982, had clearly put an end to this approach, making unavoidable a comparative assessment of the merits of various candidates.[55] In this context, the introduction of an absolute standard of competence under the *Public Service Reform Act* can be seen as an effort to release the commission from undesired constraints placed on it by the courts. As it turned out, about ten years later, the public service would go even further along this path by defining merit as "meeting the essential qualifications for the work to be performed" and stating in law that considering more than one person was not a condition of meritorious appointments.[56] In this sense, the 1992 amendment also constituted a first step in a longer process to change the general approach to merit.

Second, in order to provide for greater flexibility in the management of personnel, the *Public Service Reform Act* also introduced the concept of "appointment to level." While the standard approach of appointing individuals to specific positions would continue, an amendment to the

Public Service Employment Act would allow the commission to appoint some individuals to a class of positions at the same level in the public service, thereby allowing them to be moved from one position to another at the same level without having to go through a lengthy merit-based appointment process.

The "appointment to level" concept was not a new one. Almost twenty years earlier, the Finkelman Committee had proposed this approach in its *Report on Employer-Employee Relations in the Public Service of Canada*.[57] The idea had also been indirectly picked up by the Special Committee on the Review of Personnel Management and the Merit Principle (the D'Avignon Committee), which recommended in 1979 that the *Public Service Employment Act* be amended to indicate that merit could be determined not only for a specific set of duties but also for a group of positions.[58] With the passing of the *Public Service Reform Act* in 1992, the concept would finally be entrenched in law. Unfortunately, over the next decade, as it went about implementing the new law, the commission found that "appointments to level" were difficult to use broadly because remaining legislative and policy constraints, such as the classification system, were still position based.[59] But, at the time of its adoption, the concept seemed to hold some promise for enhancing the career development prospects of employees and providing more flexibility in matching employees with the needs of departments.

The "appointment to level" concept was also intimately linked to the idea of allowing deputy heads to deploy their employees to other jobs within their organization. In this regard, a third amendment made to the *Public Service Employment Act* sought to ease the conditions under which employees could be transferred from one position to another. Section 22 of the *Public Service Reform Act* added a new part to the PSEA regarding "deployments," defined as "the transfer of an employee from one position to another". Under the new provisions, deputy heads gained exclusive authority to make deployments to or within the part of the public service under their jurisdiction. Such deployments could be made only with the consent of the affected employee and, while under some circumstances they could result in a change of occupational groups, they could not result in a promotion or a change in the tenure of office of the employee. These transfers would be made without applying the principle of merit and without having to consider the priority rights of some categories of employees, such as laid-off workers or people returning from a leave of absence or benefiting from priority status due to previous employment in a ministerial office. The amendment would grant some flexibility to deputy heads to move employees around their organization, while expanding the options of employees wanting to move to other positions for greater job satisfaction or development opportunities.

Before the adoption of the *Public Service Reform Act*, transfers had been handled by the commission through the Transfer Exclusion Approval Order, which permitted the movement of employees within the same group and at the same or a lower level by excluding such actions from the application of the *Public Service Employment Act* on a case-by-case basis. In the past, the commission had attempted to exempt employee transfers from the application of the merit principle, arguing that it was unnecessarily constraining given that merit had already been ascertained at the time of the employee's previous appointment. But the regulatory and policy measures used over the years to try to make transfers a more flexible tool for staffing some positions had all been struck down by the courts, which insisted that transfers had to be considered appointments under the existing legislation.[60] Therefore, unless the commission used its powers to exempt these staffing decisions from the law's requirements because it deemed such action to be in the interest of the public service, the usual rigidities of the regular appointment process had to be applied to transfers, and this included holding competitions and allowing appeals. In this context, the introduction of deployments into the staffing system in 1992 might have been a measure of flexibility demanded and welcomed by managers, but it also corresponded to a long-standing preference of the commission that had been denied by the courts.

A fourth significant change brought about by the *Public Service Reform Act* concerned casual employment. Again with the objective of providing managers with a greater degree of flexibility, the act added a new section to the *Public Service Employment Ac*t that allowed the PSC to appoint any person to the public service for a maximum period of ninety days. These appointments would be exempted from all the provisions of the PSEA, except those specifically dealing with casual employment, and would therefore be conducted outside the merit system. The use of casual employees was seen as a way to meet short-term or urgent staffing needs, and it essentially created a new category of employees for the public service. While they did not have to meet the requirements imposed on indeterminate or even term employees, casual employees would not be eligible for the benefits granted to these other categories, including the right to take part in closed competitions.

Finally, a fifth change concerned layoffs. This time, the change was prompted directly by the difficulties that the government had experienced with contracting out in the late 1980s. At that time, the Mulroney government had attempted to contract out some government operations in an attempt to reduce costs and improve efficiencies. However, in some cases, staffing legislation had proven to be a barrier to contracting out as the affected employees could not be laid off. For example, in a decision that was later confirmed by the Federal Court of Appeal, the Public Service Staff Relations Board found in March 1990 that the government had violated a collective agreement by contracting out the jobs of 278 clerks at Revenue Canada. In its reasons, the board argued that the government could not lay off these employees because the decision to do so was not motivated by a real lack of work for the affected employees, one of the valid justifications under the law. The *Public Service Reform Act* rid the system of this barrier by amending Section 29 of the *Public Service Employment Act* to explicitly state that deputy heads could lay off employees whose services were no longer required due to the transfer of work or functions outside the public service.

The *Public Service Reform Act* was a wide-ranging piece of legislation. In addition to the changes described above, the statute also brought about a number of changes to the management of eligibility lists, employment equity programs, appeal procedures and other aspects of staffing and labour relations. But the five changes outlined here—the introduction of the possibility of using an absolute standard of merit as opposed to always relying on a competition among candidates, the possibility of appointing employees "to level," the introduction of deployments, the adoption of a more flexible regime for casual employees and the acceptance of layoffs due to outsourcing—illustrate clearly the overall thrust of the legislative reform: the desire to enhance the efficiency of the staffing system by introducing greater flexibility for managers to fill positions, move employees around the public service and facilitate the use of outsourcing strategies.

The content of the *Public Service Reform Act* also illustrates how the commission itself was an advocate of greater managerial flexibility in staffing. Some of the act's measures, such as the new standard for determining merit without comparing candidates, the possibility of considering the future needs of the public service in selecting the best qualified candidate in competitions or the more flexible management of eligibility lists, were not recommended by the PS 2000 Task Force on Staffing, but they were included in the legislation at the instigation of the PSC. Some of the other amendments, including the controversial creation of deployments, had been recommended by PS 2000 but were in fact measures that had been advocated by the PSC for several years. Moreover, in some cases, such as layoffs, absolute standards or deployments, the amendments contained in the *Public Service Reform Act* specifically sought to re-establish practices that the commission or the government had tried to adopt in the past but that had subsequently been prohibited by the courts.

Clearly then, the commission was not dragged into inscribing greater flexibility into the staffing legislation by the government and senior public servants. It actively sought out many of those changes. In fact, during an interview for this book, a former executive who worked on the *Public Service Reform Act* for the commission remembered how the PSC was willing to entertain even more wide-ranging legislative changes, including some relating to the definition of the merit principle, but was turned down by PCO officials, presumably due to concerns about the reaction of unions.[61] While not as comprehensive or bold as might have been expected at the outset, the *Public Service Reform Act* brought forward the most significant changes in years.

The *Public Service Reform Act* in Parliament: A Polarized Debate

Bill C-26, the bill to enact the *Public Service Reform Act*, was not well received when it was tabled in Parliament. The Liberal members representing the Official Opposition in the House of Commons considered the bill to be flawed and incomplete and tabled two motions that would have sent it to a parliamentary committee for a pre-study. Both motions were defeated by the government. The New Democratic Party also opposed the bill, arguing that it would weaken the PSC and the merit system as well as weaken public sector unions and fail to protect workers. During the debate at second reading, opposition parties essentially characterized the legislative proposal as an attack on the merit principle that was sure to create a system that would allow managers to make arbitrary staffing decisions. Government members defended the bill on the ground that it would modernize the public service, making it leaner and more efficient.

The antagonistic tone of the debate on the floor of the House was an indication of what was to come at the committee stage. The bill was referred for a detailed study by a legislative committee in February 1992 and the committee, naturally dominated by government members, held about two-and-a-half months of public hearings on it. The testimony given by witnesses who appeared before the committee was overwhelmingly critical and opinions were sharply divided between managers and employees.

Union representatives were unanimous in condemning the changes related to labour relations but also those dealing with staffing. Not surprisingly, the amendment facilitating layoffs due to contracting out were roundly condemned. But the introduction of deployments was also strongly opposed. For example, in his testimony, Daryl Bean, head of the Public Service Alliance of Canada, argued that "the government's proposal with regard to deployment [was] so tilted in favour of management and so open to abuse as to be totally unacceptable."[62] Other union leaders concurred, criticizing the bill for constituting an attack on the merit principle, weakening the PSC, and simply representing the interests and preferences of the senior management of the public service.[63] Even well-known academics, such as Gene Swimmer and Barbara W. Carroll, and social activist organizations, such as the National Action Committee on the Status of Women, worried about the weakening of merit and the PSC.[64]

Despite this barrage of opposition, the bill did have a few supporters. As could be expected, the Association of Professional Executives of the Public Service of Canada (APEX) supported the legislation. Its representatives argued that the new measures would improve the staffing system and provide more flexibility for executives so that they could adequately fulfill their managerial duties. In the end, they believed overall morale would improve.[65] The Public Policy Forum, a well-known non-profit organization interested in the public service, also supported the bill, speaking favourably of the introduction of deployments but regretting that the government had not used the opportunity to address the thorny issue of the political rights of public servants.[66]

In the midst of this debate, the PSC clearly sided with management and offered a strong defence of the new measures regarding staffing. The commission's president, Robert Giroux, was one of the first to testify before the committee in March 1992. In his opening remarks, he argued that the bill was essentially "about the reconciliation of efficiency and fairness in human resources management to better serve the people of Canada."[67] He added,

> The dynamics of today's workplace demand more flexible staffing arrangements than the present act permits if we want to give the best possible value when providing services to the public.... In summary, the Bill, as I see it, represents very much a balancing act—balancing the very real need for a more effective Public Service with the equally compelling need to preserve merit, and protect employees.[68]

Of course, this central preoccupation—the need to strike a balance between competing values in a way that would serve the interests of Canadians—again placed the commission in an uncomfortable, and somewhat ironic, position. Having recently had to fend off, inside the public service, the managerial interests that would have reduced it to a parliamentary oversight body, it was now publicly seen as being too close to those same managerial interests. As the commission itself defended the proposed amendments to the *Public Service Employment Act*, others were fighting these changes in order to protect the commission's authority and its role in the staffing regime.

In the end, owing to the strong parliamentary majority held by the Mulroney government, the *Public Service Reform Act* was adopted, with minor amendments, at third reading on November 30, 1992. After a quick review in the Senate, it received Royal Assent a few weeks later, on December 17, 1992. The legislative changes undoubtedly represented a win for the advocates of greater efficiency and flexibility in staffing and, at the time, they were viewed by many observers as an undue encroachment of managerialism on the traditional values and principles of the public service.

But for those involved in the reform process, at the commission as well as at the centre of government, there was a sense that the changes were limited, the imperfect result of arduous internal debates about how to better organize the central functions of personnel management. Eight years later, the Office of the Auditor General was dismissive of the changes adopted back then, considering them to be "minor changes," which "have fallen short of expectations."[69] Even today, many former officials whom we interviewed feel that the Public Service 2000 initiative and the subsequent adoption of the *Public Service Reform Act* were missed opportunities. Former officials with the Treasury Board Secretariat and the Privy Council Office regret that the system failed to fix the problem created by the fragmentation of responsibilities for personnel between the Treasury Board and the PSC. Former officials with the commission believe that it may have been an undue obsession with institutional reforms that resulted in the forgoing of the opportunity for more substantive legislative and policy changes. In any case, despite the positive fact that the first legislative changes had been made to staffing legislation in over two decades, much dissatisfaction persisted.

CONCLUSION

The adoption of the *Public Service Reform Act* in 1992 appears to have ended an intense period of debate about the appropriate mandate of the PSC and its role in the staffing process. Even before the election of the Mulroney government, the work of the Office of the Auditor General in the early 1980s had already brought long-standing departmental dissatisfaction about staffing to the fore. Then, the new government's rhetorical embrace of the new public management movement and its push for administrative reform renewed the age-old quest for greater efficiency and flexibility in the staffing process. As always, the PSC's appropriate role was a prominent theme in these debates.

The events examined in this chapter illustrate how, in contrast to a common misperception, the commission was more than willing to reform itself and the staffing process. While it is clear that it resisted, with success, more radical institutional reforms that would have threatened its independence as the guardian of merit and non-partisanship, it did favour significant reforms to staffing rules, seeking to ensure greater managerial flexibility. And while the efforts launched by the PSC itself to revise staffing rules may have been of limited scope, the commission collaborated actively in the more fundamental legislative changes of 1992, advocating many of them even before they became the object of system-wide attention. In short, this period illustrates how the commission cannot simply be presented as an obstacle to reforms, a perennial defender of the status quo in staffing. In fact, the Mulroney years revealed the Public Service Commission to be an active reformer, acknowledging the importance of efficiency in staffing and actively seeking greater flexibility for managers. But the commission was a cautious reformer, always preoccupied with maintaining a balance between efficiency and the competing values of equity and non-partisanship. As it pushed to build more flexibility into the legislative framework or attempted to find further opportunities for delegation, it was also clearly willing to fight to preserve its vital role as an independent agency with the necessary clout to preserve the desired balance of values.

ENDNOTES

1. Peter Aucoin (1995), *The New Public Management: Canada in Comparative Perspective*, Montreal, IRPP, 12.
2. Donald J. Savoie (1994), *Thatcher, Reagan, Mulroney: In Search of a New Bureaucracy*, Toronto, University of Toronto Press, 10.
3. Quoted in David Zussman (1986), "Walking the Tightrope: The Mulroney Government and the Public Service," in Michael Prince (ed.), *Tracking the Tories: How Ottawa Spends, 1986–87*, Toronto, Methuen, 255.
4. Luc Juillet and Matthew Mingus (2008), "Reconsidering the History of Administrative Reforms in Canada," in Jerri Killian and Niklas Eklund (eds.), *Handbook of Administrative Reform: An International Perspective*, New York, Taylor and Francis, 222–223.
5. Public Service Commission of Canada (1990), *Annual Report 1990*, Ottawa, Minister of Supply and Services Canada, 15.
6. The data on the number of employees is drawn from Table 1 of the statistical annexes of the Public Service Commission's annual reports for 1984 and 1992. The number of employees in the federal public service is defined differently by the Public Service Commission, the Treasury Board Secretariat, and Statistics Canada. The commission's data includes all the employees covered by the *Public Service Employment Act*, but it excludes employees appointed under the act for less than six months. It also excludes employees of Crown corporations, ministerial staff, employees appointed by Order-in-Council, members of the Royal Canadian Mounted Police and military personnel of the Canadian Armed Forces.
7. Donald J. Savoie (1990), *The Politics of Public Spending in Canada*, University of Toronto Press, Toronto, 127.
8. Denis Saint-Martin (1998), "Management Consultants, the State, and the Politics of Administrative Reform in Britain and Canada," *Administration and Society*, vol. 30, 557; and Savoie (1994), *Thatcher, Reagan, Mulroney*, 128–129.
9. Public Service Commission of Canada (1986), *Annual Report 1986*, Ottawa, Minister of Supply and Services Canada, 13.
10. Ibid, 61.
11. The data is taken from the appendices of the commission's annual reports. The number of employees at the PSC for each year is as follows: 1984: 2,494; 1985: 2,563; 1986: 2,419; 1987: 2,249; 1989: 2,152; 1990: 2,093; 1991: 1,968; 1992: 2,017.
12. Interview with a former senior official of the PSC.
13. Interview with a former senior official of the PSC.
14. Office of the Auditor General (1983), "Chapter 2 – Constraints to Productive Management in the Public Service," in *1983 Report of the Auditor General of Canada*, Ottawa, Minister of Supply and Services Canada, paragraph 2.38.

15   Interviews with former senior officials of the PSC and the TBS.
16   Public Service Commission of Canada (1985), *Strategy Document, 1985–1990*, Ottawa, Public Service Commission, 2.
17   Ibid, 9.
18   Ibid.
19   Ibid, 1.
20   Ibid, 2.
21   Ibid, 10.
22   In particular, about a year before the strategy document was released, the Commission had seen its policy on "non-appointment transfers" overturned by the Federal Court in *James Wilkinson v. Public Service Commission Appeal Board*.
23   Public Service Commission of Canada (1985), *Annual Report 1985*, Ottawa, Minister of Supply and Services Canada, 9.
24   Interview with a former senior official of the PSC.
25   Public Service Commission of Canada (1985), *Annual Report 1985*, 15.
26   Ibid.
27   The objectives are summarized in a memorandum on the state of administrative reforms, by D. D. Quiring (director general of the Program Development and Review Directorate, PSC) to directors of personnel, dated December 1986 (RG32, vol. 2046).
28   In the commission's documents, these reviews are sometimes referred to as "staffing efficiency and effectiveness studies."
29   Public Service Commission (1996), *Consultative Review of Staffing*, unpublished document, 9.
30   Interview with a former senior official of the PSC.
31   Memorandum by D. D. Quiring (director general of the Program Development and Review Directorate) to Branch Management Committee, entitled "Results of the Administrative Reform Policies, Procedures and Program Review," dated December 1986 (RG32, vol. 2046).
32   Public Service Commission (1996), *Consultative Review of Staffing*, unpublished document, 11.
33   Memorandum by D. D. Quiring (director general of the Program Development and Review Directorate) to Branch Management Committee, entitled "Results of the Administrative Reform Policies, Procedures and Program Review," dated December 1986, page 6 (RG32, vol. 2046).
34   Memorandum by Gilles Létourneau (director general of Policy, Staffing Programs) to Administrative Steering Committee, entitled "Administrative Reform Status Report," dated August 11, 1986, (RG32, vol. 2046); and Memorandum by D. D. Quiring (director general of the Program Development and Review Directorate) to Branch Management Committee, entitled "Results of the Administrative Reform Policies, Procedures and Program Review," dated December 1986 (RG32, vol. 2046).

35   Savoie (1994), *Thatcher, Reagan, Mulroney*, 130.
36   Luc Juillet and Matthew Mingus (2008), "Reconsidering the History of Administrative Reforms in Canada," in Jerri Killian and Niklas Eklund (eds.), *Handbook of Administrative Reform: An International Perspective*, New York, Taylor and Francis, 223–224.
37   Trefflé Lacombe (1986), Speech given by Trefflé Lacombe, commissioner of the Public Service Commission of Canada to the Annual Interdepartmental Conference on Staff Relations in St-Jovite, Quebec, September 25, 1986.
38   Ibid, 11–12.
39   Ibid, 11.
40   Ibid, 10.
41   Paul M. Tellier (1990), "Public Service 2000: The Renewal of the Public Service," *Canadian Public Administration*, 33:2, 130.
42   Ibid, 126.
43   Ibid, 127.
44   Ibid, 131.
45   Ibid.
46   Interviews with former senior officials at the PSC and the TBS.
47   Interview with a former senior official at the PCO.
48   Ibid.
49   Interview with a former senior official at the PCO.
50   Ibid.
51   Interview with a former senior official in the personnel branch of the TBS.
52   Public Service Commission (1996), *Consultative Review of Staffing*, unpublished document, 12.
53   In addition to the *Public Service Employment Act*, the *Public Service Reform Act* amended a series of other statutes, including the *Public Service Staff Relations Act*. Among other things, the new law tried to streamline procedures and increase the availability of alternative methods for settling bargaining disputes. It also formally designated the clerk of the Privy Council and secretary to the Cabinet as the head of the public service, mandating the incumbent of that position to submit an annual report on the state of the public service to the Prime Minister and requiring that this report be subsequently tabled in Parliament.
54   See the Federal Court's decision in the 1972 case, *Surinder Nath Nanda et al. v. Appeal Board Established by the Public Service Commission*.
55   See the Federal Court's decision in the 1982 case, *Attorney General of Canada v. W. E. Greaves et al.*
56   These measures are contained in the new *Public Service Employment Act*, enacted in 2003 as a result of the adoption of the *Public Service Modernization Act*. The specific provisions are contained in sections 30(2) and 30(4) of the new act.

57   In 1973, Jacob Finkelman, then chairman of the Public Service Staff
      Relations Board, had been asked by the government to review the *Public
      Service Staff Relations Act* and make recommendations on ways to improve
      labour relations in the public service. Despite its more specific focus on
      labour relations, Finkelman dedicated a section of his report's chapter
      on collective bargaining to the issue of staffing and the *Public Service
      Employment Act*. In it, he rejected several requests made by the unions,
      such as making the rules concerning initial appointments and promotions
      subject to collective bargaining, but he also urged the commission to
      consider making appointments in such a way that the appointees would
      not be restricted to a specific position, thereby encouraging greater staff
      mobility within the public service.

58   D'Avignon Committee Report, recommendation number 5.1.

59   Office of the Auditor General of Canada (2000), "Streamlining the
      Human Resource Management Regime: A Study of Changing Roles and
      Responsibilities," Chapter 9 in *Report of the Auditor General of Canada
      – April 2000*, 16.

60   For example, the Federal Court's decision in *Réjean Yergeau v. Public
      Service Commission Appeal Board* (1978) struck down the original
      regulation exempting transfers from the appeals process. Then, the Federal
      Court overturned the commission's 1981 policy on "non-appointment
      transfers," which stated that a limited category of transfers were not
      considered appointments under the PSEA, in *James Wilkinson v. Public
      Service Commission Appeal Board* (1984). Finally, in *Public Service Alliance
      of Canada v. Her Majesty the Queen* (1992), the Federal Court struck down
      the commission's exclusion approval order that exempted lateral moves
      from the merit and appeals sections of the PSEA, finding it too broad in
      application.

61   Interview with a former senior official of the PSC.

62   House of Commons of Canada, Proceedings of Legislative Committee H,
      March 17, 1992, 7.

63   See, for example, the testimony of the representatives of the International
      Brotherhood of Electrical Workers (March 18), the Economists',
      Sociologists' and Statisticians' Association (March 24), and the Professional
      Institute of the Public Service of Canada (March 25) before Legislative
      Committee H studying Bill C-26: The *Public Service Reform Act*.

64   See their testimony before Legislative Committee H studying Bill C-26:
      The *Public Service Reform Act*, given respectively on March 19, April 2, and
      March 26.

65   See the testimony of John Riddle, President of APEX, before Legislative
      Committee H studying Bill C-26: The *Public Service Reform Act*, on March
      31, 1992.

66   See the testimony given by the Public Policy Forum's representatives before Legislative Committee H studying Bill C-26: The *Public Service Reform Act*, on March 31, 1992.
67   Testimony of Robert Giroux, President of the Public Service Commission, before Legislative Committee H studying Bill C-26: The *Public Service Reform Act*, on March 11, 1992.
68   Ibid.
69   Office of the Auditor General of Canada (2000), "Streamlining the Human Resource Management Regime," 11.

MERIT AS THE ESSENTIAL MANDATE: REPOSITIONING THE PSC: 1993-2008

> For the merit system over the coming years, guardianship of values will be the predominant theme.
>
> Public Service Commission, directional statement, 1999

The formation of a Liberal government following the general election of 1993 seemed to offer the opportunity of a new beginning for the federal public service. The Progressive Conservatives, initially distrustful of the bureaucracy and steeped in the rhetoric of cost-cutting and government retrenchment, were returning to the Opposition benches in a state of disarray. The Liberals, under the leadership of Jean Chrétien, a politician expected to be more supportive and respectful of the bureaucracy because of his many years of ministerial experience in Ottawa, were back at the helm. Their detailed electoral platform, known as the Red Book, did not pay much heed to the issue of public administration, a fact not surprising in a electoral platform, but its general tone seemed more positive about the role of government in Canadian society.[1]

In fact, the Liberal party's thirteen years in power witnessed the most significant changes to the public service in decades, including in the area of human resources management. Only a few years after the Chrétien government took power, a renewed sense of urgency about the country's finances led to some of the most dramatic cutbacks in the history of the Canadian public service. But beyond major cuts in personnel, this period also saw the most fundamental and comprehensive reform of the public service's human resources management system since 1967. As we will see in this chapter, throughout the 1990s, the Public Service Commission (PSC) itself sought to adapt to a changing context: it progressively revamped its approach to delegation, placing greater emphasis on respect for core values and accountability for results, and it came close to radically reducing its involvement in service delivery and focusing more exclusively on oversight. However, with the adoption of the *Public Service Modernization Act* in 2003, those efforts were overshadowed by more profound legislative and institutional reforms: the definition of merit was modified in the pursuit of greater managerial efficiency, and the PSC lost some of its functions in favour of a strengthened focus on the oversight of merit. In sum, as it was approaching its centenary, the PSC was returning to its essential mandate—protecting the merit principle—while the very meaning of merit was continuing to evolve.

PRESERVING THE PROFESSIONAL PUBLIC SERVICE IN A CHANGING ENVIRONMENT

Despite their efforts at cost-cutting, the Progressive Conservatives left the federal government in a difficult fiscal position when they lost power in 1993; the new Liberal government found itself facing a very critical international financial press. The subsequent turbulence of international financial markets in 1994 created an even greater sense of urgency for a drastic turnaround in government spending. As a result, the need to control expenditures more effectively and reduce the size of government remained a driver of administrative reform. To deal with the situation, the Chrétien government launched a major reform initiative, known as Program Review.

Between 1994 and 1996, Program Review led to a major restructuring of the public service. Over a three-year period, cutbacks amounted to $29 billion out of annual program spending of about $120 billion.[2] While a portion of these cuts were realized through a reduction of federal transfers to provincial governments, they still had a significant impact on the operations of the federal public service. In particular, roughly 45,000 positions were eliminated—an astonishing reduction of nineteen percent of employees in the core public administration.[3] Most departments were affected by the cuts, some in particular. Transport Canada, for example, saw many of its activities transferred to local authorities, autonomous agencies or private-sector organizations. While this may be an extreme case, the department went from the equivalent of 19,881 full-time employees in 1993 to 4,258 in 1999, and its budget fell from $3.9 billion to under $1.6 billion over the same period.[4]

Program Review also aspired to be a 'rational' exercise in the redesign of government as opposed to a more traditional, across-the-board exercise in budget cuts. While there is considerable debate about whether these ambitions were realized,[5] they certainly had an effect on the process that was adopted to secure the cuts. While central agencies set expenditure reduction targets for each department, deputy heads were asked to design reform plans in order to carry out those reductions in their respective departments.[6] To do so, they were given a set of questions to guide their work. The questions were meant to steer executives through a systematic examination of their departments' programs and operations. Executives were expected to question and rethink what their departments did and how they did it, especially in light of the changing socio-economic environment. For instance, each program was to be reviewed to determine whether the public interest still required that it be maintained and, if so, whether it could not be offered as effectively by the private sector or by another level of government.[7] The end result, it was hoped, would not simply be a cost-cutting exercise but a strategic review of the role of the federal government at the turn of the century.

There is no doubt that the Program Review exercise created some challenges for the PSC. As an organization, it experienced its own share of cutbacks. Between 1992 and 1998, it downsized its staff by 960 full-time employees and its annual budget was cut by $43 million.[8] Moreover, as a central agency dealing with personnel, government-wide cutbacks of such magnitude also presented a considerable challenge. As Ginette Stewart, a commissioner of the PSC at the time, would later recall,

Program Review, with its staffing controls and employment reductions, had a major impact on the PSC. Responsible for administering priority entitlements and workforce adjustment, the PSC and its partners concentrated on providing support mechanisms for those affected by government restructuring: career counselling, resource centres, workshops, job matching and referral services to public service positions and outplacement networks with other employers. The PSC also assisted departments by participating in development and career-management programs to maintain an adaptive, competent and professional Public Service. As well, the PSC worked with the Joint Career Transition Committees, a co-operative venture by the employer and the bargaining agents to facilitate change.[9]

Special measures were also taken by the commission, in collaboration with the Privy Council Office, the Treasury Board Secretariat and deputy heads, to support assistant deputy ministers and lower-level executives impacted by the restructuring.[10]

Over this period, the PSC devoted a large part of its efforts to ensuring that affected employees were treated equitably despite the massive changes brought about by Program Review.[11] The commission worked to ensure that the rights of employees as well as the requirements of the merit principle were respected in the midst of tremendous changes. It also actively cooperated with other central agencies and departments to facilitate the movement of remaining employees and support the transitions of those who had to reorient their careers. Through these efforts, the commission demonstrated how, more than a simple oversight body, it remained an active member of the management team, working closely with other agencies to facilitate administrative changes and optimize the public service's use of its human resources.

However, in addition to the challenge of dealing with the effects of the cutbacks, Program Review had another impact on the commission: it triggered another internal process of reflection about the PSC's essential mandate and how best to fulfill it in an environment that had significantly evolved over the years. Like other departments, the

PSC was also targeted by Program Review and it received the series of questions intended to guide the internal review of its programs and spending. Ruth Hubbard, who had recently been appointed president of the commission at the time, remembers that the executive team originally found that the questions were difficult to apply to a central agency, let alone one that was also an independent parliamentary agent. But the intent of the exercise was clear and she decided to use the opportunity to engage the commission in a broader reflection on its role in the context of an evolving public service.[12]

To pursue this reflection, in addition to some purely internal discussion, the commission launched a series of learning workshops, involving a select group of senior public servants, academics and other experts. The discussions at the workshops held in the context of this Learning Series, which began in the fall of 1996, helped the commissioners explore the emerging challenges facing the public service and think about how the PSC should respond to them. One of the key issues to emerge from this reflection was the need to reaffirm the importance of a professional public service to the country's democratic governance.[13]

In the late 1990s, this concern became an important theme for the PSC's leadership. With the globalization of socio-economic relations and the shift toward a knowledge-based society, values such as efficiency, innovation and flexibility came to occupy a more prominent place in public discourse about government. In a fast-changing environment where the needs and problems of citizens were increasingly diverse and complex, governments were being called upon to quickly provide better adapted responses; but to do so they had to be flexible, results-driven, innovative organizations. The legitimate pursuit of these objectives, fuelled by the growing prominence of the new public management discourse, led to a widespread condemnation of the traditional bureaucracy and to the embrace of results-driven management as a way of reinventing the public service of many industrialized countries. On this score, Canada might not have been the most adventurous reformer, but it was part of the pack, and the culture of its public service had changed significantly over the years.[14] For the Public Service Commission, the guardian of some of the most fundamental values of traditional public administration, the potential erosion of these values in the face of the growing popularity of public management was cause for concern.

In the latter half of the 1990s, the PSC began to publicly reaffirm the importance of a professional public service, rooted in the traditional principles of merit-based appointments and promotions, non-partisanship and enough independence to allow public servants to "speak truth to power" in the public interest. In its annual reports for fiscal years 1995–1996 and 1996–1997, the commission dedicated entire chapters to "the essence of a professional public service," reminding Parliament not to lose sight of the importance of these foundational principles as it pursued public sector reform.[15] For example, in its 1995–1996 report, it affirmed,

> 'Getting government right' will mean optimizing both administrative efficiency and the traditional virtues Canadians associate with their public institutions. A vital challenge in the short and medium term—in addition to building the new Public Service through recruitment and reinvestment—is preserving the essence of a professional and politically neutral Public Service. The hallmark of that professionalism is the ability to give the government of the day the best possible advice without fear or favour, based on objective and impartial reflection on the long-term public good, to loyally carry out the orders of the democratically elected government, to obey the law and to act with probity in the public interest. In addition to being highly competent, a professional Public Service has to be nonpartisan, and entry and promotion must be based on merit. As the parliamentary agency which safeguards merit and nonpartisanship, the Commission believes it has a responsibility to remind Canadians that an institutionalized, professional bureaucracy is a cornerstone of our Westminster-based form of democracy. The final chapter of this annual report aspires to instigate a broader discussion about the importance of safeguarding fundamental democratic, ethical and professional public sector values as the search continues for more flexible ways of governing Canada in the interest of Canadians.[16]

In subsequent years, the concern about safeguarding the fundamental values of the traditional public service did not subside. If anything, it probably deepened as the public service continued to evolve.

One of the important events that brought into even sharper focus the potential erosion of the merit principle due to managerial reforms was the creation of agencies with a distinct administrative and legal status in the late 1990s. At that time, more than 50,000 public servants were moved out of the core public service to join separate agencies with distinctive employment regimes. The most notable case was the creation of the Canada Customs and Revenue Agency in the spring of 1999, which took 43,000 employees out of the core public administration. Thousands of public servants also left for the newly created Canadian Food Inspection Agency or Parks Canada.[17] While an important objective pursued by the creation of these agencies was the improvement of service delivery, the desire to make efficiency gains by escaping the more rigid staffing regime of the core public service was also a prominent goal. As separate employers under the law, the new agencies were no longer subject to the *Public Service Employment Act* and no longer fell under the authority of the PSC.

The creation of these agencies undoubtedly reflected a significant level of frustration with the staffing system among government and public-service decision-makers concerned that it constituted an enormous drag on efficiency. But the creation of these agencies was a significant blow to the application of the merit principle in appointing public employees. Before it became a separate employer, Revenue Canada accounted for about a third of the appointments made to and within the public service, a stunning proportion of appointments that now escapes the reach of the PSC.[18] As public administration scholar Donald Savoie pointed out, this innovation resulted in a two-tier public service, where one tier is seemingly presumed to be naturally more impervious to political pressure to make partisan appointments.[19] At the time that the decision was being considered, the commission's president strongly opposed it, causing some tension with the Privy Council Office, but to no avail.[20]

It is important to note that the commission's concern regarding the erosion of the traditional values of a professional public service never constituted a denial of the need for greater efficiency or managerial flexibility. In fact, its active support for legislative changes earlier in the 1990s and its endorsement of further changes in the following years show that the commission remained committed to these goals. Once again, the issue was rather one of balance. Having a public service staffed with competent and non-partisan civil servants able to advise the government of the day without fearing for their career advancement was as important for the future well-being of the country and the effectiveness of its government as having one that was innovative, efficient and capable of adapting to its changing environment. The challenge was to find ways to reconcile these legitimate and important objectives without neglecting one at the expense of the other.

In the late 1990s, as the commission struggled with this challenge, and what it meant for its future role in the public service, its response turned essentially on two related initiatives: one that sought to further delegate staffing authority to deputy heads within a stronger framework of accountability; and another that considered the radical curtailment of its involvement in service delivery in favour of a stronger oversight role.

RETHINKING DELEGATION: ACCOUNTABILITY AGREEMENTS AND VALUES-BASED STAFFING

The PSC's commitment to delegation had remained unwavering since the adoption of the *Public Service Employment Act* in 1967. Throughout the 1990s, the commission pushed for even further delegation of its staffing authority to departmental heads, with maximum flexibility for managers. However, as a result of its own experience and in response to criticism from managers (insufficient delegation and flexibility) and employees (too much delegation to distrusted managers), the commission also decided to adopt a new approach to delegation: one that would emphasize respect for the values underlying public service staffing, a less prescriptive delegation framework that would allow departments to customize their staffing systems and departmental accountability that would be based less on individual transactions and more on overall staffing outcomes. This shift in approach came as a result of two main reviews of staffing policies and practices.

First, early in the decade, the commission established a consultative committee on the Review of Staffing Delegation composed of departmental, union and private sector representatives.[21] The process was extensive: no fewer than forty-nine consultative groups were convened as part of this initiative, involving various categories of managers, employees and stakeholders. The schism between managers and employees was evident, and the commission concluded, among other things, that it had to improve employees' confidence in managers.[22] The strong union opposition to the 1992 amendments to the *Public Service Employment Act*, which provided enhanced flexibility for managers, was largely a reflection of the distrust felt by many employees. More and better accountability for the use of delegated staffing authority was needed to improve the reputation of the staffing process and build confidence.

To address this problem, the commission worked on the development of a new delegation instrument: the Staffing Delegation and Accountability Agreement (SDAA). Each department would negotiate such an agreement, which, signed by the deputy head, would become the basis for rendering accounts for departmental performance. By using broad indicators and focusing on staffing outcomes and the overall integrity of the staffing system, this approach would counter the tendency to react to individual events and, since agreements were negotiated case by case, they could be tailored to the specific circumstances of each department.[23] In this way, expectations would be clearer and more attuned to departmental requirements: something to assuage both employee representatives and managers. Moreover, departments were expected to share their annual performance report with their employee representatives and report on the feedback received.[24] Implementation of the Staffing Delegation and Accountability Agreement was delayed by the 1993 restructuring of departments and then by the 1995 Program Review, but it nevertheless progressed gradually throughout the decade. By 2001, the near totality of the core public administration was covered by the new system.[25]

A second review conducted also helped confirm this broad shift in approach. Commissioned in the summer of 1995, the report of the

Consultative Review of Staffing was tabled in July 1996. The review was originally launched in response to departmental complaints about the excessive time required to fill positions, and it was tasked with finding ways to make staffing simpler and more efficient.[26] Involving central agencies, managers, union representatives and various human resources experts, the initiative generated an exceptional level of consultation with stakeholders. At these consultations, PSC officials were struck by the intensity of interest in change that they encountered[27] and, eventually, the review led to a broader agenda for non-legislative reform, known as staffing reform.[28]

The Consultative Review of Staffing final report, which was sanctioned by the commission, strongly endorsed extensive delegation of authority to departments, but it also advocated a loosening of the constraints placed on departments for the exercise of their powers.[29] Departments needed to be encouraged to fully use their delegated authority to redesign their own staffing operations, involving employee representatives in the process. But for this kind of renewal to work, the PSC had to ensure that its own staffing framework, within which departments must operate, was not too prescriptive. The commission had to focus less on detailed rules and more on the values that underpinned the staffing system. Accountability had to focus more on results and less on process and transactions. In this way, values-based staffing, as it would come to be known, was largely premised on a well-known bargain: fewer rules and constraints in return for more accountability for achieving results.

As we can see, the general approach underpinning the Consultative Review of Staffing report had strong affinities with the approach to delegation and accountability that the commission was progressively developing over this period. Hence, it is not surprising that they became entangled together in the broader agenda of staffing reform pursued by the commission after 1997. As former commissioner Ginette Stewart observed, these reforms were founded

> on the core belief that Deputy Heads, under existing legislation, can be delegated staffing authorities specifically tailored to their needs and with fewer conditions — if the delegation is accompanied by customized delegation and accountability agreements.[30]

These initiatives also illustrate clearly the overall direction that the commission was taking during the 1990s: focusing less on the direct control of staffing transactions, moving from a rules-based to a less prescriptive, values-based staffing framework and placing more emphasis on accountability for results by departments. There is no doubt that this shift in direction tended to play up the oversight and accountability dimension of the PSC's mandate. Thus, in conjunction with the PSC leadership's growing concerns about the challenges being posed to the traditional public service, this shift contributed to a reconsideration of the commission's historical role in the delivery of staffing and related services.

RECONSIDERING THE PSC'S ROLE IN SERVICE DELIVERY: THE 1999 DIRECTIONAL STATEMENT

As we have seen, one of the effects of Program Review at the commission was that it triggered a period of intense reflection about what its role should be at a time when the public sector was undergoing significant transformation. This thinking led the commission to pay increasing attention to the fundamental values and principles associated with a professional public service in a Westminster-type parliamentary democracy, a preoccupation that was reflected in its annual reports to Parliament in 1996 and 1997. As a parliamentary agent entrusted specifically with the protection of one of those fundamental principles (independent appointments based on merit), the commission was naturally concerned that those principles and values, essential for maintaining a professional bureaucracy able to administer the law fairly and for providing competent, non-partisan advice to government, might be eroded in the new context. In an environment overtaken by management, who should care about the fundamental issues of public administration and about the unique role of the bureaucracy in a parliamentary democracy if not the Public Service Commission?

However, this preoccupation naturally raised a number of questions about the commission itself. In the new environment, where departments enjoyed unprecedented authority and flexibility, did the commission need to change in order to play its role in protecting the professional public service? If independent oversight of departmental staffing was becoming the commission's key role, was it well prepared to fulfill this vital function? In particular, to what extent was a strengthened oversight function compatible with the commission's continued role in the delivery of human resources services? These issues were discussed intensely by PSC officials as they considered the future of the organization. Then, following a series of strategic retreats held in the fall of 1998, the commissioners adopted a directional statement, which proposed a new orientation for the commission.

The directional statement, entitled *A Strengthened Focus for the Public Service Commission of Canada*, proposed to radically cut back the commission's involvement in the delivery of human resources (HR) services in order to devote itself more fully to the independent oversight of departmental staffing systems.[31] Over the years, it argued, the PSC had substantially changed how it safeguarded merit by moving away from the direct control of staffing (doing it itself) and toward more indirect forms of control (by delegating staffing to departments, prescribing how it should be done and then conducting periodic verifications and demanding accounts). But, at the same time, it had continued to deliver some staffing services and HR programs to departments. The result had been a source of some confusion and ambiguity both for departments and for employees of the commission: Was the PSC truly an independent guardian of merit, exercising oversight and demanding accountability from departments, or was it more of a service agency focused on pleasing and meeting the needs of the same departments that were its clients? Was it one of a handful of agencies offering HR services to departments or a unique agency safeguarding on behalf of Parliament the integrity of a crucial element of the HR system? As the public service was adopting a staffing model that made oversight and accountability ever more important, greater clarity was needed on these matters.

For the PSC, while the move away from the delivery of HR services would be historic and difficult, it nevertheless seemed necessary. It is worth quoting at length the directional statement's rationale:

Throughout its history, the Commission has sought to balance its
independence with the need to work with government to effectively
apply merit. One important element of early thinking *which remains
to this day and which now requires clarification* is the Commission's
program and service delivery role as an adjunct to merit. While the
Commission has already begun to change the way it safeguards merit,
moving from directly controlling and carrying out appointments to
delegating staffing authority to deputy heads, it continues, at the
same time, to deliver a variety of human resources programs and
services. Because of this, the PSC finds itself increasingly present at
tables comprising the very officials whose staffing decisions it may be
adjudicating, reviewing or auditing.

The Commission questions today the assumption that performing
these program and service delivery functions truly represents the best
means to bring about merit. It is the altering of this premise that is
the essence of this Directional Statement. With the reinforcing of
deputy head responsibilities for good people management and the
PSC's own extensive delegation of powers to them, the Commission
is of the belief that it need no longer safeguard merit through 'doing'
but, rather, through strengthening oversight.

In other words, while being mindful of the need for special attention
in areas such as senior appointments and initial entry to the Public
Service, the PSC's fundamental responsibilities would be clarified
and strengthened if it no longer delivered services in precisely the
same domains that it oversees. As a matter of principle, the PSC
cannot optimally oversee its delegated authorities while being part of
the system of program administration itself. Against this backdrop,
therefore, the PSC intends to divest itself of its program and operational
responsibilities and strengthen its focus on its fundamental mandate,
the safeguarding of merit.[32] (emphasis added)

This proposal—to divest itself of most of its program and
operational responsibilities in favour of a more exclusive focus on the
oversight of delegated authority—undoubtedly represented a bold

gesture on the part of the commission, and it certainly illustrates how the PSC has been willing to rethink its role in ensuring quality public administration over the years.

Divesting services would mean the loss of resources and employees, which, some people thought, might reduce the PSC's clout and influence in Ottawa. But it would help provide greater clarity of purpose, with the commission's energies being refocused on its core mandate. As the Directional Statement unequivocally stated,

> Simply put, the PSC is involved in too many product lines which, taken together, divert energy and attention away from the main task of ensuring that the principles it was created to maintain are indeed protected and promoted…. Modern public sector human resources management requires excellence in both the delivery of human resource services and the oversight of merit. The Commission believes the time has come for these two functions to be separated.[33]

As officials of the commission argued at the time, this separation of functions would allow the government, if it wished to do so, to create a new, truly integrated HR service provider.[34] Thus, reorienting the commission's mandate would strengthen oversight, and at the same time, if the government moved toward better integrated service provision, create an opportunity to increase the efficiency of the overall HR system.

The directional statement was not a definitive statement of policy. Rather, it painted a picture of where the commission should be heading. To become a reality, it needed to be supported by the senior leadership of the public service, not only because the separation of functions it was proposing would involve a significant reallocation of responsibilities among central agencies involved in the HR system but also because, even if legislative changes were not required, programs would have to be transferred out of the PSC and they would have to go somewhere. Support of the key actors in the system was crucial.

But, as it tried to move forward, the PSC obtained mixed support among senior public service leaders. While many senior deputy ministers supported the overall thrust of the proposal and the idea of better integrated HR service delivery, they also expressed concerns about the system's ability to effectively coordinate HR policy if the PSC were to become further removed from the management team of the public service. At the time, the Clerk of the Privy Council Office (PCO) was talking about a more corporate (whole-of-government) approach to HR management in the public service, and it was not clear whether the commission's proposed course of action would contribute to this objective. In fact, the directional statement was not received with enthusiasm at the PCO when it was officially sent to the Clerk in January 1999.

In any case, a full debate of the directional statement, as an image of the future of the PSC and its role in the HR regime, was significantly hindered because of inopportune timing. Not only was the system preoccupied by other management issues, such as Y2K and a difficult reform of the universal classification system, but the directional statement also arrived at the PCO as the Clerk, Jocelyne Bourgon, was about to leave her position. As a consequence, serious consideration of the proposal would have to wait for a new clerk to be in place. As it turned out, by the time the new clerk settled in, the debate had shifted to the need for more fundamental and comprehensive HR reform, a debate triggered largely by the release of a very critical study by the Office of the Auditor General in April 2000.

Even at the PSC, the directional statement was relatively short-lived, a victim of changing circumstances. While the commission released it publicly in the spring of 1999 and announced publicly that it would pursue "a very active, open and transparent consultation process" on its new direction,[35] the statement was in fact soon abandoned as a blueprint for thinking about the commission's future. Before the end of the year, its strongest advocate, Ruth Hubbard, had left the PSC presidency. The two commissioners who served with her, Ginette Stewart and Mary Gusella, also left around the same time.

The new president of the commission, Scott Serson, did not readily endorse the divestment of most staffing and HR services, thinking that the PSC would remain more influential and better positioned to ensure respect for the merit principle by continuing to balance both roles. And a few months later, in its 2000 annual report, the commission effectively shelved the directional statement:

> The Commission believes its leadership role in the human resources management (HRM) system will be enhanced through the implementation of the values-based approach described above. The Commission will continue to monitor carefully the interplay of its two important roles of independent Parliamentary overseer and key player in the HRM system. The issue of an appropriate balance of these roles will be revisited if there is any indication that the effective oversight of merit is impeded in any manner.[36]

Despite its limited direct impact, the directional statement had clearly raised an important issue that would not simply disappear in the following years. The more staffing authority delegated to departments and the fewer the constraints placed on them to exercise it, the more vital the commission's oversight role would become. To what extent could the commission vigorously play this oversight role, including through audits and investigations, while at the same time remaining significantly involved in operations and offering services to client departments? Was there a need to rethink the activities of the PSC to allow it to focus better on its essential mandate: safeguarding the merit principle? Because they were germane to long-term trends in staffing, these questions would soon return as key issues. But, by the end of 2000, they had already become part of a much larger debate about the need to modernize the whole HR framework of the public service.

Triggering Comprehensive Reform: the Auditor General's 2000 HR Study

As the PSC was working on redefining its own role, pursuing its delegation and accountability agenda and reconsidering its role in delivering services, the Office of the Auditor General (OAG) was conducting a major study of the human resources management regime of the public service. As we have seen in previous chapters, it was not the first time that the auditor general would take a critical look at the bureaucracy's management of its human resources. But, released as part of its report in 2000, this study, *Streamlining the Human Resource Management Regime: A Study of Changing Roles and Responsibilities*, would be a landmark, a particularly hard-hitting critique of the state of personnel management in the public service calling for fundamental institutional and legislative reforms.[37]

Written under the direction of Maria Barrados, assistant auditor general, who incidentally would become the president of a reformed PSC three years later, the report conveyed the sense that action was urgently needed to resolve some key personnel management issues, especially in light of upcoming challenges, such as the major waves of retirements and the growing need for knowledge workers in a modern public administration.[38] Extremely critical of the state of staffing and human resources management, the OAG's report observed that staffing remained "a major source of frustration" for managers and employees alike.[39] Despite repeated efforts to make the system more flexible, managers essentially viewed it as "unduly complex, inflexible and inefficient," and many employees were even sceptical that it led to fair hiring decisions.[40]

The OAG's diagnostic for the ills of the staffing and human resources management system focused largely on its excessive regulation. The report argued that much of the administrative burden on departments resulted from policies and regulations imposed by the PSC and the Treasury Board to ensure that the relevant laws, and the related and ever-expanding jurisprudence, were respected. As a result, despite successive waves of delegation of authority to departments, managers remained entangled in a web of cumbersome rules. For example, the report pointed out that the Treasury Board's personnel and pay administration manuals contained more than 12,000 pages of instructions in 1997.[41] The system's complexity was such that, according to various studies, departments had to develop policies and rules of their own to ensure that their employees complied with the requirements of central agencies.[42] The outcome was clearly inefficient: staffing a new position that had to be classified took almost eight months, and the public service employed about three times the number of HR professionals as the standard in the private sector.[43]

In order to improve staffing, the OAG advocated "substantial change—even legislative change."[44] For example, changes to the *Public Service Employment Act* would be needed to provide departments and the Public Service Commission with greater flexibility in the appointment and deployment of personnel. But in addition to these modifications, there was also a need to deal with the excessive fragmentation of the responsibility for human resources management in the public service. The responsibility and related accountability for improving human resources management needed to be clarified and, for the OAG, there was no uncertainty about it: the responsibility and accountability of deputy heads, the leaders of departments and agencies, had to be strengthened. As it argued,

> The underlying philosophy should be that deputies have the authority to act at their own discretion in all areas except where the centre has chosen to prescribe policy, and those areas should be limited to the minimum essentials. It is crucial that new responsibilities and deputies' accountability for acting on them be set out clearly.[45]

Clearly, decades of an approach emphasizing the delegation of authority had successfully presented deputy heads as primarily responsible for administering a centrally prescribed framework but had failed to make them HR leaders by making human resources management an integral part of their management responsibilities. Reforms were now needed to take these additional steps: empower them, set clear expectations about HR management and hold them truly accountable for their performance.

The role of the Public Service Commission in all this was left rather undefined by the OAG. The OAG observed that there was agreement on the vital role played by the commission in protecting the merit principle. But the report advocated a renewed dialogue with Parliament about how the commission should fulfill this function, and it stated that the possibility of legislative reforms should be part of the discussions. Consideration also had to be given to the appropriate extent of the commission's involvement in delivering services that were not central to the protection of merit.[46] However, the report did not include any explicit calls for removing the commission's staffing authority or for changing its unusual institutional position as an independent parliamentary agency also exercising executive powers of appointment to the public service. Observers looking for a clear signal in this regard were left noting repeated exhortations in favour of clarifying the division of responsibilities among agencies and a passing observation that the "reluctance to tamper with the independence and role of the Public Service Commission has been a factor [in the Public Service's past inability to resolve key HR issues]."[47] Thus, while it clearly advocated strengthening the authority and accountability of deputy heads in the area of human resources management, including staffing, the report's views on the appropriate role of the PSC were not as clear.

Initially, the report of the Office of the Auditor General did not generate much enthusiasm for reform. The Public Service Commission reiterated its support for reforming the staffing system so that it would be based more on values and less on rules. But it pointed out that, following its review of staffing in the mid-1990s, steps had already been taken in this direction. Furthermore, in sharp contrast to the OAG, the commission believed that much progress remained possible under the existing legislative framework. At a minimum, more work was needed before concluding that amendments to the *Public Service Employment Act* were necessary. Finally, in a clear attempt to caution the government against undertaking radical reforms in the search for greater flexibility, its official response to the OAG also stated that "efficiency, while unquestionably important, forms part of a larger balance of values" associated with staffing the Public Service of a democratic country.[48] Maintaining this balance, the commission argued, is necessary to ensure that Canadians remain confident in the public service.

In the higher echelons of the public service and the government, the initial response to the OAG's report was similarly lukewarm. Amongst the myriad of important issues faced by the centre of government, a significant overhaul of the human resources management regime would consume a great deal of energy, would likely prove disruptive and hardly seemed a political priority. Moreover, as the Office of the Auditor General itself reported, there were "concerns, notably among deputy ministers, about the practicality of pursuing such fundamental reforms."[49] Consequently, the government's initial response to the report was marked by a distinct lack of enthusiasm. In its official reply, the government stated that it was "considerably more optimistic than the Auditor General on such matters as collective and individual deputy minister responsibility, accomplishments in staffing reform, and the flexibility inherent in the current legislative framework."[50] Pointing out that committees of deputy ministers were already at work on such issues as recruitment and workplace well-being, it declared itself confident in the possibility of effectively modernizing human resources management without legislative change.

However, after a few months, this initial reluctance gave way to some genuine support for change. In early 2001, in its third report, the Advisory Committee on Senior Level Retention and Compensation (the Strong Committee), which advocated the development of a long-term human resources strategy for the public service, endorsed the Auditor General's recommendation for structural reform of the HR regime. Then, a few months later, the final report of the Advisory Committee on Labour-Management Relations in the Federal Public Service, the Fryer Report, also advocated significant changes to the human resources management regime, this time to the legislative framework concerning labour relations.[51] Within a short time span, the government had received consistent and strong signals about the need for institutional and legislative change.

The general election of 2000, which resulted in a comfortable Liberal majority, seemed to present a measure of political stability and commitment that would make significant reforms possible. Upon its return to office, in the Speech from the Throne read on January 30, 2001, the Chrétien government committed itself to administrative reforms that would allow the public service to attract the skilled workforce needed in a knowledge economy and society. As it stated,

> The Government is committed to the reforms needed for the Public
> Service of Canada to continue evolving and adapting. These reforms
> will ensure that the Public Service is innovative, dynamic and
> reflective of the diversity of the country—able to attract and develop
> the talent needed to serve Canadians in the 21ˢᵗ century.[52]

In this context, enjoying clear political support and responding
to growing calls for legislative changes, Mel Cappe, clerk of the Privy
Council and Head of the Public Service, took steps to set the bureaucracy
on a path of reform.

SEEKING A NEW BEGINNING: THE *PUBLIC SERVICE MODERNIZATION ACT*

The Clerk of the Privy Council's *Eight Annual Report to the Prime
Minister on the Public Service of Canada*, tabled in March 2001, was
largely dedicated to the need to build a modern, people-centred public
service in order to meet the challenges of a knowledge-based society,
especially at a time when large-scale retirements would soon create
significant recruitment challenges. In the report, Cappe announced
"the beginning of a phase of more fundamental reform," which would
lead to a cultural shift that would bring managers to see that people
management is an integral part of good management.[53] But, "today's
human resources management laws," the Clerk warned, "do not allow
us to move quickly enough on the transformation to a modern, people-
centred public service. More fundamental change is required."[54] Also in
the report, he asserted that "no matter how you look at it, it is clear that
we are not able to keep pace because our current people management
regime is too linear, inflexible and complex" and that "to keep pace
and better support the efforts of public servants at all levels, we need
to move from our incremental approach to a more fundamental reform
of the legislative framework for human resources management in the
Public Service."[55]

Once reformed, the legal framework would continue to ensure
the protection of merit, representativeness, non-partisanship and

competence, but it would also ensure that management would be responsible for all aspects of personnel management, and authority for personnel management would be pushed down as far as possible in the departments' hierarchy.

The Clerk's report and other statements, coupled with the Speech from the Throne, undoubtedly represented an unequivocal and strong endorsement of significant legislative reforms by the centre of government. Moreover, the Clerk's declaration left no doubt about the overall orientation of the reforms to come: flexibility, efficiency and transfer of authority to departmental managers were the order of the day. However, to make these reforms a reality, much work remained to be done on the specifics of the legislative changes. To do this, on April 3, 2001, the Prime Minister appointed a Task Force on Modernizing Human Resources Management, headed by a senior deputy minister, Ranald A. Quail, who would report to the Clerk of the Privy Council. At the political level, the president of the Treasury Board, Lucienne Robillard, a senior minister with a long experience of the public service, was given responsibility for looking after this initiative and ultimately shepherding the resulting legislation through Parliament.

The recommendations of the Quail Task Force, and the eventual changes that it led to, were significant and wide ranging, affecting not only staffing but also labour relations, training and development and the regulation of political activities by public servants. Many of the changes that it advocated eventually made up part of the *Public Service Modernization Act,* which was enacted by Parliament in November 2003.[56] With regard to staffing, significant changes were made to the public service's approach to the merit principle as well as to the distribution of responsibilities among central agencies and departments. The overall thrust of the reforms, in keeping with the Clerk's initial direction, was to emphasize greater flexibility in staffing rules and further delegation of authority, inscribed in the legislation itself, to departmental managers. Overall, the adopted measures clearly were the most fundamental and wide-ranging changes to the public service's human resources management framework since 1967.

In examining these changes and their impact on the Public Service Commission, two sets of issues appear particularly important: the debates over institutional reforms, dealing mainly with the independence of the PSC and the distribution of roles among central agencies, and the legislative changes that sought to make staffing more efficient, especially the new legislated approach to the implementation of the merit principle. We will now look at these issues in turn.

Institutional Reforms: A Redistribution of Roles

A key objective of the 2003 reforms was to clarify responsibilities for human resources management in the federal public service. In this regard, the reformers' main desire was to see the responsibility and accountability of deputy heads for managing their organization's personnel increased and more clearly affirmed in the law. As it has often been pointed out in the past, deputies had come to be seen as the operators of a centrally prescribed framework that left them little room for judgment and leadership. There was a sense that personnel management had often been a neglected dimension of their managerial responsibilities, a situation that was not tolerable in an environment where talented and motivated people had become the most precious resource of departments and where recruitment and retention were becoming increasingly difficult.

To address this concern, the *Public Service Modernization Act* included some important provisions. The preamble of the new *Public Service Employment Act* explicitly affirmed that staffing decisions should be made at the lowest possible level within departments: delegation of staffing authority, from the PSC to deputy heads then from deputy heads to lower level managers, was to be the core philosophy of the staffing system.[57] In the same spirit, the preamble also provided that managers should enjoy flexibility in staffing arrangements. Furthermore, the PSMA also amended the *Financial Administration Act* to transfer some of the Treasury Board's authority for personnel management to deputy heads, especially in the areas of training and development, termination and demotion and the setting of standards for disciplinary actions. The exercise of the new powers would be subject to policies and directives issued by the Treasury Board, but deputy heads would be at the helm and accountable for their performance. Finally, as a way to heighten the importance of human resources management, the Treasury Board was also tasked by the new legislation to table in Parliament an annual report on personnel management in the core public service.

While there seemed to be a widely shared consensus on the need for clearer and more extensive delegation of human resources (HR) management to deputy heads and managers, a trend supported by the PSC, there was no consensus on a second issue of institutional reform: the distribution of roles and responsibilities among central agencies with responsibilities for human resources management. As we have seen in previous chapters, the "ambivalence of central personnel management" has long been as a source of problems for HR management in the public service.[58] The HR modernization initiative presented yet another opportunity to consider simplifying and clarifying the way personnel management was dealt with centrally. And, more particularly, it again raised the question of whether the PSC should retain its executive authority over appointments or whether it should confine its role to reporting to Parliament on the results of its audits of staffing actions undertaken by departments. In the latter model, staffing authority would be fully transferred to the employer.

Like many commissions and task forces over the years, the Quail Task Force, wanting to end the historic split in central personnel management responsibilities for the sake of efficiency, proposed to change the mandate of the PSC and to turn it solely into a parliamentary agency. Not surprisingly, the commission, represented by its president, Scott Serson, argued strenuously in favour of retaining its executive authority.[59] Serson, like many PSC presidents before him, believed that the protection of merit required a strong and independent commission. In his view, a commission that relied almost exclusively on its power to take departments to task by tabling audit reports before Parliament would likely lack sufficient levers to ensure strict adherence to the principle of merit. With a more delegated and more flexible staffing model, there seemed to be an even greater need for a strong and independent body capable of exercising direct authority in the event of incompetence, defective systems or abuse of discretion. In his view, in order to prevent abuses and retain the confidence of Canadians, the public service needed a PSC with one foot still firmly planted on the executive side of the fence.

In the senior ranks of the public service, the debate about the institutional position of the PSC proved to be difficult, and deputy ministers were divided on the best course of action. As the debate intensified, there were growing tensions between the Commission, the Privy Council Office and some deputy ministers, and, at one point, the president of the commission stopped attending the regular meetings of the Committee of Senior Officials.[60] As the head of an independent agency, Serson also met with the President of the Treasury Board to share some of his concerns about the threat to the PSC's statutory authority. As in the early 1990s, there were also concerns about the PSC taking a strong public position against the reform and publicly doubting its future ability to protect the merit principle if it lost its executive authority over staffing.[61]

In its 2002 Annual Report, at a time when the Privy Council Office was still considering reform proposals, the commission had already warned against an eventual curtailment of its independence. Emphasizing the link between its institutional independence and the protection of the key values of neutrality and equity, it had stated,

> Public Service neutrality is in large part a function of the accountability of deputy/agency heads to the Commission, who in turn is accountable directly to Parliament. Deputy/agency heads and the Commission are therefore protected from direct pressure from the government of the day in making appointments. This protection for deputy/agency heads from partisan influence should be maintained in the new system…. Another possible threat to merit would be an excessive emphasis on efficiency in staffing, at the expense of the values of fairness, transparency and equity of access. At present we are responsible for ensuring an appropriate balance among all the staffing values. In a modernized system, the Commission should

> have a way to guarantee that this balance continues to exist. At the
> heart of these issues is the continuing need for an independent agent
> of Parliament, working to protect merit in co-operation with—but
> not subject to—the Government in its role as employer.[62]

In the end, after what has been described by former senior officials of the commission as a very difficult period, the Privy Council Office decided not to strip the PSC of its statutory authority over staffing. Once again, the PSC had fended off an attempt at reducing its role to one of a parliamentary oversight body.

Ultimately, in fact, as a result of amendments introduced during the parliamentary consideration of the *Public Service Modernization Act*, the commission's independence was even strengthened. First, new provisions served to clarify the commission's governance structure and the leadership position of the organization's president, turning the jobs of the two commissioners into part-time positions and officially designating the president as the commission's chief executive officer. While the president had always had a unique leadership position in the past, the exact nature of the president's relationship with the other two commissioners had sometimes been the subject of dispute. Second, amendments were made to the procedures for appointing the president, bolstering the president's unique status and independence. While still a governor-in-council appointment, the president is now appointed only after the nomination has been approved by a resolution of the House of Commons and the Senate. Moreover, appointed for a seven-year term, the president can only be removed by the government at the request of Parliament. These amendments underscored the commission's special relationship to Parliament and its distance from the political executive.

However, while the PSC was kept as an independent agency exercising authority over staffing, the comprehensive reforms adopted in 2003 still profoundly affected the distribution of roles among central agencies involved in human resources management. The most notable change was the creation of a new central agency for human resources management: the Public Service Human Resources Management Agency of Canada (since renamed the Canada Public Service Agency).[63] Under the portfolio of the president of the Treasury Board, the new agency was created by hiving off most of the personnel responsibilities long held by the Treasury Board Secretariat, with the notable exceptions of labour relations management, collective bargaining, and compensation matters.[64] Additional responsibilities, such as career development programs previously administered by the PSC, were also transferred to the Canada Public Service Agency.

Since it seemed to run somewhat counter to the oft-professed desire to simplify the central management of personnel, the creation of the Canada Public Service Agency might have been perceived as a surprising development. In fact, the Quail Task Force had not initially proposed the creation of a new central agency. But, as its recommendations were considered and debated within the senior ranks of the public service, the clerk of the Privy Council at the time, Alex Himmelfarb, came to consider the creation of a separate human resources agency as a promising step forward.[65] The creation of a separate agency, distinct from the Treasury Board Secretariat, and solely dedicated to human resources management, seemed to serve two objectives. First, while it might not simplify the system, it would serve to recognize, at the institutional level, the fundamental importance of people management to the future success of the public service. But, second, it would also allow the Treasury Board Secretariat to focus its efforts more exclusively on budgetary policy and financial management at a time when there were growing concerns about financial controls and accountability. In this sense, a separate agency would contribute to the improvement of the management framework of the public service.

As already noted, for the PSC, the creation of the Canada Public Service Agency meant the loss of its responsibilities for career development. Its career programs, including the well-known Management Trainee Program, the Career Assignment Program, the Accelerated Executive Development Program and Interchange Canada, were all transferred to the new agency. But this was not the only change in the distribution of responsibilities. As a result of the adoption of the *Public Service Modernization Act*, the Public Service Commission also lost most of its appeals functions. Under the new legal framework, while the PSC would continue to investigate complaints involving external appointments, most complaints concerning internal appointments would be handled by a new independent Public Service Staffing Tribunal.[66] The PSC's responsibility for language training, which had played a big part in the commission's life since the late 1960s, was transferred to a new Canada School of Public Service, an expanded training organization created out of the Canadian Centre for Management Development.[67]

There is no doubt that these changes considerably transformed the PSC as an organization. Some of the affected functions, such as training, had been a sizeable part of the organization and had played a significant role in the commission's recent history. But the reorganization also provided the commission with greater clarity of purpose. As it discarded its training and career development activities, the commission dedicated a larger part of its efforts to better oversight of the staffing system, a task of growing importance due to the new law's emphasis on extensive delegation of authority to deputy heads and managers. For example, in this regard, a new Audit Branch was created and, between 2003 and 2006, the number of auditors at the commission increased from five to twenty-three, a significant reinvestment in an area that had been neglected over the years.[68]

However, it must be noted that, despite the greater emphasis on delegation of staffing authority to the deputy heads, the commission has not fully shed its staffing, recruitment and assessment services in the years since the 2003 reforms, even though these services are no longer mandatory. For instance, the commission still runs a number of specialized government-wide recruitment programs and manages the Public Service's centralized online recruitment and screening system, which received over one million applications in 2006–2007.[69] Moreover, while the new staffing regime encourages extensive delegation and seeks to maximize autonomy for departmental managers, many departments and agencies will never develop a full range of staffing, recruitment and assessment services, due to their small size or the lack of availability of HR expertise. For this reason, the commission still offers these services on an optional basis and many departments continue to use them. Furthermore, even under a delegated authority model, effective centralized services are still necessary to allow the commission to withdraw, in part or in total, the authority to do staffing from any department that has been found to be inappropriately performing these delegated functions. Hence, despite a clear realignment of its functions in favour of its oversight role, the commission remains an organization that delivers important staffing services.

In sum, the institutional reforms brought about by the *Public Service Modernization Act* had the effect of recentring the commission on its core mission: ensuring that the merit principle is applied in staffing the public service. At the institutional level, it did so by re-emphasizing the commission's role as a parliamentary oversight body, shedding some of its services and strengthening the president's autonomy from the government. But, this recentring did not mean breaking with one of the central elements of the 1908 bargain: the dual personality of the commission as a parliamentary agent and an executive office possessing statutory authority over staffing. In this sense, despite the profound changes that it brought to the central personnel management system, the 2003 reforms also provided a significant degree of continuity with the commission's history.

A New Approach to the Merit Principle

While these institutional changes were of fundamental importance for the PSC and the central management of personnel in the public service, they were not the most contentious part of the legislative changes adopted in 2003. More controversial among stakeholders and more prevalent in parliamentary debates were the proposed changes to the public service's approach to the merit principle. In addition to pushing staffing authority as far as possible down departmental hierarchies, the modernization of human resources management also meant breaking down some of the staffing system's rigidities. Since 1967, court decisions had resulted in a rule-heavy system, and legislative changes were needed to allow the public service to leave behind some of these constraints. The elimination of "unnecessary red tape in staffing" was a clear objective of the legislative reform.[70] As Lucienne Robillard, president of the Treasury Board, put it, "The current system is cumbersome and outdated. The public service needs a renewed legal framework for its staffing and management practices to allow it to operate more effectively and to better meet the needs of Canadians."[71]

The approach taken was a bold one. Merit-based appointments had never been explicitly defined in statute. The Public Service Commission had been left to design selection procedures that would bring some life to the merit principle. However, as staffing decisions were challenged, the courts had progressively defined the nature of meritorious appointments, emphasizing the identification of the best qualified candidate as determined through a comparative assessment of candidates for a specific position. Despite the amendment to the *Public Service Employment Act* in 1992 that introduced the possibility of using a more absolute standard of competence, the staffing system was still largely dominated by cumbersome procedures meant to ensure that candidates were rigorously assessed and ranked, so as not to give grounds for appeals. The 2003 legislative changes sought to leave behind this approach by legislating, for the first time, a definition of merit that would be more flexible.

The new *Public Service Employment Act*, contained in the *Public Service Modernization Act*, redefined meritorious appointments as appointments where the selected person meets "the essential qualifications for the work to be performed, as established by the deputy head, including official language proficiency."[72] In other words, it would now no longer be necessary to show that the selected person was the best qualified candidate, but only that he or she possessed the necessary qualifications to perform the work. Moreover, in making staffing decisions, departments would now be able to consider additional qualifications deemed to be assets but not essential for the job, as well as take into account their current or future operational requirements and organizational needs. Deputy heads would now have the authority, which could be subdelegated, to define these various staffing requirements. Finally, the new act stipulated that it was not necessary to consider more than one person for an appointment to be based on merit and that non-advertised appointment processes could be used.[73] Overall, these measures represented a clear embrace of a more limited conception of merit—having the essential qualifications to do a job—and granted considerable discretion to managers in conducting the staffing process.

This new approach to merit was not universally well received. In Parliament, opposition parties, which generally agreed that a new legislative framework for staffing was required and that more flexibility was needed to speed up the hiring process, nevertheless expressed some concerns about the proposed approach to establishing merit. For instance, Paul Forseth, the Vancouver MP representing the Canadian Alliance Party on the file, stated,

> My problem is that the new, watered down definition of merit gives no direction to select the best person for the job within a specific competition process. Since that basic goal would no longer be required, no justification or accountability would be required to defend perhaps a sloppy selection process or even insider advantage to a favoured person…. There is nothing that will bring the whole system down faster than the informal social network of news among employees when it becomes known that a significantly less able employee was selected for promotion under the new proposed system, where this so-called winner met the basic qualifications but was clearly not the best person within any given competition. I say to the minister that she will have a disaster on her hands if she fails to fix this most basic definition.[74]

Then, Monique Guay, who spoke for the Bloc Québécois on the file, expressed similar views:

> Staffing and the merit principle are at the heart of the reform in Bill C-25…. The minister wants to give managers greater leeway. Hiring time will be shortened, but we are wondering at what cost. The employees will have to make sure not only that they meet the position requirements, as they are currently required to, but also

that they are on the good side of the boss under whom the position falls, or else they will no longer even be evaluated. There is therefore the whole issue surrounding recruiting and staffing in which some balance should perhaps be sought, within limits. I realize that the process so far has proven complex and time consuming. But could a middle ground not be found? This is something we have a bit of a problem with.[75]

As we can see, despite being fairly supportive overall, parliamentarians sitting on the opposition benches were clearly concerned about the reform's eventual impact on the pubic service if, in practice, the reform resulted in an erosion of the merit principle.

Their concerns were fuelled or echoed by concerns expressed by many observers or stakeholders. As could be expected, labour unions were particularly critical. For example, Nycole Turmel, president of the Public Service Alliance of Canada, strongly condemned the legislation. Before the House of Commons' committee studying the bill, she said,

[The proposed *Public Service Employment Act*], in its current form, represents a wholesale retreat from a public service defined by the appointment of the best-qualified individuals. Bill C-25 delivers on its promise of increased flexibility for management, but contains very little protection for employees or the principle of merit.... In doing so, the PSAC fears that the new PSEA has the potential to usher in a new era of patronage, favouritism and a lack of accountability that is inconsistent with the government's stated objective.[76]

Some recognized experts, such as Nick D'Ombrain and Donald Savoie, acknowledged the need for greater flexibility and a rethinking of the distribution of responsibilities among institutional actors but nevertheless worried about the erosion of the merit principle.[77] Ruth Hubbard, former president of the PSC, now retired from the public service, took a similar position. In an article published at the time, she endorsed the bill as "cautiously constructive" but worried that the new approach to merit might open "the door to significantly more abuse" and become "a slippery slope to mediocrity."[78] Those were hardly strong or unequivocal endorsements.

Despite these concerns voiced in the House of Commons and in public debates, the *Public Service Modernization Act* was adopted in June 2003, with some limited amendments. As we have seen, one of those changes modified the process for appointing the PSC president. Others provided for consultations among the commission, the employer and labour unions on a number of policy issues or gave the PSC more flexibility in granting leaves to employees wishing to run for political office. While these changes were useful, they did not alter the essential intent of the legislation on matters of staffing. The vast majority of the amendments accepted by the government came from the Canadian Alliance Party, which supported the bill in the end, judging that it was the best that could be achieved at the time.[79] In contrast, all but one of the 120 amendments moved by the Bloc Québécois were rejected, as were all those proposed by the New Democratic Party.

It should also be remembered that, much like the *Public Service Reform Act* in the early 1990s, the *Public Service Modernization Act* was a very comprehensive piece of legislation. For example, in addition to pushing for more extensive delegation of staffing and redefining merit, the act also provided for the automatic conversion of term employees into indeterminate status after a specified period of time, without giving grounds for appeal. The first part of the act enacted an entirely new *Public Service Labour Relations Act*, which, among other measures, established a new Public Service Labour Relations Board and mandated the establishment of departmental labour-management committees. Moreover, because of the political climate at the time, a portion of the parliamentary debates centred on the need for better protection of civil servants who disclose wrongdoing in the workplace (whistleblowing), even though the issue was not part of the bill. Workplace harassment was another issue raised by some parliamentarians. While we have not examined them here, some of these issues and measures also met with opposition and motivated several amendment proposals. However, in the end, the government resisted most of the proposals and the legislation was adopted without much difficulty.

During these public debates on staffing reform, the Public Service Commission, as it had done with the *Public Service Reform Act* in the early 1990s, defended the need for greater efficiency. As its president, Scott Serson, argued before the House of Commons committee studying the bill,

> The proposed legislation offers an opportunity to increase the flexibility of the staffing system so that managers can respond quickly to the evolving needs of Canadians. *This change is needed, and we support it.* Increased staffing authority for deputy heads and the greater discretion for managers contained in the bill is counterbalanced with measures to safeguard against such abuses as political and bureaucratic patronage. It is a significant challenge to find the right balance between flexibility and fairness.[80] (emphasis added)

In other words, while not perfect, the new act seemed to strike a difficult but reasonable balance between efficiency and equity.

Despite its support for the bill, the PSC nevertheless suggested some amendments.[81] Some of them sought to further strengthen the independence·of the commission and tighten its ties to Parliament. For instance, the commission proposed that Parliament play a greater role in setting its budget, pointing out that negotiating its annual resources with the Treasury Board, the employer of public servants, was an uncomfortable position for an independent parliamentary agency in charge of overseeing and auditing staffing by departmental managers. It also suggested that Parliament weigh in on the criteria to be used for the selection of commissioners and it requested the right to table occasional special reports on emerging issues facing the public service in its areas of responsibility. Finally, the commission also asked to be given the authority to audit departmental practices regarding the establishment of staffing requirements (for example, essential qualifications, organizational needs and operational requirements) and to take or order corrective actions as a result of audits. Some of these proposed amendments were adopted, such as the right to issue special reports and the right to audit managerial use of staffing requirements, while the others were ignored. However, the commission's proposed amendments were clearly aimed at improving the bill on the margins in the hope of striking a better balance between efficiency and fairness. They did not constitute a disavowal of the reform's essential intent or the bill's main provisions.

In the end, having survived the reforms with its staffing authority intact and a stronger affirmation of its institutional independence, the commission had reason to be comfortable with the overall thrust of the institutional reforms. While the loss of its training services, its development programs and its appeal function left it diminished in some ways, the renewed focus on staffing oversight and accountability was in keeping with the commission's direction over the last decade. Even the new definition of merit, a bold attempt at ensuring speedier, more flexible and more efficient staffing, was supported by the commission. This might have been surprising, given that many critics of the new approach were concerned about its deleterious effect on respect for the merit principle. But, having worked over the previous decades at maximizing the flexibility available under the old *Public Service Employment Act*, the commission was well aware of the difficulties that legal and policy constraints could cause, and it knew that flexibility would be needed to deal with the upcoming challenges of workforce renewal. The new approach was worth trying; it would now be incumbent upon the commission to be effective in its renewed oversight role in order to ensure that merit would indeed be respected under the new system.

Conclusion

Over the past fifteen years, the staffing system and the Public Service Commission have been significantly transformed. When the Chrétien government took office in 1993, the commission had just gone through the difficult experience of Public Service 2000 and the subsequent adoption of the *Public Service Reform Act*. Having survived this challenge to its independence and with newfound flexibilities under the *Public*

Service Employment Act, the PSC might have simply decided to focus on making the most of the new measures while continuing to ensure respect for the merit principle in staffing the public service. But instead the decade that followed was characterized by intense efforts to rethink the role of the PSC in the human resources management system.

The central issue was the need to strengthen the commission's ability to demand accounts from departments for their use of their delegated staffing authority. The commission's introduction of Staffing Delegation and Accountability Agreements, its bold proposal set out in the directional statement to move away from operations and HR services to concentrate on oversight as well as the reforms of 2003, which saw the commission actually divest itself of some of its functions and prioritize its oversight role—all these events resulted in a progressive shift in favour of the PSC's responsibilities as an independent oversight body. As the staffing system as a whole increasingly moved toward the delegation of staffing powers and responsibilities to deputy heads, the need for the commission to concentrate on its essential mandate— the protection of merit—became clear. Strong oversight was crucial if merit, a foundational value of a professional public service, was to be adequately safeguarded. This conclusion left the Public Service Commission transformed, but with a greater clarity of purpose as it headed toward its centenary.

ENDNOTES

[1]   The issue of governor-in-council appointments was, however, discussed in the platform, with the Liberals promising to review the appointment process and make appointments more clearly based on competence and more representative of the diversity of Canadian society. Liberal Party of Canada (1992), *Creating Opportunities: The Liberal Plan for Canada*, Ottawa, Liberal Party of Canada, 93–94.

[2]   Paul G. Thomas (1996), "Visions versus Resources in the Federal Program Review," in Amelita Armit and Jacques Bourgault (eds.), *Hard Choices or No Choices: Assessing Program Review*, Toronto, Institute of Public Administration of Canada, 43.

[3]   Privy Council Office (2008), *Fifteenth Annual Report to the Prime Minister on the Public Service of Canada*, Ottawa, 26.

4   Herman Bakvis (1998), "Transport Canada and Program Review," in Peter
     Aucoin and Donald Savoie (eds.), *Managing Strategic Change: Learning
     from Program Review*, Canadian Centre for Management Development,
     Ottawa, 99.

5   See, for example, the contributions by Gilles Paquet and Paul G. Thomas,
     in Amelita Armit and Jacques Bourgault (eds.) (1996), *Hard Choices
     or No Choices: Assessing Program Review*, Toronto, Institute of Public
     Administration of Canada.

6   Thomas (1996), "Visions versus Resources," 43.

7   Guy B. Peters and Donald Savoie (1998), "Reviewing the Reviewers:
     Program Review in the United States and Canada," in Peter Aucoin and
     Donald Savoie (eds.), *Managing Strategic Change: Learning from Program
     Review*, Canadian Centre for Management Development, Ottawa, 251.

8   Public Service Commission, unpublished internal document entitled *New
     Direction*, dated April 13, 1999, 3.

9   Public Service Commission of Canada (2000), *Annual Report 1999–2000*,
     Ottawa, Minister of Public Works and Government Services, 7.

10   For example, for Assistant Deputy Ministers, the PSC's ADM Secretariat,
     headed by Margaret Amoroso, worked with the Senior Personnel Advisory
     Committee to offer career counselling and identify suitable alternative
     opportunities within the public service. For lower-level executives, the
     commission implemented additional strategies, including greater use
     of diagnostic tests by its Personnel Psychology Centre to build a better
     picture of affected employees' marketability, some measures to facilitate
     the deployment of other executives to create new opportunities for priority
     individuals, and the development of new programs, with the Treasury
     Board Secretariat, to facilitate movement of employees to the private
     sector, international agencies or even self-employment. See Ruth Hubbard,
     Memorandum to the Members of the Executive Group, entitled *Managing
     the EX Cadre through Transition*, dated February 27, 1995 (RG 108, vol.
     1466).

11   A good survey of these activities is offered in Public Service Commission
     (1996), *1995–96 Annual Report*, Ottawa, Minister of Public Works and
     Government Services, 7–11.

12   Interview with a former senior official of the PSC.

13   Interview with a former senior official of the PSC. See also Public Service
     Commission (1996), *1995–96 Annual Report*, 39.

14   See Peter Aucoin (1995), *The New Public Management: Canada in
     Comparative Perspective*, Montreal, Institute for Research on Public Policy;
     and Donald Savoie (2003), *Breaking the Bargain: Public Servants, Ministers,
     and Parliament*, Toronto, University of Toronto Press.

15   Public Service Commission (1996), *1995–96 Annual Report*, 55–59; and
     Public Service Commission (1997), *1996–97 Annual Report*, Ottawa,
     Minister of Public Works and Government Services, 38–40.

16   Public Service Commission (1996), *1995–96 Annual Report*, 6.
17   Office of the Auditor General of Canada (2000), "Streamlining the Human Resource Management Regime: A Study of Changing Roles and Responsibilities," Chapter 9 in *Report of the Auditor General of Canada – April 2000*, 12.
18   Ibid.
19   Savoie (2003), *Breaking the Bargain*, 218.
20   Interview with a former senior official of the PSC.
21   Public Service Commission (1996), *Consultative Review of Staffing – Background Document on the History of Staffing*, Ottawa, unpublished, 13.
22   Ibid, 14.
23   Ibid.
24   Public Service Commission (1998), *Annual Report 1997–98*, Ottawa, Minister of Public Works and Government Services Canada, 13.
25   Exactly 97% of the public service population was covered. Public Service Commission of Canada (2001), *Annual Report 2000–2001*, Ottawa, Minister of Public Works and Government Services, 7.
26   Public Service Commission of Canada (1997), *Annual Report 1996–97*, 19.
27   Public Service Commission of Canada (1996), *Annual Report 1995–96*, 14.
28   For a broad description of the objectives of Staffing Reform, see Public Service Commission of Canada (1999), *Annual Report 1998–99*, Ottawa, Minister of Public Works and Government Services, 6.
29   Public Service Commission of Canada (1997), *Annual Report 1996–97*, 19–20.
30   Public Service Commission of Canada (2000), *Annual Report 1999–2000*, Ottawa, Minister of Public Works and Government Services, 8.
31   Public Service Commission of Canada (1999), *A Strengthened Focus for the Public Service Commission of Canada: Directional Statement*, Ottawa.
32   Ibid, 8.
33   Ibid, 3.
34   Interview with a former senior official of the PSC.
35   Public Service Commission of Canada (1999), *Annual Report 1998–99*, 5.
36   Public Service Commission of Canada (2000), *Annual Report 1999–2000*, 24.
37   Office of the Auditor General of Canada (2000), "Streamlining the Human Resource Management Regime."
38   Maria Barrados was first appointed interim president of the PSC in November 2003. She was then appointed president in the spring of 2004 for a seven-year term, following a review of her nomination by Parliament. The parallel with the experience of John Carson is striking. Carson had also played a key part in writing a landmark report advocating fundamental

changes to the personnel management system (the Glassco Commission) before being appointed to head the PSC under the reformed system.

39   Office of the Auditor General of Canada (2000), "Streamlining the Human Resource Management Regime," 5.

40   Ibid, 20.

41   Ibid, 11.

42   Ibid, 18.

43   Ibid, 21 and 17.

44   Ibid, 16.

45   Ibid, 26.

46   Ibid, 26–28.

47   Ibid, 11.

48   Ibid, 30.

49   Ibid, 16.

50   Ibid, 30.

51   Advisory Committee on Labour-Management Relations in the Federal Public Service, *Final Report*, Ottawa, June 2001.

52   Governor General of Canada (2001), *Speech from the Throne to Open the First Session of the 37th Parliament of Canada*, available on the website of the Privy Council Office at www.pco-bcp.gc.ca.

53   Privy Council Office (2001), *Eighth Annual Report to the Prime Minister on the Public Service of Canada*, Ottawa, 1.

54   Ibid, 5.

55   Ibid, 13–14.

56   The House of Commons adopted the bill on June 3, 2003, and the Senate on November 4, 2003. The act received Royal Assent on November 7, 2003. The act provided for a longer period of implementation, with the full act coming into force by December 2005.

57   In particular, the preamble of the *Public Service Employment Act* adopted in 2003 contains the following statement: "Delegation of staffing authority should be to as low a level as possible within the public service, and should afford public service managers the flexibility necessary to staff, to manage and to lead their personnel to achieve results for Canadians."

58   The expression is originally from Ted Hodgetts. He is quoted in Paul M. Tellier (1990), "Public Service 2000: The Renewal of the Public Service," *Canadian Public Administration*, 33:2, 129.

59   Interview with a former senior official of the PSC.

60   Interview with a former senior official of the PSC.

61   Interview with a former senior official of the PSC.

62   Public Service Commission (2002), *2001–2002 Annual Report: Protecting Merit and the Public Trust*, Ottawa, Minister of Public Works and Government Services Canada, 14–15.

63 The creation of the Canada Public Service Agency was not the direct result of the adoption of the *Public Service Modernization Act*. The new agency was created a few months later, in December 2003.

64 The Canada Public Service Agency was originally under the Privy Council Office before joining the Treasury Board portfolio.

65 Interview with a senior official of the PSC.

66 In addition to complaints concerning external appointments (formerly known as open competitions), the PSC is also responsible for investigating complaints about internal appointments (formerly known as closed competitions) when they were made by the commission itself because staffing authority had not been delegated to the organization concerned. The commission also investigates cases where allegations of political influence or fraud are involved. The Public Service Staffing Tribunal hears cases related to layoffs.

67 However, the PSC kept its language testing services.

68 Interview with a senior official of the PSC.

69 Public Service Commission of Canada (2007), *Annual Report 2006–07*, Ottawa, Public Service Commission, 103.

70 Lucienne Robillard, President of the Treasury Board, *Debates of the House of Commons*, February 14, 2003.

71 Treasury Board Secretariat of Canada, press release entitled "President of the Treasury Board Introduces Legislation to Modernize the Public Service of Canada," dated February 6, 2003.

72 The definition is in Section 30(2) of the new *Public Service Employment Act*.

73 These provisions are contained in sections 30(4) and 33, respectively, of the new *Public Service Employment Act*.

74 Speech by Paul Forseth, MP for New Westminster-Coquitlam-Burnaby, *Debates of the House of Commons*, February 14, 2003.

75 Speech by Monique Guay, MP for Laurentides, *Debates of the House of Commons*, February 14, 2003.

76 Testimony of Nycole Turmel, president of the Public Service Alliance of Canada, before the House of Commons Standing Committee on Government Operations and Estimates, March 25, 2003.

77 Paco Francoli (2003), "Top Experts Say Massive PS Bill a Modest Step Forward," *Hill Times*, Ottawa, May 5. See also D'Ombrain's concerns about "individual merit" in his testimony before the House of Commons Standing Committee on Government Operations and Estimates, April 28, 2003.

78 Ruth Hubbard (2003), "Public Service Modernization: Fixing the Cart May Not Suffice," *Optimum Online: The Journal of Public Sector Management*, vol. 33:2, 2 and 4.

79   For a description of the party's position, see the speech at third reading by
      Paul Forseth, MP for New Westminster-Coquitlam-Burnaby, *Debates of
      the House of Commons*, May 28, 2003.
80   Testimony of Scott Serson, president of the Public Service Commission,
      before the House of Commons Standing Committee on Government
      Operations and Estimates, March 19, 2003.
81   For a description of the PSC's position on the bill, see Scott Serson's two
      appearances before the House of Commons Standing Committee on
      Government Operations and Estimates, March 19 and 27, 2003.

CONCLUSION

> If Canada is to be reasonably well governed in the future, a
> professional, non-partisan public service will be essential. For this
> reason, the most important of the government's central agencies,
> for the long-term, is not in my view the Privy Council Office, the
> Treasury Board, or the Department of Finance, dearly though I love
> them all. It is the Public Service Commission. If the professionalism
> of the Public Service and its attractiveness to successive generations
> of talented young Canadians are to be preserved, it is essential that
> responsibility for the staffing of government positions continues to be
> vested in an agency whose independence is guaranteed by statute.[1]
>
> Arthur Kroeger, former deputy minister

In his book on the development of the American public service,
Stephan Skowronek described the establishment of the U.S. Civil
Service Commission as "nothing less than a recasting of the foundations
of national institutional power."[2] To some extent, the same claim can
be made for the establishment of the Public Service Commission in
Canada. The adoption of a merit-based staffing system, entrusted to
an independent commission, not only changed the balance of power
between Parliament and the Crown over the control of the bureaucracy,
and the balance of power between ministers and public servants within
the executive, but also entailed the adoption of new norms, such as
political neutrality and professionalism, which have shaped the identity
of the public service and its behaviour in the governance of Canada

over the last century. The historical significance of this choice and the lasting impact that it has had on Canadian government and public administration should not be forgotten or underestimated.

While the same basic institutional architecture has remained constant over the past 100 years, as we have shown in this book, the ideal of merit, along with the independence of the PSC itself, has been contested from the very beginning. The commission's independence was first criticized on constitutional grounds—political appointments being regarded as a matter of Crown prerogative and ministerial responsibility—and then came to be seen by many as an impediment to efficiency and effective management. Over the years, the dominant definition of merit and the rules used to put it in operation have been challenged on various grounds: the need for the bureaucracy to be more responsive to elected officials, the democratic equality of citizens, the need for better representation of underrepresented groups in the public service, the fundamental right of public servants to participate in the political process, the efficient use of public resources and the need for better management. As an ideal, merit has never been straightforward: its exact meaning, its practical implications and even its desirability have been disputed throughout its history. Consequently, much more than a simple search for the "best qualified," the merit system has always been an awkward attempt to balance competing sets of values and respond to some of the political demands placed on the staffing system of a public service in a liberal democracy. To a great extent, the history of the PSC has been a continuing endeavour to strike an appropriate balance among these competing values and demands, adapting as both Canadian society and the role of the public service have evolved over time.

Throughout its history, the PSC has been both an agent of change and a voice of caution, seeking to ensure that some of the core values of the Canadian public service would not be sacrificed in the pursuit of immediate priorities. For example, in the 1960s and 1970s, the PSC readily embraced the promotion of underrepresented groups and bilingualism in recognition of the growing importance of these realities for the governance of Canadian society. Since the 1970s, through the delegation of authority to departments and its contribution to legislative reforms, it has actively sought to increase managerial flexibility in recognition of growing political demands for a more adaptable and efficient public service. In these instances and others, the PSC has fully understood the need for change, and acted either on its own initiative or in response to centrally driven proposals.

However, in other instances, the commission's desire and support for change has unquestionably been measured. While recognizing the need to adapt to changing realities, in particular to answer elected officials' calls for more efficiency, it has also played a key institutional role in reminding politicians and public servants seeking reform of the importance of some of the core values, such as political neutrality and equity, that have historically been served by the staffing system. Throughout its history, the PSC has periodically acted as a brake on reformers' attempts at transforming staffing rules in order to meet the imperatives of efficiency and responsiveness. This institutional role may not be unique, but it is rather exceptional in the public service. While some other institutional actors, notably the clerk of the Privy Council, are entrusted with upholding the core principles and values of Canada's Constitution, the PSC has a unique responsibility for safeguarding the key values that the merit-based staffing regime was originally designed to breathe into the public service. Historically, the PSC has endeavoured to play this important but difficult institutional role. In doing so, it has played an invaluable role in shaping the evolution of the Canadian public service and in defining the role of public servants in the democratic governance of the country.

Over the years, the commission's independence, inscribed in statute, has been an important asset allowing it to play this role. At various points in time, the commission has relied on its statutory independence to resist political pressures on behalf of departments, to voice a dissenting opinion about proposed staffing reforms, and to resist changes that it believed would unduly compromise such core principles of the public service as professionalism and political neutrality. For this reason, while the ambivalent institutional position of the PSC—at once an independent agency exercising executive authority over staffing and an oversight body reporting directly to Parliament on the integrity of the merit-based staffing system—has been the subject of much criticism over the years, our examination of the commission's history leads us to believe that this dual personality has served it, and the public service, rather well.

It is doubtful that a simple parliamentary agency dedicated to the oversight of staffing—the preferred model of many reformers in the past—could ever have been as effective a check on political pressures for appointments or as effective a voice defending the core values of merit in public and internal debates. The ambivalent constitutional position of the commission, while somewhat unorthodox, has been a powerful asset that has allowed it to remain closer to the realities of departments while giving it sufficient independence and distance from the government, when the circumstances called for it, to fulfill its unique mandate. Staffing a public organization as large and diverse as the public service of Canada is sufficiently complex, and merit sufficiently contested, that combining aspects of regulation, service delivery and audit in an agency like the PSC has proven to be a durable invention.

Moreover, the PSC's statutory independence has provided the Canadian public service with a more resilient institutional arrangement to safeguard its merit system. The commission's independence certainly has not insulated it, or the merit system, from change. As we have seen, the PSC has changed considerably over its history, acquiring and shedding responsibilities for the delivery of various staffing services and modifying its relationship to departments significantly. The merit system has also been considerably transformed, through policy as well as legislation. But through it all, the PSC has maintained a unique degree of independence and successfully fought off attempts to curtail its authority, and, consequently, it has remained a strong and independent voice in the staffing regime of the Canadian public service.

An Exceptional Resilience

The longevity and continued influence of the PSC is particularly notable in light of the fact that its counterparts in other Anglo-American democracies do not seem to have fared as well in the face of similar pressures for greater managerial flexibility, efficiency and political responsiveness. Commenting on the evolution in the past few decades of staffing systems in these countries, noted scholar Peter Aucoin observed that the "once powerful central agencies for public service staffing and human resource management were greatly diminished in their authority, functions and influence. In every instance, they lost their exclusive authority over public service staffing."[3] In fact, Britain, Australia, New Zealand and the United States have all significantly transformed their personnel management regimes in the last thirty years and their independent staffing bodies traditionally tasked with the protection and implementation of the merit system have suffered as a result.

In the United States, the Civil Service Commission was abolished with the adoption of the *Civil Service Reform Act* in 1978. Having been elected on a promise to reform the public service staffing system, President Jimmy Carter quickly began to introduce changes that would make the American civil service more flexible, efficient and responsive to the president.[4] The Civil Service Commission's functions were distributed to a trio of new offices, including a new Office of Personnel Management, controlled by the president. While a commitment to the merit principle remained, its protection was left essentially to the new Merit Systems Protection Board, which can hear appeals and investigate alleged violations of the law. The third major organization that emerged from the 1978 reforms was the Federal Labor Relations Authority, which took over all the labour relations responsibilities of the Civil Service Commission. These reforms were a clear blow to the independence of the American public service.[5]

Australia and New Zealand have adopted similar reforms. The Australian Board of Commissioners was abolished in 1987. It was replaced by a new Public Service Commission that was entrusted only with authority for setting policy in some areas, such as recruitment and promotion, and with responsibilities for the senior management category. To enhance flexibility and efficiency, most personnel management powers were transferred to departments. Bob Minns, the author of an extensive study on the evolution of staffing legislation in

Australia, asserts that one of the reasons for the "sudden and abrupt disappearance of the Board as a powerful, central agency" was that both ministers and senior executives of the public service sometimes felt aggrieved by its public expression of independent views and believed that it encroached on their prerogatives over the management of the public service.[6] New Zealand also did away with its commission in 1988 in order to emphasize performance-based management and increase the responsiveness of public servants to the political executive. The new body, the State Services Commission, no longer appoints all public servants but rather focuses on the selection and appointment of the chief executives of the public service.[7]

Even Britain, the birthplace of the merit system among Anglo-American democracies, has abandoned its original, more powerful and independent Civil Service Commission. It was transformed into a new Civil Service Commission, composed of twelve part-time commissioners appointed by the government from outside the public service, with few powers and only modest executive responsibilities for staffing the public service.[8] While it publishes a Recruitment Code describing expected standards for merit-based staffing, the new commission does not make appointments itself, a responsibility that now falls to departments and agencies. Instead, the commission now hires a consulting firm to audit departmental staffing practices and uses its findings to comment publicly on the state of departmental staffing. According to British scholar Richard Chapman, the original commission was abandoned because its critics saw it as being out of touch, unresponsive and, in a sense, concerned with the problems of a much earlier era in government. Politicians saw it as an impediment to pursuing an ambitious reform agenda driven by the need for greater managerial flexibility. In other words, it was killed by an "increasing emphasis on a private sector approach to management in Government."[9]

In these countries, the principle of merit-based appointment has not been abandoned, but it has been changed substantially to meet the growing demand that bureaucracies be more efficient and results-oriented, more in tune with the practices of private sector management, and more responsive to elected politicians. In all cases, the historical role of the independent staffing agency has come to an end. Over the years, the Canadian public service has faced the same kinds of pressures and its personnel management regime has been transformed as a result. But as an independent agency with staffing authority, the PSC has not suffered the same fate. In comparison with the other commissions, it has remained truer to the original model. Its role has been refocused and its policies have been adapted to the new context, but it has maintained a stronger, more independent presence in the staffing of the professional public service than its equivalents in other Anglo-American democracies. The statutory basis for its independence undoubtedly explains this greater resilience to a large extent, but the willingness of its leadership to adapt to new circumstances over the years while still defending the core values at the heart of its mandate have also contributed significantly to this outcome.

LOOKING AHEAD

As it reaches its centenary, the PSC continues to face considerable, but familiar challenges. The complete effects of the *Public Service Modernization Act*, which only fully came into force at the end of 2005, have not yet been felt. The PSC is still working with departments to forge a new relationship that will see it devote a larger share of its efforts to the oversight of staffing. The new definition of merit, inscribed in legislation for the first time, also represents a historical change with uncertain implications. The commission will no doubt devote considerable attention to how this shift toward more managerial flexibility will affect the treatment of employees, as well as the professionalism of the public service. Moreover, as the public service as a whole attempts to renew its workforce in the face of an impending wave of retirements and to attract young knowledge workers in a highly competitive labour market, the commission is likely to face new pressures to adapt its practices and policies.

Only a few years after the adoption of the *Public Service Modernization Act*, the government established a high-level taskforce to look once more into needed reforms to the public service. In February 2008, releasing its second report, the Prime Minister's Advisory Committee on the Public Service, co-chaired by former clerk of the Privy Council Paul Tellier and former Mulroney cabinet minister Don Mazankowski, again took aim at the central governance structure for human resources management, describing it as "overly complex" and resulting in a "burden of duplicative and often unnecessary rules."[10] Thus, despite the major reorganization brought by the *Public Service Modernization Act*, the advisory committee has expressed the view that further structural changes are essential. This time, however, the Public Service Commission has been spared: the advisory committee has simply reaffirmed the essential role of the commission in the safeguard of merit and the non-partisan character of the public service. It has merely suggested that the remaining services offered by the commission should be operated on a full cost-recovery basis and that deputy ministers should be appropriately involved in their governance. The advisory committee has not recommended further institutional reform affecting the commission's role or independence.

Instead, the advisory committee has argued essentially for a disentanglement of the responsibilities of the Canada Public Service Agency and the Treasury Board Secretariat. The committee would like to take the 2003 reorganization further by transferring human resources-related matters to a more unified and smaller human resources central agency. In effect, the Treasury Board Secretariat would lose its responsibilities for classification and compensation policy and focus exclusively on expenditure control. With the Canada School of Public Service remaining in charge of delivering training and development courses and the Privy Council Office continuing to ensure talent management for the deputy head community, a smaller Canada Public Service Agency would be the exclusive source of human resources policy, except in the area of staffing. Continuing to rely on a strong delegation model, the agency would be expected to set expectations, provide as light an operating framework as possible, and then ensure accountability for performance from departmental heads. In effect, the advisory committee seems to be arguing for more of the same, wanting to push further, in the same direction, the institutional reforms adopted in 2003. The committee's recommendations seem to suggest that the system is at peace, at least for now, with the PSC's new orientation and its role in the human resources framework of the public service.

But in fact, given the trends across Western democracies, it may well be that the value and necessity of the PSC will again be challenged in the years ahead on the most fundamental issue that led to its creation: political control over the public service. As many scholars have observed, the past few decades have seen the politicization of the public administrations in many industrialized democracies.[11] While an uneasy tension always exists between the neutrality and independence of a professional public service and the need for a public service to respond effectively and loyally to the direction of elected officials, there has been a distinct rise in the desire of politicians to expand their control of the public service. American scholar Ezra Suleiman points out that the bureaucracy is increasingly regarded as being solely the instrument of the political party in power and that it is being transformed accordingly, increasingly deprived of the relative autonomy that it has enjoyed historically.[12] There has been a cultural shift and "the attempt to gain control of the bureaucracy by an elected government is no longer viewed as objectionable."[13]

According to Jon Pierre and Guy Peters, who have surveyed the trends in a dozen countries, managerial reforms designed to improve efficiency, from the creation of quasi-autonomous agencies to the adoption of performance-based accountability systems, have in many cases led to the politicization of public administrations.[14] It has also been observed that the face of patronage is changing: increasingly, elected officials look to reward the loyalty of key allies, including senior public servants, who share their objectives, style and ideology, irrespective of their formal partisan history or attachment. Alongside more traditional political patronage (i.e., appointments of allies from the outside), this form of politicization (i.e., internal promotion of allies) is a significant phenomenon in many countries, such as France and Japan.[15] As well, in some countries, as a result of an increase in the number of political staffers and changes to staffing legislation, many public employees no longer fall within the purview of the merit system.

While the pressures for politicization might not have been as prevalent in Canada as in some other countries, Canada has not been immune from them. At least as far back as the government of Pierre Elliott Trudeau, elected officials have sought to establish better political control over policy decisions.[16] As we have seen, it was also an important preoccupation of Brian Mulroney's government in the late 1980s. And, referring to the more recent past, scholar Donald Savoie has condemned the rise of "court government," a concentration of decision-making power in the hands of the prime minister and a handful of courtiers to the detriment of the established policy process operated by the public service.[17] He has expressed concern that political interference in program management and day-to-day operations of the public service is on the rise.[18] Marshalling a wide range of evidence and opinions, he argues that the relationship between public servants and politicians has been broken, and that the Constitution should be amended to clearly carve out a space of autonomy for the public service in the governance of the country. Legislative reform should establish without doubt that the public service has a distinct personality from the government and should give it the legal means to resist "instructions from elected politicians to perform essentially political acts."[19] Clearly, excessive politicization is also an issue of contemporary significance in Canada.

Politicization is a complex and multi-faceted issue that clearly goes beyond staffing. However, at its core, it indisputably involves the erosion of the political neutrality and independence of the public service and challenges the conception of the public service as a hierarchical meritocracy.[20] And, as we have seen, the staffing of the public service on the basis of merit has historically been a central pillar of the independence of the public service. Politicization is therefore an issue that necessarily speaks to the staffing regime and the purpose of the Public Service Commission. As Canadians and their government wrestle with the difficult issue of the political control of the public service, it may very well become necessary for the PSC to defend, once again, the value of an independent, neutral and competent public administration to democratic government.

In the context of such a debate, it will be useful to remind ourselves of the fact that one of the main reasons the merit system was adopted, and the PSC created, was to provide elected officials with a more effective tool for implementing the democratic will. The goal was to do away with the dysfunctions of patronage and endow the Government of Canada with a professional bureaucracy, effective in making and implementing policy and dedicated to serving the political will of the elected government, but possessing enough independence to allow it to "speak truth to power" and resist political instructions that would violate laws and established norms of ethical behaviour. This complex goal, far from being opposed to the interests of our elected politicians, is in their long-term interest. As Professor Hugh Heclo reminds us, the "independence entailed in neutral competence ... exists precisely in order to serve the aims of partisan leadership."[21] Politicians should be careful that, in the pursuit of more immediate objectives, they do not end up compromising the ability of future governments, and citizens more broadly, to rely on a professional public service that is able to best serve the public interest.

Institutionally, the Public Service Commission will have a key role to play in the debate. In an era of managerialism, the PSC will inevitably have to remind politicians and public servants alike that

> because a system of representative government requires officials to act as custodians of the constitutional values it embodies, it cannot frame the role of bureaucrats solely in terms of efficient management, performance, responsiveness and securing results.[22]

Through their myriad of daily tasks and functions, public servants do not merely deliver programs, they also administer laws and, as scholar John Rohr has put it, they "run a constitution."[23] This reality means that staffing the public service must be subject to constraints that, while sometimes difficult to reconcile with managerial and short-term political objectives, serve an important purpose in the democratic governance of the country.

ENDNOTES

1   Arthur Kroeger (1992), "Parting Thoughts," unpublished speech given to the Monthly Lunch of Deputy Ministers on October 2, 1992.

2   Stephan Skowronek (1982), *Building a New American State: The Expansion of National Administrative Capacities*, Cambridge, Cambridge University Press, 67.

3   Peter Aucoin (2006), "The New Public Governance and the Public Service Commission," *Optimum online*, vol. 36:1, 37.

4   Patricia Ingraham (1995), *The Foundation of Merit: Public Service in American Democracy*, Baltimore, The Johns Hopkins University Press, 76.

5   Ibid, 90–91.

6   Public Service Commission of Australia (2004), *A History in Three Acts: Evolution of the Public Service Act 1999*, Canberra, Commonwealth of Australia, 93.

7   Graham Scott, Peter Gorringe and Mikitin Sallee (1990), "Reform of the Core Public Sector: The New Zealand Experience," *Governance,* vol. 3, 138–167.

8   Richard Chapman (2005), "The Civil Service Commissioners: Supporting the Core Values of the British Civil Service and Hearing Appeals Under the Civil Service Code," *Public Policy and Administration*, vol. 20:1, 1.

9   Richard Chapman (2004), *The Civil Service Commission, 1855–1991: A Bureau Biography,* London, Routledge, 85.

10   The report has been published as an appendix to the fifteenth annual report of the Clerk of the Privy Council to the Prime Minister. Privy Council Office (2008), *Fifteenth Annual Report to the Prime Minister on the Public Service of Canada*, Ottawa, 48–64.

11   B. Guy Peters and Jon Pierre (eds.) (2004), *Politicization of the Civil Service in Comparative Perspective*, London, Routledge; Ezra Suleiman (2003), *Dismantling Democratic States*, Princeton, Princeton University Press, especially 191–278; Richard Mulgan (2007), "Truth in Government and the Politicization of Public Service Advice," *Public Administration*, vol. 85:3, 569–586; Jan-Hinrick Meyer-Sahling (2008), "The Changing Colours of the Post Communist State: The Politicization of the Senior Civil Service in Hungary," *European Journal of Political Research*, vol. 47:1, 1–33.

12   Ezra Suleiman (2003), *Dismantling Democratic States*, Princeton, Princeton University Press, 315.

13   Ibid, 214.

14   B. Guy Peters and Jon Pierre, "Conclusion: Political Control in a Managerialist World," in B. Guy Peters and Jon Pierre (eds.) (2004), *Politicization of the Civil Service in Comparative Perspective*, London, Routledge, 284–287.

15   Ezra Suleiman (2003), *Dismantling Democratic States*, Princeton, Princeton University Press, 229–240 and 244–250.

16   Colin Campbell and George Szablowski (1979), *The Superbureaucrats*, Toronto, Macmillan.

17   See Donald J. Savoie (1999), *Governing from the Centre: The Concentration of Power in Canadian Politics*, Toronto, University of Toronto Press; Donald J. Savoie (2003), *Breaking the Bargain: Public Servants, Ministers, and Parliament*, Toronto, University of Toronto Press; and Donald J. Savoie (2008), *Court Government and the Collapse of Accountability in Canada and the United Kingdom*, Toronto, University of Toronto Press.

18   Savoie (2008), *Court Government*, 314.

19   Ibid, 338.

20   Colin Campbell and Graham Wilson (1995), *The End of Whitehall: The Death of a Paradigm?* Oxford, Blackwell.

21   Hugh Heclo (1975), "OMB and the Presidency: The Problem of Neutral Competence," *Public Interest,* vol. 38, 83.

22   Paul Du Gay (2002), "How Responsible Is 'Responsive' Government?" *Economy and Society*, vol. 31:3, 478.

23   John Rohr (1986), *To Run a Constitution*, Lawrence, Kansas University Press.

INDEX

18. Luc Juillet et Ken Rasmussen
    Defending a Contested Ideal: Merit and tehe Public Service Commission: 1908–2008
17. Gilles Paquet 2008
    Deep Cultural Diversity – A Governance Challenge
16. Paul Schafer 2008
    Revolution or Renaissance? Making the Transition from an Economic Age to a Cultural Age
15. Gilles Paquet 2008
    Tableau d'avancement – Petite ethnographie interprétative d'un certain Canada français
14. Tom Brzustowski 2008
    The Way Ahead – Meeting Canada's Productivity Challenge
13. Jeffrey Roy 2007
    Business and Government in Canada
12. Nicholas Brown and Linda Cardinal (eds) 2007
    Managing Diversity – Practices of Citizenship
11. Ruth Hubbard and Gilles Paquet 2007
    Gomery's Blinders and Canadian Federalism
10. Emmanuel Brunet-Jailly (ed.) 2007
    Borderlands – Comparing Border Security in North America and Europe
9. Christian Rouillard, Éric Montpetit, Isabelle Fortier et Alain-G. Gagnon 2006
    Reengineering the State – Towards an Impoverishment of Quebec Governance
8. Jeffrey Roy 2006
    E-Government in Canada – Transformation for the Digital Age
7. Gilles Paquet 2005
    The New Geo-Governance – A Baroque Approach
6. Caroline Andrew, Monica Gattinger, Sharon Jeannotte, Will Straw (eds) 2005
    Accounting for Culture – Thinking Through Cultural Citizenship
5. Pierre Boyer, Linda Cardinal and David Headon (eds) 2004
    From Subjects to Citizens – A Hundred Years of Citizenship in Australia and Canada
4. Linda Cardinal and David Headon (eds) 2002
    Shaping Nations – Constitutionalism and Society in Australia and Canada

3. Linda Cardinal et Caroline Andrew (dir) 2001
   La démocratie à l'épreuve de la gouvernance
2. Gilles Paquet 1999
   Governance Through Social Learning
1. David McInnes 1999, 2005
   Taking It to the Hill – The Complete Guide to Appearing Before Parliamentary Committees

0 1341 1320245 8

Composed by Brad Horning in Adobe Garamond Pro 9.5 on 12.5.

The paper used in this publication is Rolland Opaque Natural 60 lb.

PRINTED AND BOUND IN CANADA.

RECEIVED

APR 1 1 2011

HUMBER LIBRARIES
LAKESHORE CAMPUS